media

MANUAL

visual effects for film and
television

media

MANUAL

Series editor: Peter Ward

media

MANUAL

visual effects for film and
television

Professor A. J. Mitchell, BA FBKS FRPS

ELSEVIER

AMSTERDAM • BOSTON • HEIDELBERG • LONDON • NEW YORK • OXFORD
PARIS • SAN DIEGO • SAN FRANCISCO • SINGAPORE • SYDNEY • TOKYO
Focal Press is an imprint of Elsevier

Focal Press
An imprint of Elsevier
Linacre House, Jordan Hill, Oxford OX2 8DP
200 Wheeler Road, Burlington MA 01803

First published 2004

British Library Cataloguing in Publication Data
A catalogue record for this book is available from the British Library

Library of Congress Cataloguing in Publication Data
A catalogue record for this book is available from the Library of Congress

ISBN 0 240 51675 3

For information on all Focal Press publications visit our website at:
www.focalpress.com

Trademarks/Registered Trademarks
Brand names mentioned in this book are protected by their respective
trademarks and are acknowledged

Typeset by Newgen Imaging Systems (P) Ltd., Chennai, India
Printed and bound in Great Britain by Biddles Ltd, Kings Lynn, Norfolk

Working together to grow
libraries in developing countries

www.elsevier.com | www.bookaid.org | www.sabre.org

ELSEVIER   BOOK AID
            International   Sabre Foundation

Contents

Acknowledgement

Everything in this book was taught to me by somebody and I hope that by passing on some of that information I am repaying at least in part all those kind people who took the time to explain things.

I should particularly like to thank Kevin Wheatley, Ken Lawrence and Terry Hylton who waded through the manuscript in various stages of completion and put in a lot of the things I missed out! I must also thank the folks at Focal Press: the series editor Peter Ward for his support, Georgia Kennedy, who somehow kept her composure with each missed deadline, and Margaret Denley, who explained and smoothly ran the production process.

Finally I'd like to thank Evelyn and Joe for releasing me from domestic duties so that the accompanying words might be written.

A note from the author

Visual effects is a complex web of interlinking subjects traversing the whole of movie making. To avoid endlessly retreading the same ground material has been ordered to most efficiently help readers to build their knowledge step by step. Consequently this manual cannot be used like a dictionary to dip into for a quick definition, but is most efficiently used by reading through from beginning to end. Information on most techniques is to be found spread throughout the text. Blue screen for instance is dealt with in every chapter, and although it has a chapter devoted to it at the end, digital technology is also evident in every topic, since it has become all-pervasive.

The best method to achieve any given 'effect' is not set in stone and there are always many alternative solutions to any given script requirement. To try to catch the flavour of this a number of very simple shots have been re-used as examples of processes ranging from the oldest 'in-camera' to the latest 'digital post-production' techniques.

Details of how to operate specific equipment or software have been avoided since they appear and disappear within ever-shorter timescales. Therefore the building bricks of effects planning have been concentrated on – and anyway operating details are very easily picked up once the underlying principles are understood.

Finally, computer generated imaging, 3D or computer animation has only been covered in its association with VFX since it is a vast subject in its own right and covered by many excellent books dedicated to that end.

1 Introduction

'Visual effects' is a relatively new term and describes what used to be more appropriately called 'special photographic effects'. When 'optical printers' started to be used extensively in the field, the term 'optical effects' was adopted for a short time; then, in the early days of television when the signal went out live, it was called 'electronic'; with the use of video post-production it became 'video'; and then, finally, with the invasion of computers, it was termed 'digital' effects. During this ever-changing background the term 'special visual effects' and then simply 'visual effects' (VFX) was increasingly adopted to describe what had once been called photographic effects. However, this term was no longer appropriate, since frequently in their preparation a camera was no longer used.

What makes an effect 'special'?

'Special effects' are created where techniques beyond the 'normal' film making procedures are used. That is to say when things might be more complex or time-consuming or involve 'special' techniques. The normal photographic (or if you prefer 'image capture') process is shown below.

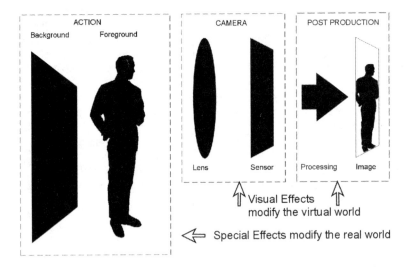

'Special' effects, as currently defined, would be where modifications are made physically to any of these elements or the interfaces between them. Thus, for example, you could set the background or foreground on fire, you could fill the space between them and the camera with smoke or dripping water, or you could physically raise the camera to a great height. These are all physical techniques and in common parlance would be called 'physical' or 'special' effects. Standing by the camera or indeed anywhere in the set these things would be easily seen and recognized by a human observer.

However, ironically, so called 'visual' effects would not necessarily be visible to the casual observer standing nearby. They can be defined as where the components of the photographic process are utilized or modified so as to alter in some non-standard way the passage of light creating the image. Thus, you might replace the background with a photographic element such as a photo-blow-up, filter the light being used on the set in some specialized way, filter or mask the lens, run the camera at an abnormal speed or interfere with the processing between image capture and presentation. All of these might be components in a process to modify the image, but with the final result being unobservable on the actual set.

In a sense, creating successful VFX involves breaking the rules to depict a distorted reality. This requires us to suspend the audience's disbelief by manipulating their perception. This is the main task of VFX and requires the practitioner to fully understand how the photographic/digital process works and thus be able to create apparently true images which in reality are fully or at least partially fake. The purpose of this book is to understand how the imaging system of film and television presents pictures to the audience so that this process can be re-deployed to give the impression of presenting reality while actually showing something else.

Why create 'effects'?

The objective of the normal photographic process is to reproduce 'reality' where that 'reality' consists of whatever is placed in front of the lens as interpreted by the cameraman and director. The aim of visual effects is to create something that does not exist at all, and further, to fool the viewer into believing in its veracity. These are two very different objectives!

There are basically three typical scenarios which call for this. The best known and most obvious is where something that does not exist, nor could exist, is created. This is characterized by the science fiction genre where imaginary robots, aliens and various space paraphernalia need to be depicted.

Slightly less obvious is the situation where, although physically possible, a scene may be simply too dangerous to photograph 'live'. Perhaps this might require performers to work amongst exploding pyrotechnics or a big dollar actress having to hang over the edge of a waterfall. Even where these things are sometimes deemed perfectly safe and the artistes are willing participants, the insurance companies may think otherwise!

Finally, visual effects can be used to 'fix' things. This might involve unintentional errors, which could require expensive reshooting but could easily be fixed in post-production. An example might be a sound boom or light being in shot during a very good 'take'. Alternatively it is sometimes easier to shoot something which is not ideal and then to fix it, rather than dealing perhaps with mechanical or other difficulties on the shoot. Examples of this might be where old buildings have modern elements which would be difficult to camouflage (such as TV aerials or modern signage) or rigs which make the shot simpler (such as safety wires for actors doing complex stunts).

Film, video, digital and string

It may not always be appropriate to shoot material for VFX purposes in the same medium as the principal photography alongside which it may eventually be cut. The decision as to which medium and format VFX elements are going to be shot with is directly dependent on how they shall be employed and what the specifications are for their final resting place. Thus, for example, if an effects shot was intended to invisibly contribute to a sequence of studio shots made on 35 mm movie film, then video'8 would be a wholly inappropriate medium to shoot those VFX components. On the other hand, if the end result were a corporate video to be distributed on VHS then shooting on 35 mm movie film would also be somewhat wasteful. These examples are very obvious, but less so is where the container for the VFX scenes is being shot on super16 film, whilst the effects components would usually be shot on 35 mm (see Formats, page 18).

Material for effects can be shot on anything: film, video or even string if that can be recorded on. The important thing is to match the recording medium with the target medium in which it will be displayed. If an effect is going to be inserted into a television screen then it could easily be originated on video, even if that TV screen will ultimately be photographed in anamorphic 35 mm. Similarly, if a computer graphic animation is to be inserted into film, video or CD-ROM, then in each case the rendering spec. would be different. In VFX every single case is 'special' and must be considered on its own merits.

Importantly, film, video and digital are all acceptable media for recording VFX depending on the final use. They can often be mixed and broadly speaking many techniques are roughly the same in all three. For example, the on-set shooting requirements for rear projection and blue screen are pretty much the same whether it is being photographed using electronic or film cameras. However, each medium is different and there are certain pitfalls to be avoided.

Film

For most cameramen and production people, film is the preferred medium. This is because of its 'look', particularly in terms of colour reproduction and contrast. But it also features incredible resolution, has an underlying grain structure and is the equivalent of a video progressive scan system: extremely important in VFX work (see page 17). The contrast range and resolution of 35 mm film far exceeds that of any current video standard, although its full quality can be scanned in to a digital system. Thus, for acquisition, even if ultimately destined to be digitally manipulated, nothing currently beats the quality of film. Film also has the advantage that it separately records the primary colours and so if it is scanned (converted into high resolution digital information) or telecined (converted into video) the colours may be much more easily and extensively adjusted. For systems such as blue or green screen this is a major advantage and film produces better results than the various electronic systems available. Finally, film's shooting speed is almost infinitely adjustable (assuming use of an appropriate camera). To speed things up you shoot slowly. But, more importantly for VFX, to slow things down you shoot at a higher frame rate. With special cameras extremely high speeds are possible, enabling such things as bullets and explosions to be slowed down to a snail's pace.

But film does have some disadvantages from an effects perspective. Because of its dependence on being mechanically advanced by a claw pulling on a sprocket hole, film is not always rock steady and can, with badly maintained equipment, be unacceptably imprecise. Because the image is physically present, dirt and scratches will show up, and they can easily creep in at any stage. Film needs to be processed before the image can be seen and checked, which puts a delay into the operation and adds an element of uncertainty to the shoot, since complex shots can't be definitively approved. Although video assist is used on most VFX shoots it is often not of sufficient quality to enable a full technical appraisal. Despite being one of the elements which contribute to film's unique 'look', grain can be a problem for effects creation. On the one hand it can show through mattes or 'fizz' on their edges but, on the other, if it has a different appearance in two elements which are to be combined, then it can intrusively show them as being separate and unrelated.

Video

Most creative staff generally prefer the 'film' look, so video is not their medium of choice. This is generally put down to film's wider ranges of colour, contrast, gamma and resolution. These are valid arguments against the 'look' of video and would also work against its use for VFX purposes such as blue screen, which is dependent on colour accuracy.

There are, however, two other elements which contribute to the film look in some people's eyes, and which make effects-work more difficult. These are grain and stability. Film has grain, which moves from frame to frame and can cause problems, whereas video (particularly of the digital kind) effectively does not suffer from this problem at all (unless excessive gain is being used). Film also has an inherent mechanical instability which can be minimized but never totally eradicated without the use of special (time-consuming and therefore expensive) stabilizing software. The video image on the other hand is always rock steady and therefore, from this view, ideal for VFX working.

The main difference between conventional video (including digital) and film is its frame and field structure. This is the major contributor to the difference in look and until just recently has tended to be ignored.

The temporal requirements of the human visual system are twofold. Firstly, for the impression of continuous motion we need to be fed more than 13 images per second. Less than 13 frames per second (fps) we see a series of unrelated static pictures, more than 13 fps we see a continually moving phenomenon. Secondly, to avoid the physiological effects of 'flicker' we need to be presented with more than 45 images per second. At less than 45 fps we are very much aware of flickering and it can have the effect of making us feel nauseous; above this speed, however, we see an apparently constant illumination (called 'persistence of vision' by the Victorians). In reality this figure varies slightly with the intensity of light and tiredness of the individual observer – but for the sake of this discussion we shall deal with the averages, as did the pioneer investigators.

In the early days of cinema a standard was adopted which elegantly dealt with these two specifications. Films were photographed at 16 fps (giving a safety factor of 3 fps above the 13 minimum, to allow for any variations). When projected, each frame was exposed three times thus giving a frame rate for the spectator of 48 fps (again allowing 3 fps safety margin above the 45 minimum). This was achieved by the simple means of spinning a three-bladed shutter wheel in front of the lens, set to spin one revolution per frame (see the figure below). The three identical exposures for each frame are known as 'fields'.

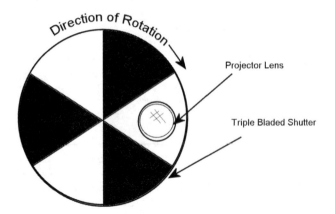

These rates are obviously very near to the minimum and, not surprisingly, 'movies' were nicknamed the 'flickers'. As film producers became large corporations and sought respectability they wanted to improve their image (both physically and socially) and so for prestigious productions they upped the speed. Without the synchronization of sound to worry about they could run any speed they liked, so they simply wrote the chosen speed on the film can and the projectionist dialled it up on his equipment. When sound, originally on synchronized disks, was introduced, this arrangement could no longer be tolerated so a standard had to be established. To do so, on a particular night all of the New York first run cinemas were polled and an average taken. It came to 23, so it was decided to adopt 24 fps as the standard since it conveniently gave the audience the speed they were used to (48 fps) when you showed each frame twice rather than three times. Given the expense of putting in sound gear this was a brilliant solution since it meant that to convert projectors all you had to do was replace the shutter's three blades with two.

When electronic television was being designed in the early 1930s they had to replicate these mathematics but also overcome the technical limits of the time. One problem was how to run the TV in someone's home at the same rate as the transmission chain. This was solved by using the frequency of the electricity supply, to which both devices had to be connected. Thus, in England 50 Hz was chosen and in the USA 60 Hz (later modified to 59.94 Hz). In both cases the frame rate was calculated by dividing the frequency in two, giving 25 fps and 29.97 fps, respectively. The trouble was that the circuitry available at that time was not able to scan the chosen 405 lines (441 in USA) fast enough to show each frame twice, and furthermore, they did not have any means of 'memorizing' a frame to simply repeat it at the receiver. Thus they came up with the idea of interlace, in which they would scan the 'odd' numbered lines in the first fiftieth of a second and then the 'even' numbered lines in the second fiftieth of a second. Thus they had all 405 lines 25 times per second, but at the same time, scanned the entire screen 50 times per second fulfilling the flicker requirements. The 'interlace' concept has been used in all broadcast television systems ever since and some high definition standards too.

For VFX this has major ramifications which cannot be ignored. In film for TV there are 25 actual pictures per second (24 in the USA), that is to say there are 25 moments of time captured. When it is transferred to video each frame is used twice, once for each field, so therefore, each frame of video represents only one instant in time. Thus, the system very nicely approximates the projection of film in a theatre where the two fields of each frame represent a frozen moment in time. Video-originated material, however, effectively presents 50 actual pictures per second (59.94 in the USA) since each field is a separate scan although at half the full frame resolution. Because of this, film on television has a stuttering appearance because objects moving across screen do so with less positions per second than the same object photographed with a video camera (see the figure below).

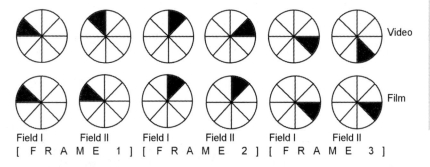

Field I   Field II   Field I   Field II   Field I   Field II
[F R A M E   1] [F R A M E   2] [F R A M E   3]

What this means for VFX is that, firstly, material shot on video will apparently move more smoothly and therefore perhaps be more believable. But if a process involves any individual frame by frame treatment, such as drawing mattes by hand, then there will be twice as many to be done for video than for film. On a budget-conscious production this could be a major consideration.

Let's say the mattes take 5 minutes each to draw and that the shot is 4 seconds long, then video would require 500 minutes or around 8 hours more labour than film, and that is just for one shot !

The second problem is that video and film cannot be mixed unless the film is run at 50/59.94 fps and then the frames are converted into fields (see below).

Film Shot at 50 fps
| frame no. | 01 | 02 | 03 | 04 | 05 | 06 | 07 | 08 | 09 | 10 | 11 | 12 | 13 | 14 |

Converted to video at 25 fps becomes:
| field no. | I | II | I | II | I | II | I | II | I | II | I | II | I | II |
| frame no. | 01 | | 02 | | 03 | | 04 | | 05 | | 06 | | 07 | |

Imagine putting an actor, shot on film against blue screen, into a video background shot, let's say with a car moving rapidly through the frame. On frame one/field I, the actor moves and the background moves. On frame one/field II, the car moves but the actor does not (the second field of the film represents the same instant as the first). On the third field (frame 2/field I) both foreground and background move together. Thus an effect would be created which is totally unreal and draws attention to the join between foreground and background (see figure below).

The character (shot on film) only moves every other frame compared with the car (shot on video)

Compositing conventionally shot film and video material is a 'no-go' area.

Two other technical aspects of the interlaced video frame 'field' and 'edit' dominance have special ramifications for VFX. Firstly is the issue of 'field dominance'. The video frame, as we have seen, is made up of two fields, the 'upper' (odd numbered lines) and the 'lower' (even). In the camera stream the upper field is captured first and the lower field second. For normal viewing these fields need to be in the same order as photographed but it is not important which field is first to be read. For example, if playback started on frame 29 field II, then playback frame 1 would be camera frame 29 field II and frame 30 field I (see figure below).

Frame 29 Field II | Frame 30 Field I | Frame 30 Field II | Frame 31 Field I | Frame 31 Field II |

This would make no difference to watching the programme since all of the frames would be temporally in the correct order. Much broadcast equipment is thus left free to synch up on whatever field is stable first.

Where equipment does determine the order, upper field first is called 'field I dominant' and lower field first is 'field II dominant'. Europe transmits field I dominant but the USA is field II dominant. Most video equipment does not care but digital systems need to be set up one way or the other and must be consistent to avoid disastrous side effects. For instance, if you had a matte and master, and they were supplied on differing field dominance, then the individual frames would never match (see figure below).

Field I Dominant

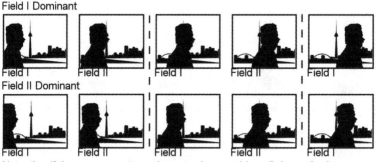

Field II Dominant

Note: that if these were matte and master they would not fit frame for frame

To get them to do so would involve throwing away the first field of whichever was second field dominant thus leaving a homeless field at the end which would have to be discarded too. The result would be one element a frame shorter than the other!

Even worse chaos ensues when a telecine transfers a film second field dominant, because then each video frame consists of a field from each of two consecutive film frames, resulting in freeze frames which have two images superimposed and therefore impossible to draw a matte for. Most old telecine machines don't discriminate between the fields of a video frame and therefore it is down to chance which way they come up. To prove this, view some off air recorded movies on VHS and then try freeze framing on a scene with fast movement, some films will be fine, but others will have an unpleasant shimmering effect and those are the ones output in field II dominance. For VFX this cannot be tolerated so check up that telecine (TK) machines to be used are set up to be first (upper) field dominant and that your post equipment is also set in this mode for both input and output.

Just to add further confusion, old systems edited between the fields of a frame whereas newer systems edit between the frames. This was because on Quad 2″ (the first broadcast tape format) cuts were originally made with a knife and mid frame. To offer compatibility with material produced in that way 'B' format 1″ tape was the same and all later equipment was made switchable. Interframe editing is what we do now and is how all digital editing systems operate but beware the switch that has been incorrectly set because of recent working with archive material or the incompetent video assistant. Field II editing will obviously result in field dominance alternating from one cut to the next – a VFX matte artist's nightmare come true.

International chaos must also be added to the overall mix. Outside the USA and Japan most of the world is at 25 fps and shoots film for TV at that speed. Cinema films universally shot at 24 fps are run at 25 fps and the slight difference in speed be damned! The USA and Japan, however, run at just under 30 fps and so their film has to be adjusted using a technique called '3/2' pulldown. Here a telecine outputs two fields and three fields per frame alternating, to make up the extra six frames needed to step up 24 fps to 30 fps (see figure below).

Original Film shot at 24 fps.

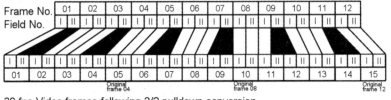

30 fps Video frames following 3/2 pulldown conversion.
Black sections indicate fields which have been duplicated.

This results in field dominance changing twice every five frames. Since video has inter-field flicker anyhow and film changes dominance because of 3/2 pulldown, the USA, Japan and other National Television System Committee (NTSC) countries had no requirement to change the field dominance with the move from early recording formats and so they remain field II dominant. Equipment to be used for NTSC broadcasters' work should therefore be set for lower (second) field dominance. This is one of the underlying reasons that effects-laden shows produced in the USA are almost without exception shot on film. To remove 3/2 pulldown to execute digital effects and then reinstate it is a very easy piece of maths and is built in to all self-respecting effects software.

There is one other digital disparity between the NTSC and phase alternation line (PAL) regions. A digital broadcast frame in the PAL 625 world is 720 × 576 pixels whereas in the NTSC 525 world it is 720 × 480 pixels. Unfortunately, for historical reasons, the pixels in TV systems are not square as they are throughout the rest of the computer world. Maintaining the height, which is related to the number of lines and is therefore fixed, a 4 × 3 aspect ratio image with square pixels would have 768 × 576 or 640 × 480 pixels, respectively. The first thing to note is that this means the 625 world has landscape-shaped pixels and the 525 world has portrait-shaped pixels. If transferred directly to a computer graphics program which does not have support for broadcast TV-shaped pixels then the image will be distorted by being squeezed horizontally for 625 or expanded horizontally for 525. As long as the work, once completed, is converted straight back to video, then opposing alterations in the apparent geometry of the image will be applied and all will look fine. However, if the image is to proceed to another world such as film or print, then compensation will be necessary and the image converted to 768 or 640 width, respectively, before commencing work. The shape of the pixels matters not a jot to the main unit but to a VFX artist using a program such as Photoshop to create mattes this is a very important consideration if everything is going to fit! One last word on international standards. The temporal conversion necessary to move from 50 fps to 59.94, plus the resolution alteration between 525 and 625 lines when interchanging broadcast programmes between the NTSC and PAL worlds, really does mess up the pictures. If effects are to be produced on a co-production the work should always be completed within one system and then the final composite converted. Attempting to achieve worthwhile effects work on standards-converted material is an almost impossible task and should be avoided at all costs.

Having said all of this, special new cameras are being developed primarily for use in the electronic acquisition of images for cinema use. These cameras, typified by the so-called 24P cameras such as made by Sony and Panasonic, use a different method of capturing the image produced by the CCD sensor in the camera. Instead of reading out the image captured for every field they collect the entire frame in one sweep. This system is known as 'progressive' scan because it scans all of the lines in one continuous pass rather than the two used by interlace systems. For viewing purposes the lines are split into two fields but, like film which has been telecined, their fields represent the same moment in time.

At the time of writing a number of features including a *Star Wars* film have been produced using these cameras and there are also some episodic television productions using the system. For effects work these cameras combine many of the best aspects of both film and video. They have the low noise and stability of video and the synchronous fields of film. They also have much better resolution than standard video although not quite that of 35 mm film. They still lack the contrast and colour range of film but, particularly in productions destined for TV use, this could be an acceptable compromise to gain many of the advantages discussed in this book.

Finally, video has a number of additional advantages for effects work. The signal is already electronic and therefore can be viewed on the set using a high quality picture monitor. It also means that there is one less stage of post-production (film has to be telecined). For certain types of effect, live tests can be made on set as the scene is being shot, so, for example, it would be possible to see a blue screen composite while shooting the foreground element. For long takes or lock-off situations the much longer running times of tapes over film magazines could be an advantage. Where really long periods of recording are required (such as in time lapse), particularly in inhospitable conditions, the output can be fed to an offboard recorder situated somewhere warm and safe and where the largest tapes can be used.

Conclusion

Film and video are both eminently useable for VFX, but currently for both TV and Film projects, 'film' still has the edge because of its higher resolution and colour characteristics. For work requiring other than normal shooting speeds, and for imagery which is going to be heavily manipulated in post, film is the best choice, although the new progressive scan cameras are an increasingly creditable option.

1 Introduction

Stocks and formats

In normal production the choice of a shooting medium is often seen as a major creative decision and given considerable thought. The job of VFX is invisibly to match the 'look' of the material with which it is being intercut, and yet, for technical reasons, it may be necessary to employ a different format from the main unit to achieve this purpose. Thus, for example, a production being shot on super16 film may be better served by having its blue screen sequences produced on 35 mm film. There are a number of technical reasons for this which are explained below, but just consider that in analogue systems such as film and (non-digital) video, every time the image is copied its quality drops. 16 mm film has a very small frame size and has to be enlarged quite considerably even for television use. This results in grain which is just this side of acceptable under normal circumstances, but the slightest additional reduction in quality can result in very obvious grain and loss of resolution. Even if done digitally the process of digitizing the film and then recording it out to film again can result in an alteration in the 'look' of the image compared with the original negative with which it is being cut. However, if 35 mm is being used, with its far superior image quality, then at the end of the chain it can be optically reduced to 16 mm, making the in-between processes apparently invisible.

There are too many processes and formats in both the video and film domains to cover in detail, but the main types and most popular systems are looked at in the following sections.

Film formats

The quality of a film image (for a given stock) is determined by the size of the frame and the number and accuracy of the perforations. The size of frame is determined by the width of the film strip and the proportions of the frame within it. The larger a frame, the less it needs to be enlarged for any given size of screen. In effects work it will often be required to use a larger frame area than the principal photography to compensate for the losses inherent in any special processes which may be used (such as using only part of the whole frame to allow stabilization work).

65/70 mm

This is the largest film size and used horizontally (with the frames side by side like still film) is best known as IMAX (or 15 perf). This format is so difficult to spool fast enough, that it has to be carried along on a bed of air for projection. It is mainly used in the theme park industry and is not really suitable for effects work given the mechanical problems of physically handling it, as well as the enormous amount of data storage it requires per frame, if manipulated digitally. Effects work for IMAX tends to be shot in a lesser format and enlarged, since there are only a couple of digital film recorders, worldwide, capable of scanning it.

The more conventional systems utilize 65 mm film travelling vertically, with the frames one above the other. This system was originally developed for the

TODD-AO process and is sometimes referred to as 5-perf because it has five sprocket holes on both sides per frame. Projection film is 70 mm wide with an extra 2.5 mm on the outside of the perfs to accommodate the magnetic stripe soundtracks used in the original system. This configuration produces a much bigger frame than 35 mm and was for a long time very popular as a means of capturing high quality images for effects purposes. Towards the end of its heyday some cameras were modified to accept 70 mm film so that camera movement data and other information could be recorded on the magnetic stripes available on the wider film. The main downfall of this format for effects is the small number of film stocks available, laboratories and other facilities to process it.

35 mm (flat/4 perf)

35 mm is of course the standard used by the motion picture industry throughout the world since the early 1900s. From an effects point of view the great advantage is that 35 mm is a complete system rather than just simply a single stock size. Because of its tremendous popularity and user base (including other industries such as science and the military, in addition to the film industry) 35 mm film is produced by a wider range of manufacturers and with a much greater range of stocks than any other format. As a result of this there are more film laboratories able to process 35 mm than any other format and there are specialist facilities who operate exotic processes not available in any other system. All of these factors are very important to VFX work since its demands are so wide and varied.

The precision possible with 35 mm beats any other system. This is mainly because its specification has been carefully honed for each specific use to which it may be put. In ordinary main unit photography this may not be a big deal, but for VFX it is an essential part of the equation. The perforations in negative stocks are designed to tightly fit the pull down claw and, if there are any, the 'pilot' or 'registration' pins which hold the film firmly in position for exposure. These perforations have squared-off corners and are designed to be tightly held for maximum steadiness. This type of sprocket hole or perforation is called 'B&H' after the Bell and Howell Company or simply 'tight fitting' or 'neg-perf'. Neg-perfs are easily damaged by ill-maintained equipment and are pretty delicate, but negatives normally will be run only a few times through carefully maintained cameras, laboratory equipment, telecines or scanners.

Not so the print material which is expected to be projected 150 times or more on equipment which may not be treated with the same love and care as a highly valued camera. So, to combat this different scenario, print stocks have 'KS' or Kodak Standard perforations which are designed to be as robust as possible. They do not fit tightly to the pins and have rounded corners to help guide badly worn claws into place. The result of this is 'weave', where the film is able to move around on the pins holding it. In a darkened cinema this is not a major issue but for effects purposes it is totally unacceptable. Where prints are specially required to be steady in telecine or scanning, then it is possible to order up print material which has been punched with 'neg-perfs'. This is a special order from the manufacturer and needs to be checked out well in advance to ensure a local supply is in place.

Through the years 35 mm has been host to many formats (see chart of sizes below). 'Full' or 'Silent' aperture uses the whole area between the sprocket holes and is four perforations high. This has a 4 × 3 aspect ratio (AR) (or 1.33:1) and was the standard format during the silent cinema era. When optical sound came in the frame was shrunk to allow space down the side for a soundtrack and this became known as Academy. The aspect ratio was maintained with the slight variant of 1.37:1.

Format	Dimensions	AR	Sound	Perfs
Full aperture	0.980 × 0.735	1.33:1	N	4
Academy	0.866 × 0.630	1.37:1	Y	4
WideScreen	0.945 × 0.511	1.85:1	Y	4
VistaVision	1.485 × 0.981	1.5:1	N	8
'Scope (2:1 squeeze)	0.866 × 0.732	2.35:1	Y	4

When widescreen systems were created the ratio was narrowed to 1.66:1 and then finally to the current 1.85:1. The quality of the image on screen remained much the same through these reductions in frame size since over the years the resolution and grain have been improved. Television is now standard-izing on 16 × 9 (1.78:1). Masking the negative or restricting the film 'gate' creates all of these ratios but of course the film is still the same size and so the frame is merely surrounded by a 'lot of black'. Many productions simply frame for the chosen ratio but shoot inside a standard Academy mask. For VFX it is highly recommended that so-called 'open gate' or silent aperture is used to allow maximum flexibility in reframing and to minimize grain. This may incur some politics since it will require talking the crew into adjusting for this and furthermore convincing the telecine or scanner personnel to alter their hard-ware and settings to capture the whole frame. But the improvement in quality and flexibility in reframing is well worth it. For instance, consider a blue screen sequence where the artiste is to be shown flying and they will be zoomed around by digital manipulation afterwards. If the actor's arms momentarily go out of frame within the chosen take, but the camera is running in open gate, then the shot can probably be rescued by reframing using the extra area of image contained in the whole negative area.

For all television and most cinema work 35 mm is an excellent medium with a certain amount of redundancy. To capture the full image quality and content of this format it needs to be scanned at 14 bit/log and approximately 4k resolution (see page 216). This is equivalent to a massive amount of data and would result in a whopping 64 MB per frame or 1.5 GB/s, which even today would be hard work. For this reason most feature film work is tackled at 10 bit/log 2k (less than half its actual resolution) as a compromise between quality and practicality. The argument goes that the actual print quality is way below the theoretical negative quality and therefore a compromise can be acceptable. For television use 35 mm is often simply telecined at the standard TV resolution of 720 × 576 (720 × 480 in the USA) even though this is considerably less than the film's real spec. This higher quality is seen as desirable since it visibly produces a better picture even when displayed on lower quality equipment, provides excellent future proofing and of course supplies the quality necessary for VFX if the production involves this requirement.

To summarize, 35 mm provides the best resolution, flexibility in post-production manipulation, steadiness and range of emulsions currently available to the film and television visual effects industry.

35 mm (8-perf/vistaVision)

Where conventional 35 mm film moves vertically through the camera at four perforations per frame, 'vistaVision' goes horizontally at eight perfs per frame. This system was briefly a mainstream format during the widescreen craze of the 1950s but fell out of favour because it required special cameras, lenses and post-production processes. Because of its superior quality, in the form of a much larger frame area, it has subsequently been rediscovered by the VFX industry for shooting 'plates' or background material to be combined with other images. By using the larger frame it ensures that if any quality is lost during the post-production it will at worst deteriorate to only that of standard 35 mm and therefore, when combined with it, will go undetected. As an example, if backgrounds are going to be projected behind artistes on a stage then a vistaVision image could manage a larger, brighter and better-resolved image than standard 35 mm. 8-perf scores over other large formats such as 65 mm by having the full range of stocks and processing facilities of 35 mm yet still providing a frame almost as large. VistaVision is approximately the same size and shape as the 35 mm still photography frame and modified still cameras have sometimes been used for shooting the format. For this same reason it can take advantage of the huge number of lenses designed for still image cameras since it shares the same field size.

35 mm anamorphic (cinemaScope, panavision 35, etc.)

This system uses an anamorphic (cylindrical) lens to squeeze the image by a ratio of (usually) 2:1. When projected, a de-anamorphosing lens is used to expand it up again. This results in a massively wide screen image. When first developed as cinemaScope the process used the whole available open gate area and therefore produced an aspect ratio of 2.65:1 (approximately) or double the standard 1.33:1 ratio. This was possible because the soundtracks were carried on a magnetic stripe along the film edge. Subsequently when theatre owners were unwilling to install the expensive new sound equipment this required, the optical track was restored, thus cutting down the width to a screen ratio of 2.35:1 (approximately). This is still the ratio of the system today.

Obviously the area of negative employed is much larger than say a 1.85:1 ratio flat recording on 35 mm, so it gives a much improved resolution. The system offers less depth of field than 'flat' 35 mm and small out of focus spots of light show up as ovals instead of the circles created when using conventional lenses. For VFX work, particularly for television, this format has a particular interest especially when used in its original full frame configuration. By shooting with a large high quality frame of width 2.65:1 a standard TV frame of 1.33:1 can be panned across it. Thus, for low budget composites, a static wide angle can be shot in 'Scope and then, in the studio, shoot a panning shot on blue screen which can be combined with it (see figure below).

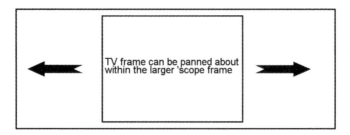

The only pitfall to watch out for when using this technique is any mismatch resulting from the slight distortion of the 'Scope lenses compared with the standard 'flat' lenses used for the other shots.

A very popular shooting variation is 'super35'. This uses conventional 'flat' lenses and the entire 'Full Ap.' frame width to create an image with the 2.35:1 aspect ratio of 'Scope. Before release printing the image is squeezed and resized (optically or digitally) to produce a standard anamorphic negative. For VFX the advantages are a large choice of lenses which are sharper and have more depth of field. The disadvantages are less negative real estate and therefore more grain, not to mention a different look.

16 mm

Outside of work produced by and for the major Hollywood studios 16 mm is the main film format used for drama in world television. Standard 16 mm has a frame size about a quarter of the area of 35 mm. It was originally designed to have sprocket holes down both sides but with just one per frame. Only one camera was ever produced with registration pins and the perforations are only available in KS (i.e., loose fitting). Thus 16 mm is not really suitable for VFX work where a lot of compositing is going to be carried out. Using modern digital stabilizing techniques the weave can be corrected. For more than just a few shots this would be as expensive as switching to 35 mm for just those same shots!

The much vaunted super16 is even worse. In common with standard 16 mm which has sound, super16 only has sprocket holes down one side, the extra space being used to create a widescreen image (see figure opposite); but of course from a VFX point of view it is catastrophic. The film frame becomes a 'flag blowing in the wind' since it is only pegged on one side. Even the latest stabilizing software cannot fix this since the weave will vary across the area of the frame.

16 mm is not even helpful to the VFX supervisor as a destination medium since nobody has film recorders that output to this format. So if the master is going to be in 16 mm then effects to be cut in to it will have to be scanned out to 35 mm and then optically printed down to 16 mm.

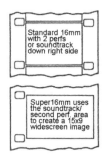

Standard 16mm
with 2 perfs
or soundtrack
down right side

Super16mm uses
the soundtrack/
second perf. area
to create a 15x9
widescreen image

Film stocks

The most spectacular aspect of film is the fact that the recording technology (the emulsion) is carried on the recording medium itself: the film. Thus you can get the benefit of the very latest advances in film imaging by using the newest film stock irrespective of the camera used to expose it. Many film recorders use B&H 2709 cameras to record their images – the latest digital technology – but filmed with cameras made before 1920 and similarly many animation houses are using Mitchell cameras from the early 1920s since these are still the steadiest around.

There is a large choice of film stocks available with varying 'looks' and sensitivities. For VFX the first and foremost aim is to match the look of the main photography with which it will sit. Once the stock used by the main unit has been ascertained it will be necessary to decide if it is practical to use it for VFX purposes or if an alternative must be adopted to match the required 'look'. Higher sensitivity or fast stocks are usually more grainy than their slower, less sensitive relatives but then the slower films are sometimes more contrasty. Each time a piece of film is copied its grain and contrast increase. Depending on the path being followed by the negative to be worked on, it may be necessary to use a slightly finer grained stock for the VFX than is used for the principal photography with which they will have to match. It is often the case that medium speed stocks are most suited to VFX purposes since these tread the line between excessive grain and contrast versus the inconvenience of an insensitive stock when trying to get as much 'stop' as possible, when for instance shooting miniatures.

VFX also make use of special intermediate stocks (see page 109) which are used for duplicating film images.

Stock numbers are deliberately not being mentioned here since they are constantly changing as emulsions are upgraded and improved. Because of this constant evolution it is very important for VFX personnel to keep abreast of the latest stocks particularly since at any given time there may be some unique materials designed for special processes. In the past there has been 5295, which was an incredible stock aimed at blue screen and miniature shooting in particular, and more recently SFX200, which was a specially modified member of the Kodak 'Vision' family designed to eradicate cross-colour fringing in blue and green screen work. This information needs to be checked at the start of every project to make sure that the most appropriate stocks are being used.

As well as special emulsions developed for the VFX industry there are also other exotic stocks often only available on special order. These include infra red,

1 Introduction

reversal, monochrome and low contrast stocks. Knowledge of all these 'special' emulsions can help to put the 'special' in effects.

Video formats

Video and digital formats are completely different from film formats. The size of a videotape has no bearing on its screen quality as would be the case with a film format. This is because the recording medium is used to record an electrical signal rather than a physical picture. The way the image is encoded within the electrical signal determines its quality and specification. Thus for VFX we are not interested in the size of the tape or disk apart from convenience factors. The variables in video recording which do affect the quality of image recorded are whether the system is analogue or digital, component or composite and compressed or uncompressed. The recording speed and capacity determine the quantity that can be recorded on a system.

Analogue systems simply record the video signal as it comes down the line. The electrical wave continuously varies in proportion to the brightness and colour of the image it carries. The signal will rapidly deteriorate each time it is copied and to be used in a digital system it must first be 'sampled' or 'digitized', which in itself will add distortions (or artefacts). For these reasons and others, it is not recommended to use analogue systems for VFX work. Analogue systems include all 1″ formats, Betacam, and semi-pro systems such as u-matic. Betacam SP and MII could be used at a pinch (see below).

Digital systems record a stream of numbers representing the image that is divided up into tiny elements called pixels. Each pixel is allocated a number representing its colour and brightness levels. In an 8 bit system each number can have one of 256 values whereas in a 10 bit system it can have one of 1024 different values. This is referred to as bit depth and determines the tonal and colour density range of which the image is capable. Too low a bit depth and you can see the individual levels as contour lines or 'quantizing', particularly in areas of subtle graduation. Sampling rate, on the other hand, refers to the number of samples taken in a given time and if too low would result in easily perceived steps along the edges of objects in the picture. Staircasing and contouring can both ruin the blending of mattes and also draw audience attention to themselves and thus derail suspension of disbelief. However, the great advantage of a digital system, particularly from an effects perspective, is that in an uncompressed environment it can be copied indefinitely without any reduction in quality. All that is happening is the copying of numbers and either you have them or you do not!

With the image divided up into known elements and each of these represented by a specific number, it is easy to make alterations to the image simply by changing the numbers. This constitutes another major reason to use digital systems for VFX work.

One word of caution, however, in broadcast standard digital systems the full range of 256 values is clipped at both ends for consistency with the analogue system and so extends from 16 to 235. If outputting to non-broadcast systems such as film or print then this range should be extended to fill the full tonal range available before any digital correction or manipulation is applied.

In a composite recording the image is encoded into a single signal whereas a component recording has multiple streams representing separate elements. The most common form of component recording is where the individual levels of the red, green and blue are kept as three separate signals. The problem with a composite image is that it is very difficult to extricate the individual components once they have been 'encoded' or combined to create it. The original advantage was of course that one only had to deal with a single data stream in a composite system, whereas component required three or more transmission paths. A composite system can be likened to 'jam', once the fruit and water and sugar have been combined: it is very difficult indeed to recover them in their original form. This is, however, exactly what VFX requires to be done. For blue screen or matching colours carefully after a complex process has been executed it is essential to be able to access the 'pure' original colours and this is just not possible in a composite system. It is therefore most important that only component systems are used for VFX work and that composite recording is avoided like the plague.

Film is in a sense a component system since the primary colours are recorded on separate layers within the emulsion – indeed the original Technicolor system had three black and white films going through a special camera! When film is scanned by a telecine machine it identifies the levels of the individual colours using three light sensitive sensors (tubes or chips) and after processing outputs separate red and green and blue feeds. These can be recorded directly but in broadcast systems are more likely to be further processed into PAL or NTSC components often referred to as Y U V. This alternative system exists for mainly historical reasons but should be understood as it is still the basis for recording techniques throughout the television industry.

Mimicking the human perception system, there is much more green in most pictures and it carries the majority of detail. For this reason the R and B signals tend to be at a much lower level and when amplified get very noisy. The NTSC and PAL colour systems had to be 'colour compatible', which meant that they still had to work on the millions of black and white televisions which existed at the time colour services started. To do this it was decided to transmit a high-resolution (for the time) black and white signal with a low-resolution colour one superimposed. The early colour cameras had four tubes, three (2/3″) colour and one (1″) black and white. It was soon realized that a synthetic 'luminance' signal was more appropriate so they created it by combining known percentages of the three colour signals and this component was known as 'Y'. The Y was mostly green so, since the percentages were known, it was only necessary to send the red and blue with it, since the green content could easily be recalculated. But R and B were low level noisy signals so it was decided to send Y-R and Y-B instead, since these were much bigger signals and therefore less noisy, but would still permit calculation of the original R G B levels.

When component recorders were first invented it was a natural choice to record these three components since they were already used throughout the broadcast chain. However, since the colour was of a lower bandwidth it was decided to record it at half the quality of the luminance. In the PAL system these are known as Y U (B-Y) and V (R-Y). This was the system adopted in the early analogue component recorders Betacam and MII but the levels were altered and known as $Y C_B$ and C_R. Colour information can be extracted from these systems and a usable chroma key can be generated from a recording made directly from the camera's onboard component recorder. However, it should be remembered that a video camera, like film, generates R G B and this is converted to $Y C_B$ and C_R in its electronics.

When digital video (DV) recorders were first introduced it was decided to continue to use this methodology, meaning that D1 and its various descendants have all adopted this system. Here, once again, the idea of recording colour at a lesser quality than luminance was given a digital twist. The sampling rate for the colour was set at half that of the luminance. Luminance was sampled at four times subcarrier frequency, 13.5 MHz and colour at half this. The formula is represented as 4:2:2. Indeed the original international committee which developed this standard had originally been going to ratify a system that was 4:1:1, which closely represented the relative sharpness of colour and brightness in the human eye and was therefore considered good enough for a transmission system. It was only at the last minute that engineers from the BBC pointed out that for visual effects processes such as blue screen this really was not good enough and the system became 4:2:2.

An understanding of these facts is important for effects workers since 4:2:2 sampling is only just good enough for chroma key and some other colour related activities. 4:1:1 is used in the DV recording systems and so although their general resolution and look is fine they are not really suited to colour-intensive work. Thus DV is fine for backgrounds but not foregrounds.

Special recording systems have been developed which can record 4:4:4 and obviously on a large project (i.e., well financed) with a lot of colour working it may be better to use such a system. But it should be noted that this is a flawed process. The $Y C_B$ and C_R does not reproduce all colours and there are holes in its range. Thus it is possible to produce 'illegal' colours which will not transmit. Worse still, the colours which this system will not reproduce can be created in R G B systems which do not suffer these problems. Computer systems are generally R G B internally and therefore it is possible when converting from the one system to the other that some colours will change or vanish! This colour change will work in both directions and therefore it is very important not to move too often between the systems. Thus, once material has been input to the computer world of R G B it should not be sent back to the broadcaster's $Y C_B C_R$ world until the very end of the work. This means that archiving of computer work cannot be on a D1 or other digital video format but should be on some data backup system.

This discussion shows why film is still so popular for large projects involving lots of effects. It can be telecined and output R G B 4:4:4 direct to the computer world and never be converted to the dirty $Y C_B C_R$ universe until project end.

Analogue/Composite and Digital/Component are not mutually exclusive pairings. There are systems using all combinations. For effects any composite system is a no-go, so therefore, as well as those already mentioned, the digital tape formats D2 and D3 should be avoided since they merely digitize the composite signal. D1, D5 and Digital Betacam are all digital and component so offer the best of both worlds and DV is acceptable for some uses but not really where high quality colour processing is required. The data created in these systems is pretty enormous. European video, for example, is made up of 720×576 pixels, each of which has three bytes of information representing the three components but with two being sampled at half the rate. This gives $720 \times 576 \times (1 + 0.5 + 0.5) = 829440$ bytes or almost a megabyte. To shift or record 25 MB/s is no mean task and therefore it has been necessary to reduce this signal size in some way. The method used is 'compression'. There are two types – lossless compression which doesn't harm the signal and lossy compression which does. Many modern transmissions and recording systems use compression to a greater or lesser degree. Digital Betacam for instance uses 2:1 compression thus halving the quantity of information it must deal with. The tiny DV format uses approximately 5:1 compression. In both of these cases the distortions or artefacts created by this compression are not particularly visible to the human viewer but the ramifications for image processing in VFX are complex.

As long as you stay within one particular scheme, then no more harm will be done, but since these different systems use different mathematical formulae (algorithms) and create different problems, then going between one system and another can create difficulties. For effects purposes it is therefore best to avoid using compression and certainly moving between systems that introduce different schemes. Transferring DV to digital Betacam and then to a computer system and then, say, back to digital Betacam again would be potentially dangerous, particularly if further work were required in the future. As with all effects projects the simple solution is *test, test, test*!

Finally, pure digital recording systems in the form of data recorders have no problems in quality terms. These devices (e.g., DTF and exabyte) are purely 'data buckets': they neither add nor take away anything from the signal – they simply record it in mathematical perfection and disgorge it when commanded so. The only difference between these systems is the cost, the speed and the convenience of the cartridge. Data recorders are not real time, but can often work concurrently whilst other work is being carried out on the workstation from which the information is being extracted. A data bucket neither knows nor cares what the format is which is being sent to it and is therefore completely transparent. This is the method which should always be used for backing up or archiving visual effects shots held on computer systems – it will however rarely match real time.

In conclusion it must be said that, if convenient, 'in progress' VFX work and elements should be held online on some server in the sky – although this will entail large disk arrays. For decent workflow a system must be created which can provide fast and safe access to all the material required and saving of what is newly completed.

Methods of creating visual effects

Effects can be created using a variety of different technological paths. Since the main 'techniques' of VFX are the same in most cases, irrespective of the technology used, these different methodologies will be briefly discussed in this section. In the later technical discussions they will only be referred to where major differences occur.

Effects can be created directly in front of the camera, be it film or electronic. An example would be a 'glass shot' where a camera shoots through a painting, or a rear projection shot where the camera shoots action in front of a projected image.

Film offers an enhancement of this process, which takes advantage of the fact that until a film is processed it can continue to be re-exposed. This technique would, for instance, permit the creation of a split-screen by exposing once with a mask across one half of the lens, and then after rolling the film back to the same starting point, re-exposing the same length of film, but this time with the other half of the lens covered. This depends on the fact that film retains a 'latent' image until it is processed – numerous latent images can be created on one length of film before it is developed and 'fixed'.

Videotape cannot be recorded multiple times but the electronic system does have its own unique technique. Since the electronic signal is instantaneously created and can travel in real time, then it can be passed through special mixing (or switching) equipment, which can modify or combine the images in real time. With two cameras fed to such equipment they could be combined into a split-screen, for instance, which would be instantly visible on any monitors fed with the output, or of course recorded for future use.

All of the above methods are done at the time of shooting, but they can be applied in post-production too. Recorded video images can be replayed through a vision mixing or switching equipment and the result recorded, just as film can be re-photographed multiple times using an 'optical printer'. Needless to say all of the video technologies can be applied to film which has been first transferred to tape via a telecine.

Finally an alternative electronic methodology also exists in the form of digital or computer technology. Here either video or film images are transferred or sampled into digital form and then manipulated or combined using computer software. Unlike most of the electronic systems using tape machines or disks and specially designed hardware these processes do not operate in 'real time' but are far more flexible and open to almost infinite development.

Many VFX processes can be created by all of these technologies. Blue screen for instance can be created for B&W film in a bi-pack camera, live through a vision switcher, in video post-production from a tape or film, in film opticals or in a computer digital system. The techniques of lighting the actors, the blue screen or indeed of shooting the background images would be the same in all cases and for this reason which of the above might be used to combine the elements is not considered in sections on this process.

2 Photography for effects

Camera parameters

The principal tools used in VFX photography are much the same as those employed for the main action camerawork; it is what they are used for that is different. Although an important part of modern film language, and one which does not unduly tax normal production, a moving camera adds significantly to the complexity and expense of effects sequences. For this reason a static camera is assumed throughout this manual up until page 179 where the various techniques used to achieve this are considered in detail.

The lens

The photographer's main resource is the lens and this is no less the case in VFX. Very careful thought must be given to the choice of lens, not just for its conventional variables such as f/stop and speed (maximum aperture) but also to its quality and the effects of the choice further down the line.

Lenses are analogue devices and none of them are perfect. They suffer from a number of distortions and, in particular, the high-quality short-run hand-built lenses crafted for movie cameras are very inconsistent.

All lenses suffer to some degree from the four principal defects of: chromatic distortion, shading, flare and geometric distortion. In normal photography these are usually not a problem and will not be noticed by the casual observer. However, in effects work, images are often combined, making comparison possible and perhaps showing up the differences between lenses.

Chromatic aberrations in most lenses are kept to some specified minimum which will not be intrusive to anyone viewing the image created, however in effects the criteria have to be much tighter. Imagine for instance a lens which focuses light of different colours in slightly different planes. Let us say that our lens causes soft red and blue edges on sharply defined subjects. In our example the subject is an actor standing against a blue screen. On one side there will be blue on the inner edge (see figure below) and on the other side there will be red on the outer edge.

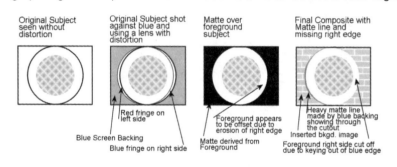

Original Subject seen without distortion

Original Subject shot against blue and using a lens with distortion

Red fringe on left side
Blue Screen Backing
Blue fringe on right side

Matte over foreground subject

Foreground appears to be offset due to erosion of right edge
Matte derived from Foreground

Final Composite with Matte line and missing right edge

Heavy matte line made by blue backing showing through the cutout
Inserted bkgd. image
Foreground right side cut off due to keying out of blue edge

The result of this is that the key detection will 'eat' into the subject on one side and will see imperfect blue down the other. The outcome will be that extra work has to be done to make the blue screen elements composite properly and indeed may culminate in an imperfect result. This is just one example, but it shows how lenses of a much tighter specification are required for effect work. This means careful selection and testing are essential.

Shading can create the same sort of problem with blue, green or any colour of chroma matting screen, since it will cause the colour to be uneven across the background. This can be corrected, but with a cost in time and money. Where a tonal matte is being used shading will create even worse problems.

The biggest headache of all is where the components of a shot are being made on different lenses with different degrees of shading. Let's imagine two elements being combined, where one is shot with a lens which has shading, and the other with a lens which is perfect. When you look at a normal shot made with a lens which has shading and a character walks across it, he will get darker as he moves into the shaded area – but this will not be noticed because the background in that part of frame is itself equally darker. However, if the shot described is created from two images, one with shading which has the actor walk across it, and a background shot with a distortion-free lens, then he will appear to get darker for no apparent reason. An even worse scenario is where a split screen is being made between two shots with these different lenses – the matte line will become visible (see figure below).

aeroplane to be removed by replacing the sky

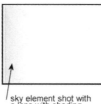
sky element shot with a lens with shading on left side

shading although not too bad on the clean shot shows up the matte line in composite

And this does not just apply to 'real' lenses; in computer-generated backgrounds the virtual lenses are perfect and so a shaded image will show up there too. To deal with this an evenly lit white card should be shot for use by digital post to create an identically shaded 'virtual' lens for the CG image.

Flare is where light bounces around inside the lens and so produces lighter patches – effectively the converse of shading where dark areas are created. All of the same problems occur but additionally flares are often coloured so they can create patches of unwanted colour such as blue in the middle of the subject matter in a blue screen shot. Flare can also cause loss of contrast and detail which again can draw attention to added elements. On the other hand, a romanticized idea of flare is one of the most popular effects to be added over a composite in post, so as to make it appear realistic – e.g., virtual circular flares from a camera looking at an added CG sunset.

Geometric distortion is where straight lines stretching across the frame look curved. This tends to increase with nearness to the edge of frame. Barrel

2 Photography for effects

distortion is a severe example where all lines at the edge of frame appear to be twisted. Again in normal photography this effect usually goes unnoticed but causes major headaches where images need to be combined. If the background is flat, but a blue screen foreground has bad geometric distortion, then as characters move across the floor they will appear to float above or sink into it. Obviously this depends on the shot, and where the image is close in will not matter, but in wide shots where lenses with different geometric aberrations are being used, it will create big problems in matching. Ironically it is in these shorter focal lengths that distortion is more likely to occur. The fact that the small targets in CCD cameras dictate wider lenses for a give angle of view is yet another factor working against video as an acceptable option for VFX photography. Using advanced computer design techniques some 'flat field' lenses have been developed in an attempt to combat this situation but these lenses are expensive and few in number.

The virtual lenses of computer systems are perfect and therefore will never be made to fit with the images from physical lenses (see figure below).

these three images would never be able to sit on top of one another without being heavily modified

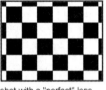  

shot with a "perfect" lens   shot with a lens with severe barrel distortion   shot with a lens with severe pincushion distortion

To match these technologies it is necessary for the computer-generated imaging (CGI) operators either to remove the distortion from the real world lens, or add the same distortion to their virtual camera. In either case this task will be made all the easier if a grid (preferably white on black) is shot with the lens being used for the live action foreground. In post, counter distortions can be added, to even out any unwanted curving in the grid against a 'perfect' comparator.

Combining shots made using distorted lenses with CGI can be easily accomplished by using white cards and grids, to define the inherent distortions, but this will not help to align elements shot using different lenses each with their own characteristics. The problems associated with shooting elements for later combination vary according to the shot. A close up of the star shot against blue screen to be backed by an out of focus waterfall location will not pose any problem even with vastly different lenses. However, on wider shots there are big problems, particularly those which show the actor's feet and therefore mean that the foreground must be 'attached' at all times to the floor.

All or any of the distortions mentioned here could reveal the matte line or cause obvious disparities. The simple answer is to use the same lens, preferably on the same camera, for all the elements of a given composite. This way everything in both halves of the image will be reproduced identically. If it is not possible then the lenses to be used should be of the same type and tested rigorously to ensure they produce similar results. If they have to be of different types, say because different kinds of camera need to be used, then to make the shot work it will probably be necessary to do the compositing digitally, and to give the compositors the necessary references with white card and grids shot for both lenses.

It is not only because of creating matched geometry in elements that are to be combined that the recommendation is to use the same lens. To make composite shots work, the individual elements must match perfectly or give the audience tell-tale clues that something is not as it should be! For this reason focal lengths and focus should match exactly, or the game is up. Imagine, for example, a simple close up of our star behind which a location shot is being added by blue screen. If the foreground is made with a 100 mm lens on 35 mm film, then focused on the artiste, the background would be well out of focus and quite compressed. If the location shot were however made on a 25 mm lens then it would be sharp and pretty wide. The composite would look unconvincing because these two types of characteristic simply do not gel. This is a simple example which could be fixed in post-production by zooming in on the background and defocusing it, but in many circumstances it would not be so easy to sort out.

Even when scaling, the same lens should be used if possible. An example would be where an artiste is to be inserted into a very wide shot of a model street (see figure below). When shooting the actor against blue it is impossible to get the camera back far enough to match the size required by the miniature.

miniature setting   actor shot against blue   foreground size reduced in
but not able to be shot   post-production to fit the
wide enough due to lens   correct perspective of shot
and studio limitations

In this case, as long as the angle is correct and there is plenty of 'air' around the actor, it is better to shoot with the same lens than to put on a wider angle and so get her approximately the correct size. In post it is easy to reduce the actor down to fit, but much more difficult to correct any disparities caused by using different optics.

Finally it should be said that it is generally not appropriate to use zoom lenses for VFX. Owing to the compromises necessary in their design, they suffer badly from distortion and, worse still, they vary as the focal length is changed. For matching, it is almost impossible to reset a zoom to exactly the same settings as it might previously have had, and so this type of equipment is best avoided.

It is important to match all lens variables between elements. This means that focus, depth of field, f/stop and focal length should all match. One of the best ways of determining this information is always to include a reference version of the shot showing an approximation of the intended composite. For example, a 'plate' for rear projection or matting behind an actor back at the studio, could have a person stand in, so that the shot can be properly framed and the correct focus and depth of field will be demonstrated. By doing this, focus will automatically be correctly set, and then the empty shot can be made safely in the knowledge that the degree of softness is right.

The shutter/pulldown system

In a film camera the shutter and pulldown mechanism control the exposure time, the frame rate and motion blur. In a video camera these are the business of the CCD chip (or, in old tube cameras, the scan circuitry). All of these factors are of major significance in the creation of believable VFX.

Film

On most cameras the shutter mechanism consists of a disc which spins between the lens and the film gate at a rate of one complete revolution per frame. This disc is approximately cut in half with one segment allowing light to pass to expose the film and the other half opaque to light and so permitting invisible pulldown of film to the next frame (see figure below).

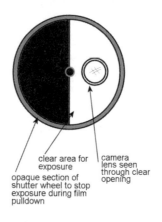

clear area for exposure

camera lens seen through clear opening

opaque section of shutter wheel to stop exposure during film pulldown

By creating this wheel from two metal sections, one behind the other, the size of the opaque section and hence the open section too can be adjusted. Obviously the larger the transparent section the more exposure that can be obtained. If the gap is exactly half of the disc (a 180° shutter) then at 25 fps the exposure will be 1/50th of a second (24 fps = 1/48th). Some cameras go up to 200° shutter angles to enable improved light sensitivity. If the shutter angle were reduced to a 90° angle then exposure would be reduced to 1/100 s and with increasingly small angles the exposure would reduce accordingly. On Mitchell cameras, for example, the angle can be continuously reduced all the way to zero so that a fade-out can be achieved – useful for effects created in-camera.

This faculty of a film camera offers some very useful possibilities to the VFX technician. Firstly it permits exposure to be adjusted without recourse to the f/stop which alters depth of field. This might be important when matching shots made on location in bright sunlight and on the blue screen stage where a large stop is necessary to gain a decent exposure and for some reason neutral density filters cannot be stacked up in sufficient numbers in the daylight shot. It also allows the frame rate to be varied without having to make an adjustment to the f/stop where speed changes are made on shot, e.g., for pyrotechnics or pictorial effect. There are a number of modern cameras that allow this to be programmed in. It does, however, effect blur (see below).

A second aspect of this arrangement is that in some circumstances VFX shots may require control of the relative sharpness of the image. The longer the exposure time the further a moving object will travel and therefore the more blurred it will be. This softness due to movement is known as 'motion blur' and is a major concern of VFX because its presence or absence is a big give away to the realism of a particular shot. If, for instance, we photographed a section of sky and then a jet plane flew through it – on analysis of single frames the plane would be very blurred although in motion it would look fine. On the other hand, if we panned with the plane, analysis would show the background blurred and the plane reasonably sharp.

Now imagine that the plane is a CGI model – if it were seriously sharp it would appear to jitter as it moved across screen and its strange appearance would immediately alert the viewer to something being wrong. The same applies to a stripped-in background behind a real plane. On the other hand, it might be that for a product shot in a commercial, crystal clarity of falling fruit, for example, might be required and this would call for a smaller shutter angle. In stop frame animation these problems become enormous. For more detail see page 42.

In addition to the shutter angle the speed at which film passes through the camera also affects the exposure. At 6 fps exposure will be 1/12th of a second (assuming 180° shutter) or at 120 fps it will be 1/240th of a second. Combining shutter angle with this we could therefore shoot at 6 fps with a 9° shutter and then ramp the speed up to 120 fps with a 180° shutter and see no change in exposure. This would need a lot of light and would result in a serious change in motion blur but does demonstrate the point.

The shooting speed is enormously important to VFX since it basically accommodates the scaling of motion. If you were shooting a miniature car, for a given lens it would obviously have to travel at a slower speed than its full size brother. A 1/10th scale car would appear to be travelling at the same speed as a full size one if it were going at 1 mph instead of 10 mph. This can easily be achieved by moving the model at the appropriate speed and shooting normally. However there are a number of special cases where this does not work.

Natural phenomena such as water and fire behave in exactly the same way whether looking at 2 miles out to sea or two feet across the bath. To scale this correctly it is necessary to run a camera shooting miniatures at a higher speed to compensate for their size and this is dealt with in the section on miniatures below. It should be noted that slowing down by playing video at slower speed (slo-mo) is no substitute for high speed photography which creates extra frames detailing the motion. Extremely sophisticated algorithms are now available in many programs to extrapolate the extra frames which are missing when slowing a shot down digitally. But no matter how good, they are no replacement for material shot at the correct speed in the first place – but they can get you out of a scrape and offer great creativity after the event.

If very sharp images are required at a medium speed (say 120 fps) but it is not practical to achieve the high light levels necessary to shoot with a small stop, then strobe lighting may provide the solution. This is very high intensity short duration light (like a still camera flashgun) which flashes at an assigned speed and can be synchronized with the camera. It is often used for 'product' shots in commercials such as cornflakes, sweets or whatever tumbling through the air. The exposure time may be significantly shorter than the time the shutter is open but very intense for that short burst. On a reflex camera the viewfinder will not see any image unless the strobe is set to run at twice the exposure rate. For composite shots like blue screen, strobe lighting systems such as unilux must not be mixed with conventional continuous output sources. Say a blue screen were lit with normal light and the product moving through frame in front of it were illuminated with high intensity strobe then (see figure below) a motion-blurred silhouette of the subject would cover the backing with a sharp non-motion-blurred image somewhere within the larger silhouette. Keying in this circumstance would be next to impossible.

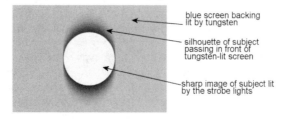

blue screen backing
lit by tungsten

silhouette of subject
passing in front of
tungsten-lit screen

sharp image of subject lit
by the strobe lights

Just as slowing down the scene is accomplished by speeding up the camera and then playing back at normal speed so speeding up the shot is created by slowing down the camera. This, too, is important in VFX because complex shots such as stunts or scenes involving mechanical rigs may have to be shot more slowly and then sped up to make them appear to be happening realistically. An example might be where a character is hit by a moving car. This can all be done at say quarter speed to permit safe and accurate operation of the scene and then sped up again in post-production. This speeding up in post is, of course, just a matter of running the film at the normal speed. Let's say you shoot at quarter speed (6 fps) then, if run at normal projector speed of 24 fps, the shot will have been sped up by a factor of four. Motion blur will be correct because with the action going at quarter speed it will only travel a quarter of the distance per frame than it would at normal speed and since the camera is going at a quarter also, they cancel out.

These days it is so easy to speed up material when using video/digital post-production, a scene such as described above would often be shot at normal speed with the action played at quarter speed and then simply sped up by a factor of four in post. This is tricky, though, because unlike running a film camera slow this method will alter the motion blur. Since the objects are photographed at normal speed their blur will be that of the slow movement they are doing. Even when sped up this will still be much less than that of a faster-moving object. In such circumstances motion blur would have to be added digitally to compensate for the alteration made in shooting. Thus if you can do it, it is still preferable from a realism point of view to shoot at the correct camera speed for the shot. On the other hand to shoot normally or faster than normal and change speed in post is preferred by many because it leaves open the option to experiment and eliminates the need for deciding in advance (or to be uncharitable, of knowing exactly what you are doing!).

For graphical styles these tools are extremely useful and, on music videos for example, offer fantastic creative opportunities. A typical effect is to run the camera at a slower frame rate with widest shutter angle and then in post-production restore it to normal speed by step printing (i.e., if it is shot at 12 fps each frame is printed twice to restore speed to 24 fps). The result is a stuttery appearance but with incredible motion blur, smearing the subject in a most artificial but fluid way.

Finally, shutter and shooting speed become a major issue when shooting special processes such as projection or motion control. In systems involving another frame-based medium it is essential to preserve synchronism between exposures. Thus, for example, if we were projecting an image and then photographing it (as in rear projection) the stationary phase of the projector would have to exactly coincide with the shutter open phase of the camera and the exposure time could not exceed its length. If, as with most projectors set up for this purpose, it did not have a capping shutter then if the camera exposure (i.e., shutter angle) were too long it would catch either/both of the film pulldowns on the projector. If the projector does have a shutter then the two shutters should be precisely phased together.

The same applies to shooting a video monitor. Exposure on the film camera must coincide frame for frame with the scanning of the tube. If synch is slightly out then a dark bar will slowly roll up or down the picture (coinciding with the lines not being picked up by the film). For television use the solution is to shoot at the broadcast speed (e.g., 25 fps in PAL countries) and use a feed of synchs from the video source to control the camera. Shooting other speeds is a complex matter and discussed at length under process projection (page 133). The simplest modern solution is simply to use LCD screens, which have a long decay rate and therefore can be shot at a wide range of speeds without ill effect or, of course, to insert a picture in post-production.

Alternatively systems such as motion control which involve movement raise other problems. If multiple passes are being made with the camera moving

2 Photography for effects

identically on each pass then it is imperative that the shutter wheel be in exact harmony with the move, otherwise when it comes to combine the images they will contain slightly different frames because of parallax (see figure below).

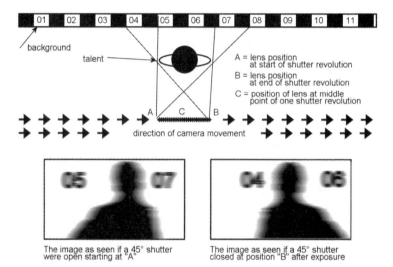

The image as seen if a 45° shutter were open starting at "A"

The image as seen if a 45° shutter closed at position "B" after exposure

Thus a computer-controlled camera must include one axis of control for the shutter position to guarantee that it is coincident at any given point of each pass.

It should be remembered that on reflex cameras what you see through the finder or on the video assist is precisely *not* what you will get. If a gun shot flash is less than 1/50th of a second when shooting at normal speed and you see it in the viewfinder then it will not be recorded on film (see figure below).

TIME LINE	ACTION	CAMERA STATUS
1st 1/50th second light goes to viewfinder	presses trigger	film advancing
2nd 1/50th second light goes to the film gate	gun fires	viewfinder blank
3rd 1/50th second light goes to viewfinder	flash of light	film advancing
4th 1/50th second light goes to the film gate	smoke	viewfinder blank

image as seen in the viewfinder

image actually recorded by the film

Similarly a clear picture from a projection system will almost guarantee that you have nothing on film! This is because the image is fed either to the film or the viewfinder but not both at once!

Video shutter and speed

The CCD (charge coupled device) imager used in modern video cameras works in a totally different way to film. Put simplistically, the light sensitive picture elements (cells) of the CCD chip build up a charge proportional to the level of light falling on them and its duration. At the end of each frame or field's exposure cycle (depending on type of CCD) the charge is shifted away from the exposed chip to the reading system and any residual charge on the chip is flushed clean. Exposure time is therefore based on the period between the end of flushing and the start of shift. Almost all video cameras have a fixed frame rate so there is a maximum time that this period might be – usually pretty close to the frame or field rate (i.e., at 25 fps each field would have almost 1/50th of a second). Faster speeds are possible by shortening the collection period to say 1/100th or even 1/1000th of a second, which might be useful in sports footage to be freeze framed. On some models a physical shutter is required to blank off the light while the charge is shifted away. Since the camera is part of an entire system only specialist machines with their own non-standard recording systems can run at any speed other than the standard broadcast speed for which they are set.

There are a few specialized high-speed systems available for sporting use but they are very expensive and limited in availability. Currently there is one (Panasonic) varispeed HD system available, but it only goes up to a maximum speed of 60 fps (which is its normal running speed). It is this area above all others that has limited the use of video in VFX and, indeed, commercials' production. Speed changes are essential and a system which to all intents and purposes cannot do it, is not really a viable alternative. Although some of the slo-mo and digital varispeed algorithms are very sophisticated they cannot compete with the true varispeed of film systems.

At a pinch where only a small amount of speed up is required it is possible to convert the fields of a video system in to frames. This doubles the number of temporal exposures but of course it does halve the vertical resolution. However, on a busy shot with movement and perhaps pyrotechnics this may be an acceptable compromise, especially if some additional motion blur is added.

Filters and lens attachments

In normal production practice it is common to use additional elements on the front or back of the lens. These are most commonly methods of controlling the colour or resolution. Since VFX are often colour- and/or resolution-dependent for their success, extreme care has to be taken in this area.

Accurate colour is essential in all VFX whether immediately dependent on it or not. For example, blue screen shots must have accurate colour to work at all efficiently, since the quality and saturation of the blue determine how well the key is made, and unbiased non-blue colour on the subject is essential if it is going to sit invisibly into the background image. Processes which are not colour-dependent, such as split screens, also need very pure and precise colour to avoid pinpointing the effect itself (e.g., revealing the existence of the split) or of drawing attention to the effect shot (e.g., not exactly matching the look of the shots on either side of it).

This has a two-pronged effect on the choice of filtration. It demands that film stocks are correctly balanced for the illumination type so that the colour reproduction is as accurate as possible. But, it also insists that filters which deliberately distort colour reproduction should not be used. Thus for instance the use of an '85' filter to balance tungsten film in HMI lighting is essential, particularly in a blue screen scenario, but use of a chocolate or pink grad filter would be totally out of the question.

Obviously it is very important that VFX shots, particularly of the invisible variety, match exactly those surrounding them. Thus if all of the shots in a sequence are made with a chocolate filter then the effects shots themselves should maintain this style and demonstrate a colorimetry slued in exactly the same way. But shooting, say, a blue screen through such a filter would be totally inappropriate if a good key is to be created and therefore we are faced with a dilemma. The solution for all such situations is to shoot completely 'clean' without any distortion and then add a matching colour manipulation in post-production after the effect has been accomplished. In the example of a chocolate filter it should be left off for the blue screen and preferably background photography and then, once the combined image has been created, the chocolate filtration should be added to the entire composite. This has the double advantage of not only allowing maximum quality for the matte process but also of creating the effect across the entire image including the demarcation line between foreground and background and thus contributing to its concealment.

'Shoot clean, add image enhancement after' is one of the major rules of effects photography but it will only work if post-production can successfully emulate the camera effect being deferred. It is therefore extremely important that sufficient information is provided to enable the effect to be recreated in post. To do this, examples of shots with and without the effect should be provided and, with a coloured filter, a reference shot of a white card with and without the effect. These before and after shots should include both the background and foreground elements of the composite as well as any other appropriate scenes. This avoidance of filtration should be taken very seriously since it must be realized that many well made filters actually stop almost all light of a particular wavelength from passing through and therefore the damage cannot be undone in a telecine or scanning bay. For instance a chocolate filter will actually stop a lot of blue light from passing through and so to achieve a blue screen post-production colour grading may not be able to restore an adequate amount of blue since there is nothing there to actually enhance. Remember, filters 'remove' light, they do not add it. A red filter *removes* cyan, it does not add red!

The other popular form of filtration used in principal photography is diffusion. Many cinematographers use this to enhance the 'look' of romantic scenes to help ageing actresses and to 'blow out' in-shot illumination. Although many modern keyers, both hardware and software, are said to be able to deal with soft keys, and indeed despite the fact that keys are often softened to make them more effective, it is not a good idea to shoot scenes to be composited with a softening filter on the lens. Using our example of a blue screen the fact that edges are softened will mean that there will be no definitive setting for the crossover. A soft foreground subject edge will mean that at some point it will be not quite blue enough to key but still bluer than normal, resulting in a range of settings making the matte bigger or smaller but never exact (see figure below).

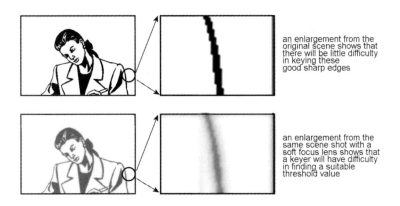

an enlargement from the original scene shows that there will be little difficulty in keying these good sharp edges

an enlargement from the same scene shot with a soft focus lens shows that a keyer will have difficulty in finding a suitable threshold value

As with coloured filtration the best approach is to shoot clean and sharp and then add a matching diffusion across the entire composite once it is combined. More so than in the case of coloured filters, this will do a great job in covering up the join between foreground and background. Even if a reasonable key can be created with a diffused foreground, the relative hardness of the key line compared with the images to be combined, could show up as a strange and unrealistic effect highlighting the subject. A bright light on the background, which would spill across onto the subject if it were really there, would simply stop at the matte line whereas, if combined in post, would cross over just as it would if the entire image were real.

It goes without saying that good reference material should be provided, such as a white grid on black and some shots of bright points of light with and without the diffuser.

Other image enhancements

Just as with filtration any other methods used in principal photography to skew the image should be avoided in the shooting of elements for composite photography. Thus, for example, bleach bypass/ENR/silver retention should not be used when shooting material which is colour-reliant, since the desaturation and colour skewing which might result could endanger the successful execution of the effect. Other chemical processes such as cross and push/pull processing and optical systems such as flashing (in camera or lab) should also be avoided since all of these effects could complicate keying but can be successfully emulated in post-production.

2 Photography for effects

41

Temporal manipulation

The VFX department is often called on to supervise photography that manipulates time. Sometimes it may be temporal distortions specifically defined by the script such as 'the years passed by'. On other occasions visual images requested from the effects department may simply be best produced using such techniques, for example, as 'the flower withered and fell out of the maiden's hand'.

There are three basic 'in camera' techniques involved here: timelapse, where real world time is speeded up (usually very substantially); stop motion, where a synthetic time frame is created (usually for animation); and timeslice, where time is slowed down or completely frozen to allow three-dimensional scrutiny. These techniques are often undertaken by the main crew or by specialists, but also form an important part of the VFX toolkit.

Stop frame/motion animation

One of the best loved and earliest VFX techniques, stop frame animation was used in many of the great effects classics, through *The Lost World* (1925), *King Kong* (1933) and *Clash of the Titans* (1981) to the present day when its techniques are being re-applied to computer graphics such as *Jurassic Park* (1993).

Stop motion photography basically involves an animator taking one frame at a time whilst altering the subject between each exposure. A miniature dinosaur lumbering across a model forest floor could typify this. After a frame is recorded the dinosaur is advanced by one frame's worth of movement and another frame is exposed. Slowly but surely an entire sequence can be built up using this frame by frame procedure.

Extremely well engineered miniatures are required for this process since they must be capable of the smallest most accurate movements and yet be very stable and rigid. Most commonly, stainless steel armatures are built with the necessary movements incorporated into their construction and are then covered over with latex or other pliable materials and finally painted with the necessary textures. However at the other extreme a lot of stop frame animation is also practised using plasticene or clay figures (claymation) which can easily be moulded and distorted from one frame to the next.

Before starting a stop frame sequence it is important to guarantee that nothing apart from the animated subject matter is going to alter. All non-moving lamps and fixtures must be rigidly secured so that neither movement nor its shadows will become apparent. Lamps should all have new bubbles put in them so that there is minimum chance of their colour or brightness deteriorating let alone one blowing during the sequence. A clear path for the animator should be assured and easy access to the frame advance button (preferably on a long chord to avoid touching the camera). The advent of digital post-production has made this work much simpler since it is now perfectly safe to have various rigs and support devices in shot during the animation process which can then be removed in post. For this reason a 'clean plate' (a frame without the animating subject present) should always be supplied to make easy the cleaning up process. If the shot incorporates a move then a motion control camera or field head should be used to permit an identical pass for post-processing.

Since the subject matter in these shots is completely static the image created is crystal sharp and the resultant movie can have a flickery appearance. This is because there is no motion blur as would be expected if the subject were really moving. This can be covered up in three ways. If the camera is moving in the final shot then it is best to make the move whilst the shutter is open. This will create motion blur over the entire image but this will help to cover up the fact that the subject has none of itself. An alternative is to motorize the models and have them make a slight movement during exposure – this has been dubbed 'go-motion' by ILM who first used the technique in *The Empire Strikes Back* (1980) and *Dragonslayer* (1981). Finally, and for stop frame work this is the simplest method, the motion blur can be added in post-production using suitable software. Moving anything on a miniature/stop frame set is perilous so any technique that distances movement from the set has to be a good idea.

Technically stop frame animation is very straightforward. With a film camera a special animation or stop frame motor is all that is required. This is designed to fire the shutter and advance the film by one frame when activated. It has to be set up so that its cycle ends with the shutter closed – once in the correct synch it will stay that way. These motors usually permit multiple frames to be exposed on an activation since for safety reasons some animators like the security of multiple frames for each image. In post-production such sequences require step printing to eliminate duplications.

Video suffers from the problem that the tape cannot be kept against the heads for long periods, so each frame has to be edited on to the end of the sequence. Some DV cameras have an animation mode specially designed to do this, but for most work, the solution is to either let the tape run all the time and pick out the relevant frames, or record on to a hard disk with a computer controlling the system. Some editing programs provide this facility.

Stop frame is a time-consuming and painful technique. It is often not desirable to halt once a shot is underway and it may then take 30 or more hours to complete. The results can, of course, be stunning, as in the films of Ray Harryhausen, but in the modern economic climate this is a technique not popular with producers, and does suffer from some built-in inadequacies such as the rippling effect that is very difficult to avoid in hair, finger prints in clay and how to deal with liquids, aerial effects and so on. But on the other hand the organic control which the animator can apply and the 'touchy feely' nature of the process are much loved by many converts.

It has been said that such techniques are totally superseded by computer graphics, but in actual fact a combination of the two has proved a brilliant solution for certain sorts of shot. Conventional armatures are built but instead of dressing them in say the body of a dinosaur, they are rigged with tiny sensors which can feed any movements made to a computer animation program. Stop frame animators work these physical models as before, but instead of exposing a frame of film after each adjustment, they capture the information describing what they have done. CGI models of the creatures are built, and the stop frame data is then used to control their animation. This permits the expertise of animators to be used, but

2 Photography for effects

gains all of the advantages of using computer models with their superior hair and motion performance.

Timelapse

This technique is effectively an automated version of stop motion, which shoots at a very low but constant frame rate. Instead of shooting studio-based models it is usually used to capture organic motion or natural phenomena. Individual frames are recorded, at pretty normal exposures, but with large intervals in between. The interval could be anything from a few seconds to hours or even days. The concept is to rapidly speed up events otherwise impossible to easily observe, such as a flower growing, blooming, wilting and finally withering, or clouds rapidly speeding by, or the erection of a large building. Sometimes the event can be orchestrated, as in the assembly of a large construction, other times it may be completely uncontrollable, such as the building of a bird's nest.

Although simple in concept and straightforward in theory, timelapse can involve some very complex planning. Firstly the timing of the shot must be determined. Here there are two major considerations, the time the event being recorded will take to complete and the screen time production would like it to fill. Imagine a shot for Euro TV (25 fps) that must last 4 seconds on screen; it will require 100 frames. The time for the event should then be divided by this shot length to estimate the interval between frames. Thus for a plant which has a life cycle of 25 days we should allow a quarter of a day (6 hours) between each frame. This is a nice simple example because our plant is being grown in a greenhouse which is constantly illuminated for the shot. The exposure could be a normal 1/50 second at whatever stop although this would then create a very jerky, steppy result. If a smoother, more flowing and graceful movement is required then perhaps some motion blur should be introduced. This could be done in post-production (preferable) but it could also be achieved with a long exposure time achieved by slow film, small aperture and heavy neutral density filtering (obviously low light would not be good for the plant's growth).

However, if our shot was of a building being erected and it took say 100 days to build then that would mean we would expose just one image per day. Over three months the quality and quantity of light is going to change appreciably and therefore a number of extra decisions shall need to be made. Will exposure be varied or kept constant? If the latter, then the image could take on a shimmering effect as it varies in brightness from frame to frame. But if the former then it should be done by varying exposure time, since changing aperture could affect the look of the shot and it might appear to 'breathe'. The exposure could be adjusted by shutter angle, neutral density filtering or exposure time. All of these could work but involve other decisions depending on the equipment being used and the shooting method adopted (will the camera be attended or completely on auto?). Having made these decisions it is necessary to decide at what part of the day it shall be shot: at the same time each day – which will result in the light appearing to move across the shot, which can be a very nice effect with shadows smoothly wiping across the frame; alternatively it could be calculated to offset the exposure by a daily increment so as to maintain a light level (for example by going half an hour after sunrise).

Other technical issues must also be resolved such as whether a high shutter speed or long exposure time serves the shot best, whether to use any filtration at all and what film speed and colour temperature to use (is the shot day or night, dusk or dawn?).

But above all there is also the complexity of camera placement, lens length and framing. If you are shooting a hole in the ground where a building will eventually appear it will be necessary to decide on how to cover the two radically different extremes – the empty start and filled up end. So, is the camera locked off (most timelapse shots are) and therefore how much room must be left in the top of frame for the building to grow into? This obviously must be calculated with reference to the architect and builders. Alternatively, will the camera be tighter and pan up with the building as it grows. This is very tricky to work out so that a smooth pan will be created. The pan can be made manually by each day tilting up the camera by a predetermined amount previously marked-up on the camera head. The camera could also be motor driven and controlled by either a computer or special mechanism designed for the purpose. Alternatively, it is shot on a wide locked off angle and the frame enlarged to permit movement within it.

Apart from photographic issues, placement and organization of the shot will also have to be dealt with. Where and how can the camera be mounted to gain access to the required image? Will a specially built tower have to be constructed or can the equipment be mounted on an existing structure? What is its exposure to the elements and therefore will it have to be in a sealed weatherproof housing with temperature and/or humidity control? Is easy access possible and, if on film, can reel changes be avoided or, if required, then a system capable of allowing such changes without moving anything will be necessary. If video is being used, will the recording media be at the camera head or at some more hospitable location nearby and more easily accessible?

Finally special arrangements may be necessary for the site operation. In the example above, for instance, with just one frame per day, people would pop on and off in single frames which might not be acceptable. Therefore it might be necessary to agree a certain time each day when the site would be clear – obviously this might predetermine the time of exposure to be in the middle of a meal break or other convenient time.

Timelapse, whether on a large scale, such as depicting a building site, or a small scale, such as recording the life cycle of a chrysalis, can be tackled using a variety of formats and techniques. The most convenient is a film camera controlled by an intervalometer – a specialist control box which manages the variables such as interval between exposures, camera shutter and pulldown. The intervalometer needs to be used in association with a stop frame motor. Most rental companies have suitable models for the camera types they supply.

Video is more of a problem since unlike film the tape cannot be left in contact with the heads for long periods. Thus it is necessary to edit in the single frame recorded at each cue point. To avoid errors such as tape dropout it is customary to record a number of frames for each exposure. Other decisions also need to be made depending on the circumstances of the shot, such as whether to shut down the system between exposures or to leave it in standby and whether the recorder should be at the camera head or remote.

Apart from some DV camcorders which have a built in intervalometer function most cameras and recorders cannot be programmed to do this. Thus a custom controller or computer with special control software will be required to govern the process. A far better approach is to record on to hard disk and for this option a number of editing programs (such as Adobe Premiere) include the necessary control functions and a far superior integrated approach. In cases where the total event time is short – less than 2 hours – then it may be simplest to leave the system recording at normal speed for the duration and then extract the necessary frames during post-production.

It is also possible to use still cameras loaded with large magazines. These can be controlled by an intervalometer and offer the advantage of a much larger frame. Conversely they will have to be transferred to a digital system for assembly into a sequence of matching frames. Registration is not always all it might be in stills cameras although specialist units are available at a 'price'. The advantage of a larger frame for TV use is that a locked off shot can be made and then with appropriate enlargement a move can be added afterwards.

Timelapse can be used for a vast array of subjects to produce both photorealistic sequences such as we have discussed or for surreal or abstract imagery by shooting natural phenomena such as clouds and water or specially created subjects such as growing crystals or other chemical reactions.

Some timelapse assignments are extremely difficult and require a fair degree of expert knowledge. This particularly applies to the areas of macro, micro and insect photography. There are a number of specialists working in this area such as OSF (Oxford Scientific Films) of the UK and it may be best to subcontract this type of work to such companies particularly as they may have the required shot in their extensive libraries.

An additional variation on timelapse is the so-called 'pixillation' in which an artiste is filmed in the same manner as a stop frame model. The technique appears to show a person apparently shooting around the frame in an extremely jittery and incoherent way. This is achieved by recording frames at intervals which may be timed or more usually are manually fired in the same way that stop frame animation is achieved. An example would be for a frame to be taken as the subject jumps, he/she would then move to the next position and jump again during which another frame would be taken. This would be repeated for the character to follow some chosen path and on film or video he/she would appear to jerkily float around 'above' ground. This is not to be confused with pixelation in which the image is broken up into coarse squares of colour as if it were hugely enlarged to show the individual pixels.

Timeslice

Sometimes this is also known as Bullet Time, Frozen Time, Still Array or Timetrack. Although a relatively new technique it employs methods going all the way back to Muybridge (1830–1904) and despite using conventional cameras it is only with the benefit of digital post-production that it has become practical. Initially devised with nature subjects in mind it was embraced by the commercials industry and made world famous by *The Matrix* (1999). Timeslice in its most common form will capture a moment in time using multiple cameras. If these cameras encircle the action then playing one image from each camera in turn will allow the viewer to apparently travel around a frozen subject.

Thus, for example, the scene might show an athlete jump into the air, at which point the image freezes and the camera appears to describe a full 360° circle all the way around him (see figure below).

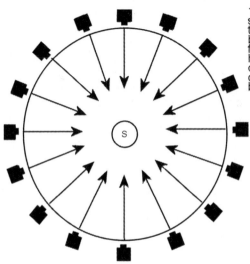

16 Cameras surround the subject "S". To create a timeslice they fire together but will only provide 16 frames or just over half a second - double or treble the number of cameras shown would be more typical.

This effect is created by shooting with an 'array' of lenses – one lens for each frame of the sequence. These lenses may be on separate cameras carefully aligned to match the required viewpoints or be on a specially built camera-rig. The positioning of these lenses must coincide precisely with the physical locations and orientations of the single lens on a movie camera, were it to make the required move in real time without the temporal effect. Indeed if the cameras in the rig were to be fired exactly 1/25th of a second apart then the result should precisely reproduce a conventional track along their path. However, to achieve the bullet time effect, all of the separate lenses must expose their frames at the same instant.

Timeslice is a very effective technique and can produce eye-popping results but it does suffer from some inherent problems. Alignment of the cameras is very difficult and tricky techniques such as the use of laser sights are required if any chance of success is to be assured. Most awkward and dependent on digital post to fix, is the fact that lenses are imperfect analogue devices which do not match one another very accurately. Thus to fit the images together the sequence has to be loaded into a digital effects system and painstakingly each frame has to be manipulated to match those before and after it. The curvature of the lens and other distortions have to be dealt with including exposure variations due to shading. Additionally still cameras do not very accurately align their images and so this will also have to be adjusted too. Finally the actual alignment of the cameras on the subject may be slightly inaccurate and this too will have to be sorted out.

A second problem also plagues timeslice shots with more than just the smallest move and this is the fact that it is almost impossible to avoid having some of the lenses in the view of others. To deal with this the sequence is often shot against blue or green screen with the lenses shooting through small ports or even nets painted in the relevant colour. Again digital post-production comes to the rescue with these intrusions being painted out by hand.

Setting up timeslice shots is a complex and time-consuming job and sorting them out in post is also a difficult and slow process. This results in the shots being necessarily expensive to implement but the results can be terrific. Most commonly stills cameras are used because of their mass production and relatively low cost. They also boast a larger frame that helps in the reframing which will almost inevitably be required. Some systems permit automatic wind-on of all the units whilst others are single shot only. It is quite common to place a film camera at the start and/or end of the array so that one can have normal footage that freezes, tracks around the subject and then recommences normal speed at the end of the sequence. Low cost DV cameras can also be used and have the advantage of capturing every frame throughout the sequence so that the image could change from normal speed to frozen and back again at will, whilst all the time moving around the array. Unfortunately these cameras have extremely poor lenses, require careful synchronization and considerable attention in post to make them match at all reasonably. A number of specialist companies have built special rigs for creating these effects and these offer as their main advantage a slightly faster rig time, although most of them still need substantial sweetening in digital post.

Miniatures

Many effects involve the use of 'models': specially made representations of objects which, for some reason, cannot themselves be used. For example, a cream cake might be required in a motion control (MoCo) pack shot, but would melt under theatrical lighting – so a real-size replica is used. Another MoCo shot might be of an electric shaver, but the actual product is too small, and requires a double- or even triple-sized model to facilitate the required photography. A futuristic city might need to be shown and is built as a model many times smaller than the real thing, or a futuristic car is photographed at one-twelfth scale (i.e., one foot is represented by one inch). All of these examples are 'model' shots, but the last two can also be classified as 'miniatures'. Strictly speaking, miniatures are model shots, but given the special conditions necessary to shoot small-scale subjects it is best to differentiate between the two. Shooting real or giant-sized models employs pretty standard techniques, but dealing with miniatures is a whole different ball game, and therefore, the two should not be confused. Nowadays the question as to whether a large model or a small miniature should be used, has had the third and increasingly popular variant added, of using computer-generated models (see page 239).

When planning to shoot a subject in miniature it is important to nominate a scale correctly. This will always involve a compromise between cost and convenience. The larger the miniature is, the more detailed and perfectly finished it can be, but the more expensive it might be to photograph. A building constructed at one-quarter scale is going to be much more expensive to light and will involve a far bigger backing than one at one-twentieth scale. The smaller scale will simply be much more manageable. However, there comes a point where the cost starts to rise again, as the detailing becomes more difficult at increasingly reduced sizes. Small defects, which would be trivial in quarter scale, become increasingly evident as they grow in size relative to the miniature if its scale is reduced (e.g. to 1/48th size). A further problem is where mechanical or electrical elements are involved. Our 'building', for instance, would have a minimum size if it were to contain its own lighting, since the heat from the lamps would need to either dissipate naturally or have fans to cool it.

Planning must also take into account the practicality of shooting the miniature. A 20 foot square model landscape for instance would not be best built on the studio floor. This would involve everyone crawling around on their hands and knees and make camera placement very difficult, except for extreme high angles. Much better to raise it up on trestles which allows for easy access to the front, back and sides, and from below, to sections in the very middle, access for easy wiring and other service feeds, comfortable working height for operators and simplicity in positioning the camera if it is to shoot at 'ground level' from the edges.

The required behaviour of the model will influence its construction and size. If it is to involve pyrotechnics or water then it must be over a certain minimum size for the effects to appear real. If it is to contain services such as lighting, motors, miniature projection or video screens then it must be large enough to house the necessary equipment. If it is to move then it must be big enough, with sufficient mass to enable the necessary gags to be played. Additionally careful thought must be given as to how a moving model shall be motivated. Will it be animated frame by frame (stop motion), pulled by wires or even be self-powered by having some form of internal mechanism? If the latter, shall it be controlled by wires, by radio or by pre-programming? This choice has ramifications all the way to post-production.

For instance, wire work may be successfully camouflaged on stage, but with digital matte work so efficient it is often more cost effective to have wires in shot during the model photography and then remove them using digital wire removal (see page 234).

Finally the realities of shooting will also affect the model's size. Dependent on the shot's closeness to miniature elements, depth of field and focus will need to be considered. There comes a point when the model is just too small to allow focus to cover it adequately and for the lens to be physically placed in the required position.

Having decided on the scale and design of the miniature, the next stage (following construction, a concern of 'special' effects and not what we are focused on here) is the actual photographic procedure to be used.

As with all branches of visual effects photography the main task is to fool the audience into believing that the miniature is a full size 'real' entity and this comes down to matching. If the miniature is to be combined with live action material, for example a futuristic building to be composited into a real location, or actors to be blue screened into a model, then the 'matching' will entail co-ordinated lighting direction and quality, similar focal length and image qualities such as filtration. If the miniature is a stand-alone shot then it should match our expectations of an equivalent 'real' shot. Whatever the particulars, it must match in with those with which it will be intercut if part of a sequence, and with other similar shots elsewhere in the movie if it is 'standing alone'.

Photographically, matching the look of full-scale scenes is not as easy as it might seem. Unlike, say, blue screen compositing where you can usually employ the same lens, camera and settings, it is not always physically or photographically possible.

The main problem with miniatures is the scaling down of distances and therefore of depth of field (DoF). Let's say we are shooting a model car. The real car is 12 ft long, 18 ft from a wall behind it and with a 25 mm lens we position the camera 15 ft from the front of the car. At f/2.8 and focused on 25 ft this would keep everything in focus from 13 ft to 184 ft, so the whole car and the wall behind would all be in focus. Compare that with a miniature car of one-sixth scale. The car is 2 ft long and the camera is 2¼ ft from it whilst the wall is 3 ft behind. At the same stop of f/2.8 and focused on 2¼ ft we would have a DoF from 2¼ ft to 2¾ ft, which would mean that short of the wall being out of focus so would be most of the car. Increasing the stop to f/12.5 and focusing on 3½ ft would provide the necessary 2¼ ft to 9 ft approximately. This example is using a big model which would require quite a large environment, so realistically, one-twelfth or smaller scale would usually be used.

In this example most of the variables have been kept the same to demonstrate the point – that, with scaling, DoF becomes a major issue. In the real world all of the many variables involved would be considered and employed. It should be noted that to shoot at f/12.5 rather than f/2.8 would require almost five times the exposure. Extra exposure can be obtained by increasing light level, using faster stock (or more gain) or increasing exposure time by running the camera at a slower speed. Faster stock or increased gain will result in more grain or noise and a different look from material shot with the preferred choice and this may not be an acceptable option. Increasing exposure time would be possible on a static shot or using a motion control system if the camera moves, or in a stop motion scenario – it would not work for a scene were there was real time movement. Finally increased light level (usually the chosen option) might not be acceptable for financial reasons or practical considerations, such as the subject not being able to tolerate the consequent heat levels.

A combination of all the above might be considered, plus pulling off any filtration in use and increasing the camera shutter angle if not fully open.

An additional tool is to use wider lenses, although if matching with shots created at full size and more normal focal lengths this too would change the look and could give a clue that something were different. For a given distance setting and stop, all lenses give the same DoF, but since a wider lens gives a wider field of view it is possible to move the camera in to maintain a common subject size. Doing this of course increases perspective and causes the background to appear to be further away. If the set-up is relatively static and controllable then it may be possible to adjust the subject-to-background distance to at least partially compensate for this and also, by bringing them closer together, lessen the DoF necessary to maintain sharpness. Finally, for a given angle of view, wider lenses are necessary when using a light receptor of smaller size. Thus for a given image 16 mm will have more DoF than 35 mm and similarly a 1/3″ CCD will have more DoF than a 2/3″ CCD. In most circumstances this would not be a recommended route, but given that the smaller formats usually come in a smaller form factor too, there could be times when this would be a solution.

Having solved the DoF problems we come to the important question of pictorial matching. The quality of light in the miniature must match that expected of a real scene and yet with smaller subject matter the standard luminaires may suddenly prove problematic. A daylight exterior scene for instance, in the real world, will have a point source (the sun) surrounded by a huge overall soft light (the entire hemisphere of sky). With a small-scale miniature even a 'pup' suddenly becomes a very broad source compared with the sun in the real world, unless it is pulled back a long way which, of course, diminishes its luminosity at the reflective surface. So for miniatures where hard shadows are required either very powerful lamps pulled back a long way or special solutions are needed. If the miniature stage is relatively empty of people it may be negotiable to open the lens on a spot (taking the necessary health and safety issues into consideration – e.g., everyone wearing some sort of eye protection) or to obtain plain (optically flat) glass to replace the lenses in fresnels – although these frequently shatter, so great care must be taken with this option. If a large miniature is in use and the expense can be taken, then an old style arc lamp provides the sort of intensity necessary with a very small source size.

Large areas of softness can obviously be created with light bounced off white reflectors or light punched through diffusion materials such as trace, frost or spun. However, there is a trade-off between the diffusion which cuts down on light output per kilowatt and the intensity necessary to get a deep stop. Multiple evenly spaced out soft sources such as Chinese lanterns or space lights are another way to go, but these can cause soft but still visible multiple shadows – always a give away in studio 'exteriors'. In reconstructing the appearance of exteriors it is essential that all shadows travel in the same direction, so if multiple hard sources do have to be used then this must be carefully attended to. If practical, the easiest solution to realistically lighting miniature exteriors is to shoot them outside under the real sky and sun – sometimes it is even possible to use the real sky as the background.

With small specialized miniatures it may be necessary to extemporize in the selection of light sources. Small low voltage halogen lamps are often pressed into action and for very small hard sources tiny mirrors such as used by dentists or in bird cages can be utilized very effectively by reflecting light from a larger source off set (see figure below).

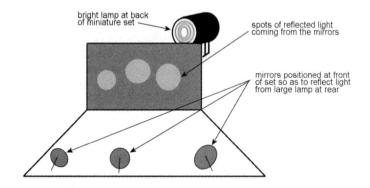

bright lamp at back of miniature set

spots of reflected light coming from the mirrors

mirrors positioned at front of set so as to reflect light from large lamp at rear

Where lights are required within the miniatures, either small lamps such as 'pea' lights can be used or light sourced below the miniature can be conveyed up inside it by either mirrors/reflectors or glass fibre bundles. In dealing with in-built lighting the important factor to balance out is heat versus brightness. Although miniature sets are often created specifically to be burnt down it should only happen when the production team ask for it!!

A final consideration in lighting miniatures is how to accentuate as much as possible the 'mass' and dimensionality of the subject matter. It is important to create strong modelling and decent contrast so as to maximize texture and detail. Flat frontal lighting will simply draw attention to any indefinable but easily discernible clues to the true size of the subject.

Matching the angle that would be expected in a full sized scene is another tricky requirement. Imagine a street scene from a normal human viewpoint at ground level. This might be, for example, around five feet. With a miniature of one-twelfth scale the lens height would drop to five inches and at 1/24th scale the lens would be a mere 2½″ from the base plane. Unless this coincides with the very edge of a model built on a platform it will be very hard to position most film cameras and quite a few video cameras with the lens at this height. A consideration in choosing scale, obviously the larger the model the higher the lens may be positioned from the surface. Where the scale is small, a mirror or inclining prism can help if the angle is not too difficult, but use of such apparatus requires an optical correction in post-production.

If using normal lenses, mirrors or prisms, and the camera needs to pan, then it may be necessary to mount the camera on a nodal point head. The problem is that if the lens is quite large and positioned close to objects within the miniature then when it moves it will actually appear to 'crab' because of a phenomenon called parallax. This is the effect responsible for the fast passage of telegraph poles outside a train window compared with distant cows on the hillside. If you close one eye and pan your head side to side with a finger held out and aligned with a distant object the finger will move across it (see figure below). This is equivalent to a normally balanced camera.

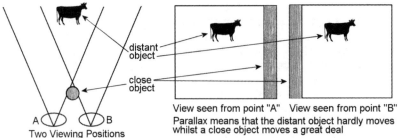

distant object

close object

A   B
Two Viewing Positions

View seen from point "A"   View seen from point "B"
Parallax means that the distant object hardly moves whilst a close object moves a great deal

However, if you do the same exercise but now pan your eyeball without moving your head the two will remain coincident. This is the equivalent of centralizing a camera pan head under the nodal point of the lens. This is the virtual point where the light crosses within the lens and pivoting at it will mean that all objects, whatever their distance from the camera, will remain coincident. Use of nodal point mounted cameras is an important tool in many VFX processes.

For more difficult scenarios where the lens is required to be right inside the miniature and perhaps must also move around within it, some form of optical relay system such as a periscope, endoscope or 'snorkel' will be required. In all of these the principle is similar, with the image being relayed from one end of a tube to the camera at the other end.

In a periscope, mirrors are used with the camera looking sideways either down or into one end of a tube (see figure below).

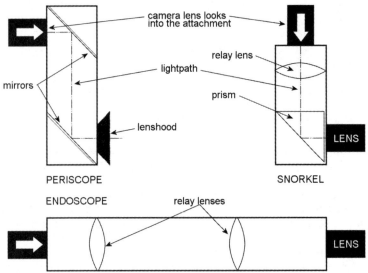

camera lens looks into the attachment

relay lens

lightpath

mirrors

prism

lenshood

LENS

PERISCOPE

SNORKEL

ENDOSCOPE   relay lenses

LENS

2 Photography for effects

53

With an endoscope the optical relay system brings the image from one end of a thin tube to the camera looking down from the other end. In a snorkel (or pitching lens) the camera looks down the tube and receives light optically relayed from a lens at the opposite end and at right angles to the tube (see figure on page 53). In all of these the system permits the camera to be positioned well clear of the miniature (usually suspended above it) and permits the much smaller lens to be closer to the datum and in a much tighter space. These systems usually have very small stops typically larger than T/8. The magnification is so great that the smallest movement will show up, so they need very careful mounting. For the greatest stability and ease of positioning it is usually best to attach the camera to a motion control rig. A major headache when using such rigs is to avoid their shadowing the subject and picking up flares.

Natural phenomena do not scale. Aerial effects such as fog, gravitational effects such as free-fall motion and the movement of water, and physical effects such as fire, all behave in roughly the same way irrespective of the size of the canvas. The presence of any of these in a miniature will significantly affect the shooting method.

The atmosphere contains tiny particles even in the purest of air and these create the aerial perspective through which we see the world. These particles scatter light as it passes through the air and so the further into the distance we look the more diffuse are the details. Thus in a wide exterior scene with distant mountains we would expect them to be slightly more diffuse and indeed lighter than closer objects such as a foreground fence. The problem is that this effect operates in the same way for any 'body of air', and therefore, in a miniature landscape with the mountain ten feet from the fence, you will get the same diffusion effect as generated from ten feet in the 'real' landscape, that is to say none at all. The real mountains are of course diffused by a 2 mile body of air! The absence of this diffusion is a give away, and its synthetic addition to the scene will help tremendously in advancing its believability. With just a simple wide shot, without major foreground elements, then a diffusion filter might be used. However the problem with this approach is that it creates a uniform effect over the whole image.

Real haze will increasingly diffuse the image with distance and is therefore a variable effect. In the theatre this effect can be recreated using a series of gauzes at various distances into the setting. This technique may be used in model photography too, but is obviously dependent on neither the subject, nor the camera moving through the set.

The most useful solution is to use a fog machine, which will create the same conditions as real haze. However, it is important (and difficult) to maintain a constant level and to avoid obvious wafts of smoke drifting across the stage. Thus the best approach is to fill up the studio and try to get the smoke as even as possible and then to constantly top it up. On large complex sets it may be practical to automate this process by having sensors controlling smoke machines which trickle feed the atmosphere; on small sets the secret is to 'wall in' the set with poly (foamcore) or flats and minimize the number of personnel and movement.

Fire and pyrotechnics behave in the same way irrespective of their size. You cannot have miniature fire! Thus to shoot these subjects in a miniature context, for example, a building being blown up, the largest model practical both physically and economically should be used. In smaller-scale scenarios fire, flames and smoke will apparently move more quickly than in a larger-scale context – just imagine the effect of a gust of wind on a small bonfire 6″ high compared with one 6 ft high. To compensate for this it is often necessary to shoot at a higher than normal speed. There is no hard and fast rule here and indeed the context of the fire may dictate a conflicting adjustment, but in general it is best to slow down fire effects by a small amount, such as by shooting at 30–40 fps.

On the other hand, pyrotechnics used in miniatures will often need to be slowed down substantially to see the effect at all. The problem is that with, for instance the blowing up of a building, the mass of wood and masonry will be totally different in a model where a beam of one-sixteenth scale will only weigh one-sixteenth and therefore behave in a totally different manner to the real thing. Here, substantial increases in camera speed are often necessitated. Again the speed change is dependent on the closeness of the shot and so wide shots would typically be at speeds over 100 fps whilst closer shots might be up to 50 per cent more. It should be remembered that it is very easy to chop frames out to speed up a shot in post-production so, if in doubt, shoot at a higher speed (i.e., slowing the shot down more) and then speed it up by the necessary amount in post. Audiences are used to seeing explosions, in particular, at slightly slower than normal speed (so that they can savour the moment) and it is therefore quite acceptable to exaggerate effects of this type.

One important side issue concerning fire/flames in miniatures is that these can be very bright and, particularly if slowed down, can be over-exposed to the point of showing up as just a white hole in the frame. The only way to deal with this is to establish by testing what exposure will best render the fire effect and then lighting the miniature to that level. This could require a higher exposure than might otherwise have been used which, added to the necessity of shooting at higher speeds, means substantial quantities of light could be required.

Like fire, water too cannot be scaled – it behaves the same whether in the bath or the Atlantic Ocean. A large ship moving in the sea would behave in a totally different manner to a small-scale model bobbing about in a fish tank. It is just not possible to produce small waves nor to alter the mass of a miniature. For this reason it is necessary to use as big a model as can be afforded and in the largest tank available. Although there are a variety of tricks such as putting wetting agent into the water to reduce the surface tension and adding detergent to increase white foam these will never cover up the effects of scaling objects related to a water surface. It is absolutely essential to shoot miniatures associated with water at higher speeds and once again testing the specifics of a given shot is essential, since there are so many variables involved. Wind machines, wave machines and dumps (chutes down which large quantities of water may be dropped) will all help to create the necessary atmosphere, and a spillway (low wall over which water constantly flows out) at the back of the shot will avoid the necessity of having to matte-out the back wall of the tank. A blue, green or projection screen, or a painted sky backing may be positioned behind this.

As mentioned the problem of the non-scalability of water is only part of the difficulty and the mass of miniature vessels is equally important. This issue is the same for all types of miniature and is basically dependent on the laws of motion which are consistent for any size of object. Thus gravity works in the same way whether a stunt-artiste is leaping off a full sized building or a marionette is being dropped off a miniature. The fact is that the miniature will have a smaller mass and will be dropping a smaller distance. But motion is dependent on mass and acceleration at a constant speed of 32 ft/s so the scaled miniature would behave in a totally unrealistic way. Similarly, for a model car to move across a miniature setting it will need to have its speed adjusted to appear to be correctly travelling. Fortunately in this case there is a mathematical formula for working out the camera speed necessary for a given scale.

$$\sqrt{\frac{D}{d}} = f$$

where D is the distance travelled in feet for full size, d is the distance travelled in feet for the miniature and f is a factor increase in operating speed.

Thus scale of 1/64 increases speed by ×8 giving 200 fps for television and 1/24 gives a speed of 125 fps which is the maximum speed of most standard film cameras and therefore providing a practical limit scale of 1/24 for most miniatures. Some 16 mm cameras can reach 200 fps but for anything faster than this, specialist cameras such as Photosonics, which can rev up 300 fps and beyond, will be required and involve very costly hire and stock rates.

One last factor which has to be considered in all of this is the situation with motion blur. Shooting at higher speeds automatically results in faster shutter speeds which can give a very jittery effect. Running at a moderate 100 fps produces a shutter speed of 1/200th of a second which will produce a very sharp image with little motion blur compared with that produced at 1/24th of a second. This can only be remedied by using the maximum shutter angle (which won't help much) and adding motion blur in post-production. In many respects shooting at high speed suffers from a number of the problems also found in shooting stop motion at the opposite end of the shooting speed scale!

Visual effects shooting toolkit

Palm-held computer
For rapid calculations of timelapses, angle of view, etc., palm-held computers by Psion, Palm Computing or Handspring running a cinematography software package are essential and can be obtained from either http://www.davideubank.com or http://www.zebra-film.com

Spot meter
This is the best way to check out the evenness of blue or green screens. Reflected light meters are better to use for this than incident models, because of the variable absorption of screen material and the difficulties of accessing all parts of a large screen.

Viewing glass
Tiffen make both blue and green viewing (or, wrongly, 'pan') glasses. These consist of a very dense colour filter which when looked through will instantly

reveal any variations in the density of the screen and also offer the advantage of being very discreet when visiting the set!

Inclinometer
Essential for working out the camera's angle of tilt relative to the horizontal.

Measuring devices
VFX involves a lot of measuring such as to match foreground and background camera positions and for CGI combinations. The simplest of these is a tape measure but since distances may be quite large (e.g., measuring a set) it is good to have the heavy duty sort used on building sites or cricket matches in addition to a small steel tape for checking out individual elements.

A high-tech addition is a laser measuring device such as made by Leica and Bosch. This projects a small red dot and on activation gives a very accurate distance between it and the device. The advantage over the sonic variety is that distances to very thin objects can be rapidly read off. A small white target (plastic, card or even paper) should be carried in case the subject is too dark to reflect or to provide a point where there is nothing to aim at. This device is particularly suited to quickly reading distances between camera (particularly when it is not easily accessible) and various points in the set or when measuring up a large area.

Referencing aids
Mirrored, grey and/or white globes for capturing lighting and reflection references. An off-white card for recording a lens' shading and general colour defects. A white-on-black grid to record lens aberrations such as barrel distortion.

Some fluorescent yellow tennis balls and ping-pong balls to be used as tracking markers – for bigger subjects special constructions will be needed. One-inch white, blue and green camera tape can also be used, particularly for sticking on chroma screens; carry all three – the floor crew will always run out of the one you particularly need!

Still camera
A still camera with a wide-angle lens to take reference stills which can be knitted together to show the whole setting or annotated with measurements. This camera should have a fast lens so that images can be taken in studio lighting conditions without the use of a flash. This is essential if the actual set lighting is to be shown for reference purposes. The best practice is to use film of the same ASA/ISO rating as that being used for the shoot, and then exposing with the stop set by the cameraman – this should get as close as possible to the look which will end up on film or tape. The best film stock is that being used to shoot the movie; a short length can be loaded into a stills cartridge and most labs are happy to process these if alerted in advance.

An alternative or addition to a 'film'-based still camera is a digital camera, which has many advantages such as instant gratification, the ability to load into an on-set computer and do tests, and even e-mail the images back to base. Care should be taken here though, since the resolution and colour may not match the system being used for the 'real' job. On the other hand, digital stills taken on set (and video too) have often been integrated into the final comp!

Documentation

It is essential to record precisely what is being done and how. This information will be a lifeline to the post-production artistes and should be as complete as possible. The best way to guarantee this is to have a set of pre-printed forms that include tick boxes and spaces for all the important data which might be required (see example opposite). Of course the ultimate way for the post team to gain information is to have an on-set representative and this is always to be recommended.

Episode		VFX Shot		Date			
Scene		Element No		Time			
Slate		Preferred Take		Notes by			
Take		Roll No		Storyboard			**VFX DATA**

Shot Information	Setting						INTERIOR	EXTERIOR
	Time of Day	DAY	DARK	DFN	DAWN	DUSK	LOCKED	MOVING
	Director						SOUND	MOS

CAMERA	Camera Body No		Cameraman	
	Speeds FPS		Stock	
	Shutter Speed		Shutter Angle	
	Format		Aspect Ratio	

LENS	Lens No		Type	
	Focal length		f/stop	
	Focus setting		Filter used	

POSITION	Elevation		Subject Dist	
	Inclination		Screen Dist	

VISUAL EFFECTS	Method: (eg: blue screen)	
	Element Description: (eg: fgd)	
	Shot Description: **[DIAGRAM OVERPAGE]**	
	Characters In Shot:	Shot Lgth: (eg: 2/s)

3 Imaging without a camera

Normally the territory of video art and experimental film, abstract and non-representational photography may be requested from a VFX unit. Subject matter requiring this sort of work includes: control, monitoring or futuristic displays within a setting; abstract and biological backgrounds into which actors are matted (e.g., in a dream, or suggesting some future process such as transmutation); to create exaggerated natural phenomena such as clouds or fire; to devise transitional image-bites; or to supply backgrounds for titles.

Imaging without a camera can be defined as image creation systems that do not employ a lens. Photographing ink being dripped into a tank would not fit into this category, but dripping it onto blank film would. Chemical, physical and various electronic techniques can all be utilized in this exotic and usually fun aspect of VFX.

Film

Film images can be created without using a lens, either by direct application onto blank film or by using the chemical processes of exposure and development to create an original photographic image on conventional film stock. In either case the techniques can be employed on a frame basis (making them very similar to stills photography) or ignoring the temporal aspect of film completely and creating a continuous image which will be segmented on display.

Direct application

This process is most commonly executed by hand and does not involve the photographic process at all. Painted or drawn directly onto the film, images can be static or animating on a frame by frame basis, randomly created between frames, or even may ignore the intermittent nature of film entirely.

The simplest method is to use opaque film and scratch away the emulsion to create transparent markings. Different densities and colours of opacity can be created by first exposing the film to various levels and colours of light and then processing. Either specifically drawn elements, which are deliberately planned and animated, can be scored or totally random elements can be scribbled. The film can be wound across serrated elements such as stones or even dragged across the floor and jumped on! The results will give random white flashes against black, like lightning.

The most common technique is to paint directly onto blank transparent film (usually 35 mm or 65 mm). This method was made famous by Norman McClaren and Len Lye in their experimental films. For animation it is necessary to paint each frame separately, the results of which will have a shimmering, pulsing and boiling appearance since it will be impossible to register precisely the figure from one frame to the next, particularly when comparing the 35 mm 'canvas' size of $1'' \times \frac{3}{4}''$ with conventional animation cells of $10'' \times 8''$. Given the nature of the image it should be noted that it is generally not possible to alter a frame once it is painted – apart from totally cutting it out.

There are three basic techniques possible. Opaque inks can be used to produce a purely black or silhouetted image against a bright white ground. Special transparent colour dyes may be used to give full coloured images. The product of either of these techniques may be used as a negative to produce white on black or full colour prints, in complimentary colours to those originally drawn.

There are a variety of methods for applying the paint but, generally speaking, water colour, oil paint, felt tip pens, transparent paints and inks (particularly Chinese stick ink and India ink) may all be used. Oil-based paints may be removed with turpentine but concentrated watercolours based on aniline dyes are the best for photographic materials since they actually sink into the emulsion. Etching inks are also good for eating away coated films but if you use them, make sure that your rulers, pens, etc., are acetate-resistant otherwise they will be dissolved!

Various aids may be used and, by the very nature of the process, will impose their own 'look' on images. For example, stamps may be used to apply the same shape to consecutive frames, or stencils are prepared to define specific areas to be washed or outlined and, if so desired, these can be made quite accurate by punching registration sprocket holes down their sides. This technique was used in the old (pre-1911) Pathecolor process in which black and white film was hand-coloured. Again, this stencil process may be used in effects to hand-colour specific parts of the frame – say, a sky or 'aura'.

Photogrammetry

In stills photography, photograms are typically made by setting semi-transparent or solid objects on raw photographic paper and exposing it, or by creating shadows over a piece of photographic paper during exposure. Exponents of the technique also use multiple exposures, moving light sources and all the tricks available in processing. These are truly photographs created without the use of a camera.

First used by Fox Talbot (photogenic drawing), and pioneered by Christian Schad (Schadographs), it was Moholy-Nagy who termed them 'photograms'. Man Ray, who called them 'rayographs', was first to add motion to the effect in *Retour à la Raison* by sprinkling nails, dust, pins, springs and drawing pins down a length of film and then exposing it – ignoring totally any cinematographic conventions including the necessity of frame bars. On projection the result can be likened to a snow storm of silhouetted objects.

For geometrically more regimented images it is possible to use a reference for frame by frame exposure. This might employ silhouette cut-outs in contact with the film or small shadow-making objects adjacent. Multiple exposures employing vignettes or light stencils and coloured gels (often created using conventional photography) can also be employed, perhaps in combination with projected lights

3 Imaging without a camera

and patterns. Although light stencils may seem a million miles from conventional photography they share many common elements with the humble contact printer through which all cinema films pass prior to being watched!

Chemical applications

It is possible to apply various chemicals to raw or exposed film stock which modify it in an unusual manner. One method used by 'fine artists' is to apply some form of photo-resist (e.g., rubber cement) which limits processing and can subsequently be removed by a solvent. This technique allows a pattern to be pre-determined before exposure, or between exposure and processing, and can produce very peculiar results, particularly at the edges of the resist where partial processing occurs. Other similar methods may be used, including the application of 'fixer' to specific areas of the film, drying it and then, following exposure, processing and fixing the film normally. The pre-fixed areas will, of course, not be affected by processing.

Reducers may be used to 'eat away' areas of the emulsion, for example on the processed negative, to increase density of image or as a positive to decrease density. Subtractive reducers take away silver density all over the image thus changing density but not contrast, whilst proportional reducers decrease image density in proportion to the silver present and thus reduce contrast. Farmer's Reducer (potassium ferricyanide, sodium thiosulphate and water) is the most famous, although more modern commercially produced solutions are also readily available. The unconventional use of Farmer's Reducer is, however, to employ it before processing (or even exposure) to etch away selected areas of the photosensitive emulsion. Those who have experimented with the methodology have proceeded in much the same way as described for painting on film, above.

Non-photographic photography

There are numerous methods of creating images other than by conventional photography and all of them may be used for VFX. The humble photocopier, for instance, can be pressed into service, taking a sequence of images which can then be manually registered and re-photographed onto tape or film. Other image-sensing systems such as thermography (heat imaging) or sonar photography (sound imaging determined by the time it takes pulses to return to the sensor/transmitter following reflection), X-rays and even Kirlian photography may be adopted by the FX department if they fulfil some special pictorial requirement. Kirlian photography is where a high voltage/low current is passed between two metal plates which sandwich the subject matter and a piece of photographic film. The results are very unpredictable, but can be extraordinary, with fuzzy shapes and spectacular lightning bolts across them.

Although they can be very successful, the methods discussed in this section are extremely unpredictable and in our commercial world it is often preferred to create abstract images using a combination of live-action shooting and post-production techniques (such as shooting backlit smoke and then colourizing it afterwards). Although modern methods are seen as more controllable these more touchy-feely effects have the advantage that they often throw up unplanned images which lead to entirely new lines of experiment – this happens more rarely when using flexible software which demands that the user knows exactly what he or she wants.

Video

Abstract and graphical images may be produced in countless ways using video technology. Here, 'video' is treated as analogue picture-making circuits, not to be confused with 'digital' techniques which are those created using computers.

Where the creation of an image on film without using a camera is limited in its usefulness and usually involves time-consuming manual operations which are unrehearsable, video can be manipulated in almost infinite ways and synthesized to fulfil a clearly defined and precise set of requirements. Because video is an electrical signal, it can be created by the use of appropriate circuits.

Designs, particularly for displays, can be created with a barrage of video equipment, most of which exists as standard in the traditional TV studio. The video switcher (vision mixer) contains many tools useful for producing graphical effects. The wipe (shape) generator is designed primarily for wiping between two pictures or combining them in a split screen but, in league with the matte (colour field/background) generator, can produce an almost infinite range of pulsing, sliding or static coloured patterns. The colour generator usually has three knobs controlling its output. The controls can be either primary colours (Red, Blue and Green) or saturation, luminance and hue, which in either case allow any broadcastable colour to be mixed. Most switchers enable their wipe shapes to be modulated and so undulating movements can be introduced also. Even such a simple set-up as a circle wipe with white inside and black outside whilst positioned half way through its range and with a fast spinning modulation could happily sit on background monitors supposedly 'on the blink'.

An advance on the simple colour generator is the so-called colour synthesizer, which is basically a multi-layer matte generator that substitutes chosen colours for selected tonal or chroma levels in a reference image. Thus, if you had a three-level device it could be set so that everything white in the control image would be made red, everything black into blue and everything grey into green. A full-tone black and white image would thus create a very contrasty multicoloured version of itself. These systems usually allow the 'threshold' to be adjusted so that the boundaries are soft or hard and thus, with careful setting, posterized effects are possible in the style of Jimi Hendrix posters. However, with the right subject matter, otherworldly alien landscapes can for example be created, such as those at the end of *2001: A Space Odyssey* (1968). These were created using laboratory techniques but similar effects can be very easily created on a humble vision switcher. If the level controls are 'driven' by sound then the colour can pulse with the drumbeat or other musical elements – this is a somewhat overused element in music videos.

Another piece of equipment found in TV studios which is just made for on-set screen fodder is the character generator or capgen. Although designed to create end credits, subtitles and the like, quite complex animations can be created using these machines and thus can create computer control screens, the data in robot viewpoints or simulations of video camera viewfinder readouts. Although these things can all be done on stand-alone computers, a capgen will be able to do the job very quickly.

VideoSynthesizers were, at one time, quite popular but, like the 'moog' synthesizer in music, have been almost totally displaced by computer systems. The videosynth was conceived as a machine that could paint with light – except it would be on a video screen. This had long been a dream and various units were built in the 1970s and 1980s which attempted to be the video equivalent of audio synthesizers. These devices boasted shape generators, colour generators and 'keying' systems so that many layers of colour could be built up simultaneously. The results were like electronic, and somewhat more controllable, versions of the 'oil' wheels used at discos. Only one mainstream commercial system was produced (by Fairlight) and nowadays these are avidly sought after by collectors. Although expensive and complex these were barely professional systems and are definitely for enthusiasts only.

Digital

Nowadays most image creation that does not use a camera will be done on computers or proprietary digital hardware (which is, in reality, a customized computer system). General-purpose graphics/VFX systems such as Paintbox (Quantel), Inferno (Discreet Logic) and even After Effects (Adobe), running on a humble PC, can create almost any effect that can be thought up. This flexibility is both the extraordinary advantage of these systems as well as their Achilles heel. With an almost infinite versatility the options available are mind-boggling but require user input at every level – the system does not really 'talk back' to the operator. Thus if you are mixing colours, you must choose the desired colour and there is very little or no element of chance. Pouring two pots of paint together on a sheet of glass will create at least some unpredictable results and the chance effects in the swirling, random result could inspire experimentation in a totally new direction. However, the flexibility of such systems does outweigh these considerations and, at any rate, it is always possible to integrate the two approaches by experimenting with some physical elements to get ideas and then photograph or scan them into the system to take advantage of the digital tools. Certainly all of the chemical/electronic effects described above can be emulated in a digital environment and the results may be combined in ways that are just not possible in the world of physical effects.

All types of computer systems can be used to produce non-representational or graphical sequences. Two-dimensional (flat) images can be originated within paint, typography, titling, graphics and animation software. Taking in video or film and manipulating them or combining multiple elements can also be used to generate unrecognizable imagery. Examples might be where graphical shapes are jumped around the screen and blurred, or natural phenomena such as sea waves are warped, distorted and coloured to create vague, indistinct images for background screens in an alien spacecraft or futuristic process. Alternatively, there are all manner of programs or plug-ins for effects software that create random shapes such as Mandelbrot figures.

Finally, the most obvious source of creative computer imaging is full 3D graphics systems such as Alias/Wavefront Maya or 3D Studio Max. This enables three-dimensional models, which are recognizable or totally abstract shapes, hard or soft, mechanical or organic, to be built and then animated to create defined or indistinct images for use in any manner of displays or as backgrounds. The discipline of computer-generated imaging (CGI) is so vast that it exists as an almost separate industry and therefore will not be covered in detail here (see further reading on website page).

3 Imaging without a camera

4　Front of camera

The very earliest and simplest effects were created in the camera. Playing with the actual controls available is the first line of attack. This basically means cranking the camera more slowly for speeded-up motion and more quickly to slow things down. Another option is to open up or close down the iris, thus making light or dark shots, respectively. The remaining control is focus and the only effect possible with this is to make the subject soft. These are the only options using the standard controls of a motion-picture camera.

The next line of attack is to look at the subject pictured by the camera. The simplest trick possible – since it requires no special or additional equipment – is to stop and start the camera on shot and, during the pause, alter the subject in some way. This was the basic technology behind many of Georges Meliés trick films. For example, to make a magician disappear, he acts out his role up to the point of disappearance and, at that moment, everything and everybody that are in frame will freeze. The camera is stopped and the magician exits frame. For a bit of excitement, a pyrotechnic might be positioned where he had been and then, simultaneously, the camera starts running again, the pyro is fired and all the other elements in the scene 'unfreeze'. When the resulting film is viewed the magician will disappear in a puff of smoke. The fact that some of the other elements in frame may move slightly will not be noticed by the audience who are distracted by the small explosion; in magic circles this is known as 'redirection' or 'misdirection' and is an important ingredient of successful VFX too. Obviously, this effect can be done 'in camera' by starting and stopping the film or, in the case of video, by doing a pickup edit. The advantage of this technique is that the result is complete in the rushes and is first generation.

Nowadays, despite these advantages, most people would do the effect as a 'run-on'. In this scenario the camera would be left running and, on cue, the magician would leave frame. Once he was clear, the pyro would be fired. In post-production the middle section of the magician's exit and the pause before the flash effect would be cut out. This technique has the advantage of allowing a choice of exactly in which frame to vanish the magician and which to come in on the explosion. Using the in-camera method does not necessarily guarantee precise co-ordination of these factors. Using video cameras or a video tap on film, it is possible to replay the recorded picture and line up any moveable elements to fit exactly their pre-effect positions. Quite often the replay can be frozen on the last frame of the outgoing shot and the outline of actors, etc., can be drawn on the monitor using felt tip pen or chinagraph pencil. When using this technique, remember to take into account the parallax effect of the thickness of the display's glass – a slight movement of the head can misalign the drawn lines and subject.

This same stop/start technique can be used for all manner of effects. It is possible to move the subjects about in the set so that they appear to jump position and objects can change from one thing to another. For instance, a magician can be seen to put a glass ball in a glass container, make a magic pass at it and, whoosh, it becomes a live rabbit. To achieve this, the camera can be stopped/started or left running and a substitution made. If the latter, then the footage of the assistant dashing in and swapping items can be cut out and, indeed, in post it is always possible to add some sort of flash to cover up the jolt between sections. It is in combining old techniques such as substitution with new techniques such as digital manipulation that quite sophisticated script requirements can be achieved economically and efficiently.

Substitution tricks effectively fit into the 'speed' classification because they involve use of the camera or video tape recorder (VTR) motor by slowing down to a speed of zero and then speeding up again. All other simple front-of-camera effects depend on the use of additions to the basic camera. These effects date back to the start of cinema but are still every bit as effective today using the latest digital imaging systems. They involve physical additions which go in front of (or in some cases behind) the lens. In all cases, when looking through the camera (assuming it has through-lens viewing, as in reflex and rackover cameras) the effect can be viewed live. All front-of-lens effects share the advantages of first generation results and the completed effect being visible on replay or rushes. These effects are not dependent on expensive post-production manipulation, although like all modern work they can easily be combined with it.

Optical effects

Not to be confused with laboratory effects done on an optical printer these use optical attachments which go in front of the lens. The intention of such apparatus is to modify the light path between subject and lens. There are many such accessories available for hire or purchase but frequently they will be constructed for a particular shot.

The rotating lens is a typical example of this family. Using internal mirrors or prisms it fits in front of the normal lens and, when activated, gives the same effect as if the camera were rotated around the optical axis. The advantage is that the lens can be just slotted in front of the camera rather than dealing with the considerable problems of physically rotating the camera which, even if it were small and light, causes problems for any connecting cables or for monitoring the image.

Such equipment can be used for either static shots that need to be made at one or more strange angles (e.g., upside down) or those where the image actually rotates during the take. Disadvantages of this system are that there will be a limit to how wide-angled the camera lens can be, there can be vibrations in the image and, in most cases, the results will be slightly soft. If the shot is seen only in motion, the resolution problem can often be ignored, as can minor vibrations. As with so many of these 'old' techniques the effect can be achieved quite easily in post-production but, irrespective of the focal length used, the image will need to be zoomed in slightly (to avoid seeing black borders as it rotates past the 90° position). This results in a slightly tighter shot and some loss of resolution (just like the optical effect!). The camera lens can have a zoom and may zoom in whilst the image is being rotated in either the optical or post-production methods.

Like all effects this can be combined with other effects, such as filming an actor lying on a blue screen via a rotating lens. If the camera starts in close and zooms out whilst the image is rotated, and the artiste extends his arms and legs, then, with a static background looking down a cliff side, we will get the classic shot of a character falling to his unseemly death. Rotating lenses come in various sizes and with either manual or motorized control. Assume a fair amount of light loss.

Kaleidoscope and tunnel lenses can be used for a variety of effects. In both cases the 'lens' uses one or more mirrored elements to distort part or all of the image.

In a tunnel lens a long tube is attached to the lens and the inner wall covered with a reflecting material. Looking down the tube we will see an extremely distorted version of the scene at the end of it, with a circular 'normal' window on the scene in the middle. Colours and movements in the subject will be reflected in the distorted barrel section, and the size and sharpness of the demarcation line will depend on how far the taking lens is zoomed in. As with all of these attachments the normal lens may be zoomed during the shot.

Kaleidoscopic lenses employ three or more mirrors to produce a multifaceted graphical effect, with the repeated images being made up of the subject on which the lens is focused variously inverted or reversed. Multi-image attachments can be either of two kinds: lenses or prisms. In the former type small negative lenses are inset into a larger positive lens (see figure below) and in prisms a positive lens has facets cut into it so that it effectively becomes a multifaceted prism. The number of inset images is determined by the number of lenslets and the amount by which the taking lens is zoomed in.

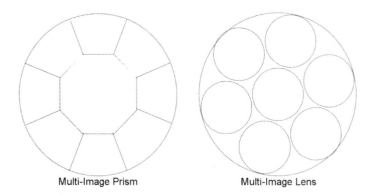

Multi-Image Prism   Multi-Image Lens

These multiple imaged effects are used in montages and dream sequences to represent the viewpoint of the mentally ill, aliens or robots. They are also frequently used as background for titles and, in the case of the multi-image lens, to represent (probably wrongly) the image seen by a fly.

There are two types of 'fisheye' lens: one where the optics are designed to fill the image format, usually referred to as an extreme wide lens, and the other where it is circular and surrounded with black (see figure below).

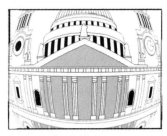

Extreme Wide Angle   Fisheye Lens

Where the fisheye (or bugeye) is an attachment it is possible to zoom in or out from the image circle and even to make it reduce right down to a small distant disc which can be even further reduced in post. These lenses are particularly useful for capturing on-set reference material for the post-production crew.

Despite manufacturers putting all their efforts and millions of dollars in R&D into creating the most colour-accurate, flare-free and sharpest lenses possible, an entire category of attachments is directed towards doing quite the opposite. It is often a script requirement to show the image of a damaged mind, one coming out of unconsciousness, sinking into it, or simply the view of someone who has lost their glasses. This is a convention frequently used because it tells the audience visually when it is seeing the character's viewpoint.

A very popular way of distorting the image is to use a 'cylindrical' lens, which basically squashes the image across one axis. This lens is basic to the construction of the anamorphic optics used in widescreen systems. 'Scope lenses have the advantage of superior corrected optics and therefore the image, though distorted, will still have good resolution and colorimetry. Basically the trick is to use one of these lenses if the film is not an anamorphic widescreen production, in which case everything will appear squashed when displayed without the use of correction. However, if the production is itself in 'Scope then the trick is to take off the anamorphic lens for the effects shots. This will result in these shots being expanded to double width when corrected for viewing. This was particularly effective in Robert Wise's *The Haunting* (1963).

Instead of a cylindrical lens a prism can be used – this will have a similar effect, although the degree of distortion can be varied by altering the angle of the prism to the lens. This type of attachment will also result in chromatic and geometrical aberrations, not to mention varying focus. Colour fringing of a similar type but without the geometrical distortion can be achieved using a diffraction grating (disc). This is a thin piece of plastic or glass with very fine lines etched across it, somewhat like the construction of a star filter. The hills and valleys of the grooves act as small prisms and hence the colour will be broken up into rainbow-like halos around brighter areas of the picture.

One additional device which can be used with many of these attachments is a filter rotator or motorizer. Usually electrically driven, this allows such optical devices as kaleidoscopes or multiple lenses to be rotated in front of the standard lens viewing them.

For all of these effects it must be said that, particularly where the image needs to be 'weirdly' distorted, it is possible to stick anything on the front of the lens. Beer glasses, old flower bowls, beautifully faceted crystal decanters – they can all produce the most beautiful effects and have done so. Customized attachments can also be made such as by taking Perspex and immersing it in hot water until it becomes pliable and then bending it into a shape which produces the desired effect. It should be remembered, though, that if any of these devices are to be used in conjunction with compositing effects such as blue screen then they should be tested first. Most will make the subject's edges too soft to key properly and therefore it would be better to shoot clean and then add a similar-looking effect after the compositing has been done.

Filtration

Although the use of coloured and diffusion filters are a standard part of photography, whether it is for effects or not, they can, like most things, be customized both in design and use to produce much more specialized effects. It might be, for instance, that extreme diffusion of image and colour is required – way beyond that which would be permissible in normal photography. An example might be where alien creatures which are made up of light energy are required in a scene for a very low-budget sci-fi series. Small lights on the ends of black sticks, shot against black drapes, could be animated by the operator holding the assembly and composited over the main action. But just mere flashing lights would be a bit uninteresting, so a very heavy filter could be made up to diffuse the lights and give them a totally unique appearance. For example, a thin piece of Perspex or transparent gel could have quite thick lines drawn across it with coloured felt tip pens. As long as these would be soft when looked through by a camera then the resulting blurred explosions when the light flashed would be very unusual once added to a completely sharp and otherwise normal scene.

In the discussion of miniatures we have seen how important aerial diffusion is. Special ways of applying diffusion in varying degrees to different parts of the image are a useful effects technique. Often for effects purposes it is more useful to use smoke, with its variation in density with distance, than a conventional fog filter. It may also be that an effect works best when confined to a specific area of frame. For example, in a teleportation scene we might wish to see the traveller go stand on a dais, a beam of light comes up, the image burns out, goes soft and then the figure vanishes. Here we might have some smoke in the setting. The artiste enters frame and goes to the dais at which point a bright spot comes on and beams down from above. It is shown up by the smoke and its intensity is increased till it blows out. We now quickly slip in a diffusion filter cut to fit just over the teleport area, the light is dimmed partially and then is faded up again to full power. The actor now leaps out of frame and once the frame is empty lighting is faded out again. Now, with the two pauses, where the filter is inserted and the artiste clears the set cut out, we can cross-fade from the first section to the second and then to the third for what, on screen, looks like quite a complex overall effect.

Selective filtering is best done by fixing small sections of gelatine filter to glass or by applying a diffusing material such as Vaseline. There are two extremes in this technique. Either the filter is very close to the lens so that the filter and demarcation line are totally out of focus or a large sheet of glass is used and placed such that it is in focus as well as the scene viewed through it. In this case the filter material will be much larger and will have to be accurately cut out to fit the element with which it must coincide (see figure below).

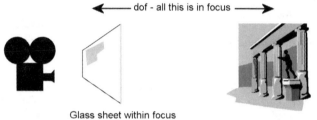

←——— dof - all this is in focus ———→

Camera   Glass sheet within focus and with filter stuck to surface   Distant scene also in focus

When using this technique it is important to make sure that no stray light is hitting the sheet of glass, as this could illuminate dust or marks and also may cause flares. It should also be very carefully checked for reflections and, if necessary, have a black tent built around it and the camera, with support and operators covered in black. Needless to say, the clear portions of the glass should be spotless and blemish-free. Finally both camera and glass should be rigid and vibration-free through being both mounted on sturdy bases and having sandbags or stage weights holding them down firmly.

Of course, once we have reached a situation where the filtration is to be on a large glass, it is possible to employ other more accurate and flexible methods. The best is to actually paint the necessary tones on to the glass. This used to be very difficult but now a picture monitor can be placed right beside the glass and the colour effect can be literally painted over the subject whilst looking at the camera image. An example of how this might be used would be where there are perhaps a number of display screens in the set which need colour compensation and which the actors do not cross. It may be easier just to paint colour-compensating transparent paint over these than to 'gel' them up, with all the problems of reflections that can often involve.

Masks and vignettes

All of the techniques considered above have utilized the standard tools and controls of photography. From this point on in the discussion the procedures being considered are outside of standard technique and will create images that boast additional features above those built into the setting or locations.

Early film making was influenced by Victorian stills photography. As with painting before it, the early photographer was not bound by a particular size or shape of image. Indeed many early photographs were presented in oval or circular frames or, whilst in a rectangular frame, the actual image was printed in a soft oval area within it. Such soft-edged borders were known as vignettes. It was only in later years that industrial methods started to dictate that everything should be presented in standardized sizes such as 'quarter plate', 10″ × 8″, etc. Because of the requirements of film distribution/exhibition it had to be standardized right from the start and so was locked into the 4″ × 3″ 35 mm format we still use today.

However, this did not stop cameramen from photographing their subjects according to the styles of the time and, for example, 'vignetting' close-ups around the edges. This could be done by having a card cut into the required shape and brought sufficiently close to the lens to be very soft. This requires a careful calculation to correctly size the vignette to get the right fall off and also offers the choice of a black or white card, to determine whether the subject gets darker or lighter around the edges. An alternative was also developed where, instead of a card, a translucent material would be used so that the image would truly blur at the edges. When black or translucent materials are used it is important to ensure that there is no stray light falling on the camera side – otherwise slight blemishes might be shown up and the illusion of it not being part of the picture would be lost.

When film makers became storytellers these tools were developed beyond their purely decorative origins. There were two uses possible, one was to use the vignette symbolically to provide information and the other was to use it to direct the audience's attention. Masks (i.e., cutouts which were kept in focus) may be used to suggest a keyhole or binoculars by being cut out in those respective shapes (see figure below).

Early use of masks to symbolically represent binoculars and keyholes

Vignettes (soft) or masks (hard) could also be used to concentrate attention on an element in the picture. For example, a triangular mask might be put around a wigwam or the picture made into a long thin rectangle to focus on a lone figure running along a hill top.

When this technique was taken to its logical conclusion the effect would be moved so that, for instance, from a full unmasked frame a circular mask might close in to eventually surround the heroine forlornly clutching her dead child.

This effect is created by having a large iris diaphragm (like the one inside a lens) mounted in front of the camera and adjustable so that the mask can be aligned as required. The effect is known as an 'iris' and the blades can be made of opaque or translucent material and painted any colour. The 'iris in' and 'iris out' became conventions often used at the start and end of a scene but became ubiquitous as the start and end of the movie, to the extent that this technique is used nowadays to suggest 'old' film. However, it should be pointed out that it was used in exactly the same way as the zoom lens is often employed today. It can be argued that the 'iris in' is indeed much closer to the way that the human vision system focuses in on a subject, compared with the optical zoom in, which is something we do not do!

Much more complex shapes and effects can be created by painting them on glass. Once again a small piece of glass close to the camera can produce soft effects and a large pane positioned further away can create sharp. On a panning shot the mask will have to be connected to the camera if it is to move with the shot, or free standing if it is to be fixed to the subject but not the camera. A gun sight, for instance, would be expected to move with the camera whereas a vignette representing an old photograph of a Victorian family is something we would want to zoom through. In the latter example it would be necessary to fit the camera to a nodal point head so that the edges of the vignette did not drift with respect to the subject contained within it.

Vignettes and masks can still be used today, even though there are simple post-production methods of producing much the same shot. However, with physical on-set effects you get a first generation result which can be instantly seen on the set and assessed through the viewfinder. On low-cost productions or student films this may be a major advantage, particularly when time may be more available than cash. Finally, the use of masks even where post-production effects are going to be added may still be necessary. One particular example is used almost daily on sets around the world and this is where additional elements will be added to a set digitally but, within the area to be replaced there is a very bright backlight shining directly toward the camera. This will almost certainly produce a nasty flare and therefore should be masked out. A conventional 'French flag' may not be practical since it can only mask a rectangular area and so a spot of black paint on a sheet of glass in front of the camera might be more suitable.

The glass shot

Otherwise known as the glass painting, Hall Process or (erroneously) glass matte or matte painting, the glass shot takes the mask painted on a sheet of glass to its logical conclusion. We have seen how masks or vignettes painted on glass can add borders and other pictorial embellishments to the picture. The next stage of complexity is to make these additions to the frame representational instead of purely graphic. For example, let's say that we have a wide shot of a farm with fields stretching off into the distance and require a silhouetted fence in the foreground. If the camera is focused on the distant hills then, with a sheet of glass positioned at the hyperfocal distance (near point still in focus when focused on infinity), we can actually paint the piece of fence on to the glass. This is made possible by the two-dimensional quality of motion pictures. So long as nothing passes between the glass and the lens, and the glass is in focus, then an object painted to be the correct size for the scene when viewed through the lens will appear to be actually in that scene. Thus the silhouette of a fence painted on the glass will appear totally believable, even if a cowboy and his horse pass by in the scene beyond (see figure below).

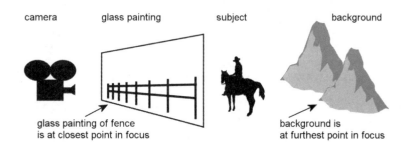

camera   glass painting   subject   background

glass painting of fence
is at closest point in focus

background is
at furthest point in focus

This minor change actually represents a fundamental leap in our effects capability, for now our mask has become a modification to the picture content itself rather than just an external decoration. However, once we have made this philosophical leap it is a small step to move on to creating photorealistic additions to the scene.

The next stage is to light the camera side of our glass and paint details into the image thereon. In the example of the fence we now paint in the texture of the wood and expose it as required to blend in with the scene (see figure below).

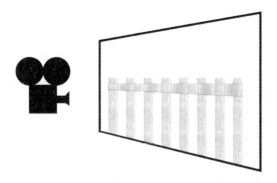

Glass painting is a fundamental technique of VFX and can be applied to the latest digital equipment just as easily as it was to film prior to the First World

War. Basically, if opaque paints are used (or are painted over an opaque base paint) what one is effectively doing is covering over detail in the real image with imaginary additions. This is a replacement technique and is the first of many in the VFX arsenal which permits falsification of real images.

There are three basic situations served by a glass shot. Firstly, it can be used to extend settings such as in the studio where only the bottom floor of a large building can be built but for wide shots we need to see the entirety (see figure below).

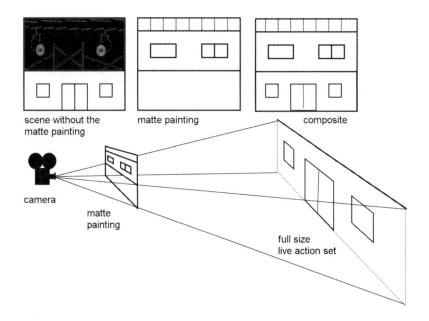

scene without the matte painting

matte painting

composite

camera

matte painting

full size live action set

The most common example of this set extension usage was in early sound films, where ceilings were added to sets often for wide shots of ballrooms with gigantic chandeliers hanging in their midst. Secondly, glass shots can also be used to depict the impossible. This could be of either extreme: the very old location, which no longer bears any resemblance to how it looked, or the science fiction scene, picturing a hypothetical future. In either case a partial studio set or a location can have the ancient or futuristic details added to the existing fabric. A final use for glass shots is to fix or salvage the existing scene. Here we could wish to remove modern aerials from a medieval rooftop, road signs from a road or camouflage equipment such as lights or sound booms.

Although a simple enough concept, the actual setting up of a glass shot can become quite complex and certainly needs great care. The glass must be optically clear and free of blemishes that would cause distortion to the subject matter behind. Before use, the glass should be tested to see if it introduces any coloration, since much glass has a very slight tint, usually green, which may need to be corrected – remember the painting is not affected but the scene behind is. This means that if a colour correction were added in post-production then it would adversely affect the painted element. To correctly compensate either, the painting must be adjusted to match the distortion introduced by the glass (most easily done by filtering its lighting), or the camera should have compensating filtration and the painting made looking at the resulting image (either through the viewfinder for reference, on a video monitor or by eye through a piece of the filter material). It is not a good idea to attempt to add complementary filtration to the far side of the glass since it is difficult to avoid reflections on such a large piece of filter material and, if outdoors, to avoid it being rippled by the wind. Additionally the glass should be quite thick and rigid so that there is no chance of it bowing or distorting in a high wind.

This dictates that the frame be pretty substantial too. The size of the glass is largely down to taste but must always be large enough to fill the frame whilst still being in focus. The distance from camera will depend on the DoF for a given subject distance and f/stop, and the angle of view for the lens will determine the minimum size for the glass. For example, a 25 mm lens at f/5.6 has a hyperfocal distance of 14½ ft. Focusing on this will provide a DoF extending from 7 ft to ∞. On 35 mm academy ratio a 25 mm lens focused on 7 ft will have a field of view 4½ ft × 6 ft, so that would be the minimum size of glass for this set-up; in fact this is a pretty good standard size to work to for the user of average height. It is a good idea to have the frame pivoted in the middle so that it can be tilted slightly to aid work both at the painting and photography stages. If it can be fully rotated then that is an added bonus since it allows easy access to the opposite side as well.

All of the precautions concerning steadiness, reflections and stray light that applied to masks also apply here. It is best to have control over the lighting so that the exposure on both painted and real elements can be balanced, and obviously the light on the glass must be even and from the side (best set at 45° to either side and/or top and bottom). Obviously, the lighting should be arranged to have the same colour temperature as the full sized scene. So, for example, if it is outside, then the lights should be HMI or, if tungsten, then suitably filtered to match the main set. Having the lights on a dimmer is an excellent option although care has to be taken with the colour temperature.

Finally, it goes without saying that the person who does the painting needs to be a skilled artist and particularly expert at photo-realism. Since a lot of scenic painting, be it on backdrops or glass, is still being done, there are quite a few specialists working in this area and, if the work is at all complex, then such a person is well worth the fee they charge. Many specialists in painting on glass have actually developed a sort of realistic-impressionism which, when looked at on the set, looks very painterly and stylized and yet, once on film, looks totally believable. Some directors like a slightly more stylized approach even in realistic films – this could be described as a sort of 'super-realism' and is best demonstrated by the work of Albert Whitlock and particularly his creations for Alfred Hitchcock such as seen in *Marnie* (1964).

Depending on the complexity of the subject matter, glass paintings can take quite a time to create. There are basically three ways to deal with this. The painting can be created off-site using reference material, such as photographic enlargements of the location or designer's elevations if it is to be a studio set. When this is done it will be necessary to modify the painting once on site, and a usable image will only be possible if precise information about lens angle has been supplied. If the angle of view does not match then the painting will never 'fit' properly and the 'modification' made on set will probably entail completely repainting the whole thing! More common is to paint the glass on site using either a viewfinder (this may be a video camera or a director's finder precisely positioned) or, if possible, the actual camera to be used for the shot. Since the glass painting is usually a wide shot and may be needed for a number of sections of the scene it will probably be convenient to have a camera set up in this position and recordings of the wide shot made at various times during the filming. In this scenario it is not a problem to make the extra camera available a few hours before the shot is needed. Since the glass and scene are shot simultaneously there is no need for a special register pin camera and thus the unit's normal second camera can happily be used.

The procedure for creating the painting is straightforward in theory but quite tricky in practice. Because of parallax the precise registration of painted elements and real elements sitting behind will only occur in one place in space, which is where the camera lens will be. Even standing in front of the glass the difference between a person's two eyes would be enough to put out the registration. Thus it is far easier to set up using a video camera, where a monitor will be completely accurate, than with a film camera and video tap. The latter would never be usable for assessing colour or lighting and would only be passable for drawing construction lines. Where a film camera must be used then it will be necessary to have an assistant to help in making reference lines and points. These are best done on the far side of the glass using wax pencils or crayons (which can be removed later with a suitable solvent). Many artists like to use construction lines corresponding to the main parts of the existing setting so that large blocks of the painting can be made without having to refer to the monitor or through the viewfinder. It is also possible to use a non-grease marker such as watercolour paint on the camera side of the glass. A popular technique is to work out the area to be painted and block it out using matte black or emulsion, which is not a problem since the image being hidden will very rarely have any bearing on the pictorial content of the painting. Obviously if there are any construction lines such as verticals to be maintained across the demarcation line, then these will have to be drawn on top of the masked area using pencil, chalk, etc.

Once the construction lines have been put in place the painting itself can be made. A variety of materials can be used, most notably oils and acrylics, but choice of medium is a personal one. One of the major factors in this work is that of efficiency of detail. There is no point in creating a level of detail which is beyond the resolution of the taking medium. Where video resolution is only between 500 and 600 lines there is little point in producing an image with three times this quality. The most important function of the painting is to create atmosphere and believability. This does not necessarily mean total realism but, on the other hand, if the shot is a low angle and looking up at a tall building, and the lines of perspective suddenly bend a third of the way up, then the audience will suspect something is amiss. Similarly, a change of colour or texture would draw attention to the demarcation line.

It is very important to choose the 'join' between real and painted image. Making a soft blend across the join is a standard procedure and can be very successfully accomplished. However, it is a far better policy to try to find some features in the subject which can be followed (see figure below).

live action full scale

matte painting

composite

An arch or window line, particularly if shaded, can help hide this join and make it much easier to achieve and ideally this should be planned well in advance. For the actual content, good reference material should be provided, such as paintings or photographs of the original feature which is being reconstructed or a collection of preferred images from the director or designer if the image is to be wholly fictional.

Glass shots are not rocket science but do require careful planning in advance if they are going to succeed with minimum fuss. A lot of materials, including some quite bulky/heavy ones, are required on set and this sort of work cannot be improvised on the day. For a setting, careful liaison between the design team and VFX are necessary so that suitable demarcation lines can be built into the constructed elements and, if an exterior location is being used, then thought will have to be given to considerations such as direction of light through the day and where the sun will be at the time of the take. Obviously any shadows depicted in the painting will need to go in the same direction as those in the setting. The 'real' sun is on the move all the time and this must be taken into account! Placing of the actors is also an important consideration. The extensions to a real setting will have to be such that the artistes do not cross the boundaries between the real and the painted worlds.

For example, if a ceiling is being shown in the painting then the actor cannot come forward to the point where the top of her body would be hidden by the effect (see figure on next page).

Basically these shots should be considered as a sandwich, where the actor is between the background set and the foreground painting – movement between these planes should be carefully choreographed.

Finally, the style of the glass shot should fit in with the rest of the film. Framing, colour and filtration should all match the shots surrounding it. As with all effects, the shot should 'match' the rest of the sequence of which it forms a part. Since the foreground painting and background live action are both photographed

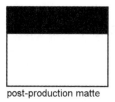

post-production matte

foreground overlapping matte line

foreground correctly positioned

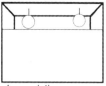

glass painting

unusable composite with subject's head cut off

final composite

together, there is no problem with using filters or other camera styles such as overexposure or laboratory techniques. The important thing is for the shot to look a part of the overall scheme of things.

In the 1930s glass paintings started to be added in post-production to avoid the inconvenience of shooting them live on the set. Subsequently they have been replaced largely by so-called digital glass paintings (see page 230) which, of course, do not use glass at all! However, some production teams still like the idea of doing the effect live and indeed on some low-budget productions it makes a lot of sense. Because of this, it is worth mentioning some of the refinements which have been added to the technique.

As noted, the real world features aerial effects which cause the image to become indistinct with distance. This will happen in the live action part of a glass shot and so, if the painting is to sit in realistically then it, too, should depict this phenomenon. The effect can be achieved by being painted into the image or by filtration. The filtration can be achieved by using a filter close to the lens or by layered filtering so as to increase the effect with apparent distance. A second pane of glass with a diffusing medium sprayed on to it can also be used. Varnish, mounting spray or even white paint can all be used to this end.

The main enhancement to what is basically a still frame and static effect, is to add movement, bringing the scene to life and making it more believable. This can be either movement within the painting or of the camera looking at it. Movement within the image can be created by having elements either on the front surface, or behind and seen through transparent sections of the painting. Lights within the painted image, for instance, can be created by having small bulbs mounted behind the painting and showing through small holes or by sticking on pieces of translucent gel and backlighting it. Elements such as fire or crowds in a stadium can be created by placing flowing material behind small holes in the painting and blowing it with fans. Small objects such as cars can be cut out and pulled across the image on wires and, indeed, cotton wool clouds have often been used in this way. Effects such as rippling water can be created by having lighting effects play on the front side of the painting.

4 Front of camera

Movement of the camera is dependent on the problems of parallax discussed earlier. Obviously the glass is relatively close to the camera whereas the live action is a substantial distance behind. Thus the set-up suffers from 'telegraph pole' syndrome as discussed in the section on miniatures (page 53).

There are two solutions to this problem. One is to use a nodal point head as described earlier and the other is to paint on a sheet of specially curved glass or Perspex which exactly mimics the motion of the camera head when panned (see figure below). The latter will only work for the camera panning and will not work for it tilting up and down, whereas a nodal point adjusted head will permit movement in either direction. One other method of obtaining a pan for use in normal television (particularly 4″ × 3″) is to shoot in an anamorphic format and then pan across it in the telecine transfer to tape.

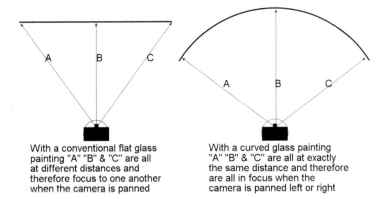

With a conventional flat glass painting "A" "B" & "C" are all at different distances and therefore focus to one another when the camera is panned

With a curved glass painting "A" "B" & "C" are all at exactly the same distance and therefore are all in focus when the camera is panned left or right

Photo cut-outs and hanging miniatures

Instead of painting a photo-realistic image on to glass it is perfectly possible to stick a cut-out section of an actual photograph in its place. This technique is most commonly used in a reversal of glass painting practice. Whereas in a glass shot the real part of the image is usually the live action, in photo cut-outs it is the photograph that will usually show the 'real' part of the shot. Say an artiste is to be shown moving between the trees in a large wood, a photograph of the location could be taken and sections cut out of an enlargement to correspond to where the actors must appear. With the photo mounted on glass, a small section of set built to coincide with the cut-out areas and all the precautions about DoF and so on adopted from glass shots, this will give a realistic rendition of the actors moving behind the trees (see the figure opposite).

If a photograph of a large building is being used then the design department should be able to use the shot itself to build a precise matching section on the stage. These procedures are the reverse of glass painting where the creative work is in painting the foreground synthetic elements. In the cut-out technique, the creative work involves building/painting elements in the live action element.

Some quite sophisticated shots have been created in this way and with careful planning it can be very inexpensive. The use of cut-outs is particularly suited to graphical effects. It is sometimes possible to dispense with the glass altogether and mount the photographic material on board or card and to support this in front of the camera by other means.

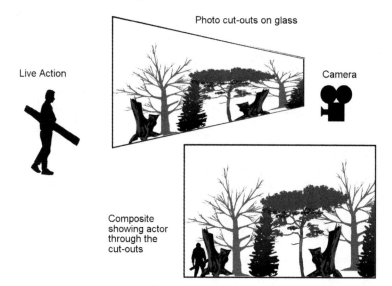

Photo cut-outs on glass

Live Action

Camera

Composite
showing actor
through the
cut-outs

One further technique, which is very complex but offers a number of advantages, is to build to a precise scale a miniature, which extends the existing set or location. This is then photographed with the same focal length lens as will be used on the set, an enlargement of suitable size made and mounted in front of the motion picture camera. Calculating the precise positions, distances and framings requires extreme care but the advantage is that if a number of different angles will be made and/or with different lighting conditions then the ability to reuse the model will make for savings.

Nowadays, as with glass paintings, it is usually far more cost effective to lay the photographic material over live action in a post-production environment where there is the advantage that modifications can be made to the photographic material, whilst looking at the shot as a whole. The foreground or hanging miniature simplifies this last technique by omitting the whole photographic stage of the process and places the miniature itself between the camera and set (see figure at top of page 82).

This has tremendous advantages in terms of matching the live action and additional elements since, as with a glass painting, the model can be modified whilst looking through the lens. It can also be lit in tandem with the actual setting and thus shadow direction and contrast can be matched perfectly. In exterior scenes lit naturally, the setting and hanging miniature will automatically match since they are lit by one single source – the sun! Producing the model for a hanging miniature is reasonably easy if it is to be combined with a physical setting since the plans and elevations for the entire setting can be produced as one piece. The full size set and miniature elements can then be extracted and scaled accordingly. It is absolutely essential that lines of perspective and verticals are accurately constructed in both the standing set and model.

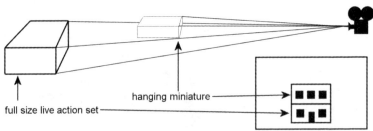

correctly aligned a hanging miniature should merge perfectly with live action

One trick that can help with DoF and the size of the miniature is to use 'forced' perspective. An old theatre trick, this involves exaggerating the perspective in such a way that the various planes reduce in size more rapidly with distance than they normally would. When such a construction is viewed from the correct position the set-up will look perfectly normal (see figure below).

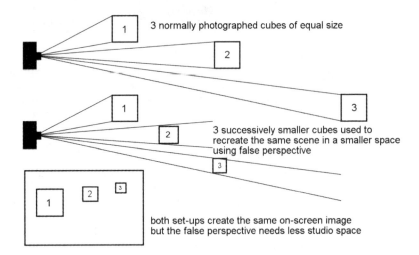

both set-ups create the same on-screen image but the false perspective needs less studio space

This technique is sometimes used in full sized sets to show a long corridor or street disappearing into the distance. In this case, if a person were to walk down that street they would apparently grow in size as they progressed. In a number of cases where this technique has been used and characters were required to be seen moving about, adults, small people, children and then midgets have been placed at various planes to match the perspective. This latter technique was used in the famous final shot of *Casablanca* (1942).

These 'miniatures' will often be quite large (see the section on miniatures, page 48) and in DoF calculations it is important to make sure that the whole miniature, including the plane closest to camera, are all in focus. A glass painting obviously has only one plane of focus but in all other aspects, including the possibility of panning the camera with a nodal point head, a foreground miniature can be set up and used in exactly the same way as a glass shot.

The technique tends to be known by the term 'hanging' miniature since it was originally used mainly for putting rooftops or ceilings on sets and was therefore hung in front of the camera. Depending on the content, such models can just as easily be positioned below or to the side of the camera, and in many cases the live action may be revealed through a small aperture such as a door or window, or the miniature may be as simple as a single sculpture.

The other great advantage of foreground miniatures is that they can contain mechanical devices such as clocks or flashing signs and quite complex movement from small cars travelling across them to miniature people, as in the famous chariot race sequence of *Ben Hur* (1925). It is even possible on larger miniatures to include elemental phenomena such as water in a waterfall or fire in a burning building, but obviously all of the worries previously discussed in the section on miniatures need to be considered.

Mirrors

Mirrors play an important role in VFX photography and also form the basis of some specific processes. The use of mirrors depends on three basic principles.

Light reflected in a mirror is reversed in one plane. This means that, looking directly into a mirror, the image shown will be reversed left to right but will still be correct top to bottom. With a mirror mounted in the ceiling and a camera looking up at it the image will be inverted top to bottom but will show a normal image side to side. A mirror will never both invert and reverse an image at the same time.

The angle of incidence equals the angle of reflection. This means that in a plan view the angle at which light hits a mirror will be the same as the angle at which it bounces back off (see figure below).

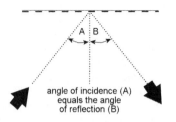

angle of incidence (A)
equals the angle
of reflection (B)

This means that, for example, if you see an unwanted light reflected on a surface, put your head just in front of the lens and look at the line from your eye to the reflection, then imagine that line rebounding at exactly the same angle from the plane of the glass: you will have your lamp.

The third, very simple, rule is that focus on a subject reflected in a mirror will be the sum of the distances between camera and mirror plus mirror and subject. You would never focus on the mirror, where all there would be is dust or scratches, neither of which we want to draw attention to.

One other consideration is that there will be a slight loss of light on each reflection, which is the combined effect of the inverse square law by which light level falls off with distance and the fact that most mirrors will only reflect back a percentage of the light falling on them. Most mirrors are pretty good and specialist reflectors such as 'mylar' film will achieve as much as 99.5 per cent. For the majority of situations this will present no problem but, for some effects dependent on multireflections, the distance covered could rapidly build up, as can the 1–2 per cent light loss incurred at each bounce. An example of this is the 'hall of mirrors' effect in which a figure is repeated off to infinity by shooting through two parallel mirrors, made famous by *Citizen Kane* (1941) (see figure below).

There are three main considerations when shooting with mirrors. The image reversal which is endemic to mirrors can be obvious (for example because the hero has a right-sided parting) and not necessarily wanted. This problem can be dealt with by (a) ignoring it in circumstances where the audience would not notice, (b) reversing scans on a video camera or flopping film (viewing it from the reverse side), (c) shooting through a prism or big mirror close to the camera, (d) reversing the image in post-production (most common approach nowadays), or (e) altering set, costume and/or makeup to reverse it (e.g., changing the artiste's parting for the mirrored shot!).

A second problem with mirrors is internal reflections. These occur where light reflects off both the front surface of the glass and the reflective coating at the back. For wider shots this is no problem but for effects which employ a mirror very close to the lens and which show highlights this can be very undesirable. The solution is to use a front-silvered mirror. These are made for the effects industry and other specialist trades and employ a highly reflective coating on the front side of the glass. This completely does away with the problem of multiple reflections but suffers from the disadvantage that the coating is quite soft and so is very delicate and requires careful handling.

The final difficulty in making mirror shots is the sheer complexity of the calculations necessary to work out sizes and positions of mirrors relative to subject and camera. Sometimes the best approach is to use small mirrors and paper models to see what exactly will really happen.

Mirrors can be used as an aid in the photography of effects and this mainly takes the form of transporting light from subject to camera, or from lamp to subject. As we have seen, light may need to be reflected in to miniatures using small mirrors and similarly they may need to be used to get the lens into very small spaces. On full sized sets mirrors may also be used to get the camera in to dangerous or awkward positions, such as when taking a shot looking along a railway track with the train bearing down on us.

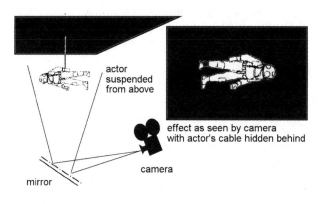

actor suspended from above

effect as seen by camera with actor's cable hidden behind

camera

mirror

A frequently used gag is to have the camera at floor level looking up (see figure above) and then suspending characters from wires to suggest floating in space or with a set built on the ceiling. The figure hides the wire, which is behind it, as in the airlock sequence in *2001: A Space Odyssey* (1968).

However, if the sequence involves pyrotechnics or water which shoots towards the lens (actually falling under gravity) then it is good practice to have the camera level and shooting upwards via a mirror. When doing down shots it is also often much easier and safer to shoot down through a mirror than to try and rig the camera looking vertically down.

Large mirrors can also be used to get much wider angles than otherwise possible in small cramped stages. The mirror effectively allows the camera to be put in a position beyond the studio walls. This can be useful for shooting large-scale miniatures or for creating the large distances necessary when using rear projection systems (see figure on page 134).

Mirrors can be used as effects in themselves. The most obvious are fairground (circus) mirrors, which produce all sorts of grotesque distortions. These effects can however be created to order by using flexible plastic materials such as mylar or mirroflex. These materials have incredible reflectivity and when stretched tight produce excellent conventional mirrors but which can also be distorted in any conceivable way. The sort of trick that can be played is to have a stretched mirror and play a scene via the reflection but without shooting off (i.e., so that the audience does not know it is looking at a reflection). At the relevant dramatic moment the mirror can be pushed or pulled from behind at the point corresponding to the heroines face which will distort in a most extraordinary way whilst the rest of the image remains clear. These materials can be rippled to produce water-like effects, vibrated to give earthquake effects or mounted in airtight boxes which can have air pushed in or drawn out to form convex or concave lenses.

Conventional mirrors can be used for the 'hall of mirrors' effect as described and to produce many interesting kaleidoscopic and abstract images. They can also be used to produce transitions live on the set. There is really no reason with digital post-production to do an ordinary wipe using a mirror by having two scenes played at right angles and then, with the mirror placed so that one scene is reflected, pulling it out to reveal the other immediately behind (see figure below).

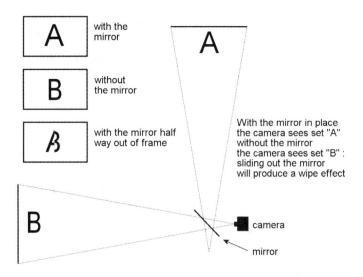

However, some ingenious and more exciting possibilities are still worth considering, such as the explosion transition. Here we have the set-up as described above with the two scenes at right angles but, instead of simply withdrawing the mirror, it is exploded either with a small charge, by putting pressure on it from the sides or by shooting it out with an airgun. In all cases it is best to score the back of the mirror in advance to ensure that it cracks in the required fashion and it may be worth shooting at high speed to get the maximum effect. This can only be done as effectively using 3D CGI, which would be quite expensive for just the one transition.

Special processes using mirrors

Beam splitters

A special type of mirror, known variously as a beam splitter, partial reflecting, half-silvered, semi-silvered, two-way, 50/50 mirror or pellicle, has a special coating which permits approximately half the light falling on it to pass through, with the remainder being reflected in the normal way. These are quite difficult to make and are consequently expensive. They are also fragile and the surface coating (most usually titanium) is very easily damaged and must therefore, bearing in mind their price, be treated with more than the usual respect. Although often described as 50/50 (meaning 50 per cent transmission (T), 50 per cent reflectance (R)) many of them are not. Most common in the cheaper varieties is 40 per cent T, 60 per cent R, whilst Chromium Deposit Mirrors are about 70 per cent T, 35 per cent R. Titanium, which is very expensive, comes out pretty near to 50/50, as can pellicles, which are not mirrors as such but consist of a very thin plastic sheet.

A number of VFX utilize the particular qualities of beam splitters, although for some effects normal plate glass will suffice. With ordinary glass it will be necessary to ensure that it does not have distortions which will show and that it is not too colour-biased (a lot of glass has a green tinge). Obviously with a 50/50 mirror only half the light will be transmitted and half reflected so this will introduce a light loss of 50 per cent and therefore require exposure compensation of one stop. 50/50 mirrors are used in a number of specialist processes such as FAP (page 137) and Schufftan (page 89) but may also be used in some simpler techniques dating back to the Victorian theatre.

Pepper's ghost

This effect is named after Dr Pepper, who used it to create stage effects. In the original configuration a large sheet of glass was arranged on stage at an angle which allowed it to reflect a small set clothed in black drapes which was off to the side of the stage. It was used in scenes which were pretty dark and staged such that the audience would be unaware of the glass. At the relevant moment a light would illuminate the 'ghost' which might be standing with a candle in hand and wearing lighter coloured clothes. To the audience the figure would appear out of thin air and have a translucent quality, with anything behind the glass showing through. This effect can obviously be used with great success when photographed, since the various positions can be optimized to the lens.

There are many refinements which can be made to this technique. Props and furniture draped or painted black can be positioned in the dark set to coincide with elements in the main set, so that an actor in the dark set can sit or otherwise interact with them. Instead of actors, objects can be made to fly about by operators dressed in black moving them on black poles. Of the effects so far discussed these are the first and simplest, permitting two live-action scenes to be combined and, for low-budget productions, offer a chance to cut costs by doing the effects live and being able to see the result on set.

Beam splitters can also be used to produce ambient or miniature composites. Where a beam of light is required it can be airbrushed or created with a real beam of light on a card and reflected into the scene using a half-silvered mirror (see figure below).

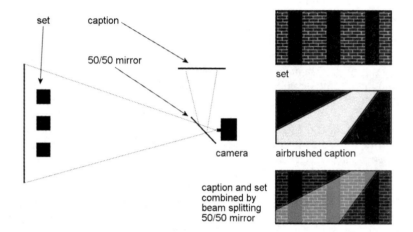

More importantly it permits miniature elements to be combined with live action sets in a more flexible way than in the hanging miniature. Here the real setting is viewed through the glass and the miniature element reflected in it. It should be remembered that the miniature element will have to be built in reverse, since it will be flipped by the mirror. This will require that there are dark patches in the setting into which the reflected miniature will be fit; however the great advantage of the technique is that the miniature can be further from the camera and therefore will be more easily placed within the DoF. It will also be much easier to light in a small separate set. The mirror will be out of focus and therefore not evident to the viewer.

Image replacement using mirrors

With their ability to relay an image from one place to another mirrors can also be used to create 'solid' effects without the transparency problems associated with using beam splitters. The simplest examples of this are where mirrors are built into miniatures and reflect full-scale live action elements. Thus a model of a space station or famous ancient building might have a window replaced by a small mirror and, at the appropriate place across the stage, a section of set built in which people can be seen moving about within the structure. DoF would have to stretch between distance to model, and distance to model plus distance from model to setting.

Once you know the rules it is easy to break them and so the converse of this can be applied, as in the great Marx Brothers' comedy *Duck Soup* (1933). Here an empty frame was built in a wall through which could be seen a complete inversion of the set on the camera side. In the shot it looks like a mirror with a normal reflection in it. Now two actors, one on either side, act out exactly the same movements as if one were the reflection of the other – at some stage they do something different and this is the basis of the gag. Very effective, yet simple technically and not using a mirror at all.

Finally it is possible to use a mirror or part of a mirror across a section of the camera field of view, to combine two elements at right angles to one another in the studio. In these circumstances the mirror edge is out of focus and indeed so is the demarcation line between the elements and no exposure loss is incurred in either half of the composite. Additionally there will be no requirement to black out the relevant sections of either setting. Using a nodal point head the camera can once again be panned or tilted. This technique can be used to combine a full-scale setting and miniatures, artwork, projected images or even the main set itself. This latter is where the mirror is placed below the lens and used to reflect the upper part of the image, thus creating an amazingly reflective floor – a favourite shot in 1930s musicals.

The main advantage of using a mirror to combine two elements is the soft demarcation and the fact that both can be quite distant from the camera and therefore within DoF. All of the considerations looked at earlier in this section will have to be taken into account, since this combines the techniques of miniatures and glass shots with other reflective processes.

Schufftan process

This is named after Eugene Schufftan (changed to Shufftan when he moved to the USA) who developed the technique in the 1920s whilst working at the German UFA Studios on films such as Fritz Lang's *Metropolis* (1927). The process initially used a front-silvered mirror and in later versions a 50/50 mirror.

In the original technique, a front-silvered mirror was placed at 45° to the camera lens with a full-scale set directly in front of the camera and a model (at right angles) reflected in the mirror. The set was built to coincide with a section of the miniature in which live action was to appear (see figure on page 90). A section of the mirror surface was then removed to coincide with the area of real setting to be combined with the miniature. In this arrangement the camera sees through the hole to the live action and surrounding it observes the reflected miniature.

This produced fantastic results because the two elements are both at full exposure and can be totally independently built and lit. The line of demarcation will be out of focus and can be any shape necessary. The result is first generation and can be observed through the viewfinder live. The technique is able to combine a real setting or location with a miniature, photograph, painting or other graphic or, indeed, any combination thereof.

The disadvantage is that it is quite difficult to set up. The first task is to ensure that the two elements are constructed so that they will fit. This requires careful draughtsmanship in the design department. Assuming that the elements are scaled correctly, they need to be aligned. This involves initially setting them up at the correct distances and orientation which needs to be planned in advance. Once this is done the camera and mirror need to be adjusted. This is where things get tricky, since the framing needs to be set to the element which takes up most of the frame (usually the miniature) but the live action element will often be that which is least easy to move.

4 **Front of camera**

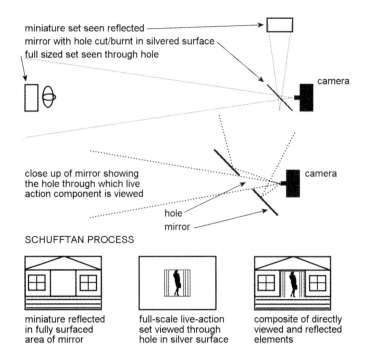

miniature set seen reflected
mirror with hole cut/burnt in silvered surface
full sized set seen through hole

camera

close up of mirror showing
the hole through which live
action component is viewed

camera

hole
mirror

SCHUFFTAN PROCESS

miniature reflected
in fully surfaced
area of mirror

full-scale live-action
set viewed through
hole in silver surface

composite of directly
viewed and reflected
elements

The best procedure is therefore to line up the miniature, which will require the mirror in position, and mark the approximate position of the area to be replaced on a monitor. Now remove the mirror and adjust the camera to place the built set in this position. Next, with everything locked down and the built set's position accurately marked on the monitor, the mirror can be replaced and the miniature moved to precisely locate with the marks. At this stage the mirror can be slid in and out to accurately show registration. Alternatively a half-silvered mirror or plate of glass can be put in to give a live view of both elements super-imposed on top of one another. While doing this, remember that left and right mean the opposite in the two sets, since one is reflected and therefore built in reverse to the other.

Once all is aligned it is necessary to remove the silver in the area corresponding to the insert set. To do this the coating can be scratched with a pin or stylus to delineate the area to be removed. Because the mirror is at 45° there may be extreme keystoning (i.e., horizontal or vertical distortion) of the image reflected in it when outlined on its surface. Thus a rectangle could become a rhombus. When the area to be removed has been marked out the surface may be etched away with nitric acid to leave a clear section through which the lens can see the live action set. The line of demarcation can be as complicated a shape or shapes as required and will, of course, be out of focus, thus creating an excellent blend.

Modern materials can be pressed into service to simplify this technique. For example plain glass can be used and, when marked up with the position of the demarcation line, can have a cardboard mask positioned and then sprayed with a reflective coating. Alternatively the mask can be used to cut an aperture in a sheet of mylar film and this can then be aligned and stuck to the glass plate. One aspect which does need more attention than on glass shots is vibration, since any movements will be magnified by their path through the mirror.

A cost associated with this technique is the destruction of a front-silvered mirror for each set-up. This can be avoided in a modified approach which uses a 50/50 (beam splitting) mirror. Line up is exactly as with the conventional process but a half-silvered mirror is used. Once everything is in place a mask and counter mask can be used to stop the unwanted sections of each element from reaching the lens (see figure below).

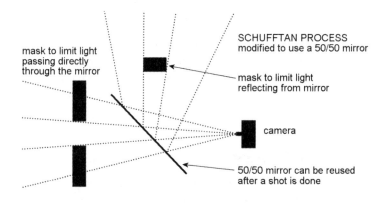

mask to limit light passing directly through the mirror

SCHUFFTAN PROCESS
modified to use a 50/50 mirror

mask to limit light reflecting from mirror

camera

50/50 mirror can be reused after a shot is done

The masks can be set back from the mirror where they can be perpendicular to the focal axis and therefore will not suffer from the keystoning problems involved in applying the information directly to the mirror surface. A special rig can be built with the mirror in a box with two glass sides on to which the masks can be attached or painted. This technique has the advantages of not destroying a mirror, placing the masks slightly further from camera so that they can be sharper if required (for example following a complicated line such as castellations) and are infinitely adjustable until the desired effect is attained. On the down side, this approach involves a loss of a stop because of the 50 per cent nature of the mirror and there is room for multiple reflections within the three glass surfaces.

Schufftan requires all of the same considerations as glass shots but allows for the flawless combining of one or more live action elements with other visual components such as miniatures. The effect is even easier to set up with modern electronic cameras and is still an excellent tool for use on low-budget or student productions where line-up time is not the major problem.

4 Front of camera

5   Composite photography

On a modern production it would be unthinkable to set a camera or stage aside for a day, just to do one glass or Schufftan shot. Thus the technically more complex, but also time-efficient, multicomponent or composite shot has become the norm. Here the separate elements are photographed at different times and places according to production convenience. Typically this allows the live action to be shot quickly on a stage with the actors and, later, the more time-consuming elements such as models or paintings can be added under more controlled conditions.

Elementary combined image techniques still offer first generation quality and end up on a single recording. But, in addition to the considerations involved in a glass shot, they also require much more complex planning to ensure that all the necessary elements are collected in the right places, by the right people, and at the right times.

Mixes and supers

The mix, dissolve or cross-fade is where the density of one image reduces down from normal to zero whilst a second image simultaneously rises from zero to full. In other words, while one image fades out (down, in TV) the other one fades in (or up). Mixes are usually synchronous with the respective fully up and down states being coincident (see top figure opposite).

Such a mix used to be called a lap-dissolve since the images 'overlapped'. If the mix were stopped in the middle when the images were approximately 50%/50%, we would have a double exposure or superimposition (super, in TV). However, in the creation of a 'super', the respective levels can be anything up to 100 per cent of both images. We have seen how this double-image effect can be crudely created using a beam splitter, but with the disadvantage that both elements need to be shot simultaneously. These effects can, however, be produced by many other methods, both in-camera or post-production, and using film, video or digital-specific technologies.

Film multiple imaging
Mixes and supers can be created on film using its 'latency' properties. Film's sensitivity to light and ability to record it continue until it has been 'fixed' in the laboratory. If a piece of film is exposed but not processed, it will contain a 'latent' image, but the emulsion continues to be light sensitive. Let's imagine that we photograph a white dot against a black background, rewind the film to the same

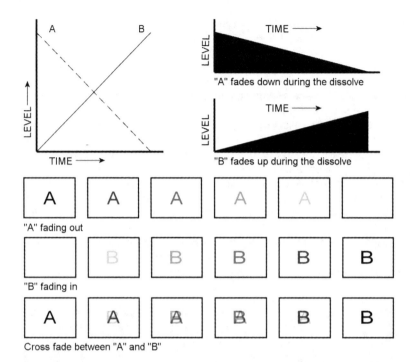

"A" fades down during the dissolve

"B" fades up during the dissolve

"A" fading out

"B" fading in

Cross fade between "A" and "B"

start position, rephotograph the dot in a slightly different place, and then repeat the whole procedure again (see figure below).

1st exposure

2nd exposure

3rd exposure

Latent image

When the film is processed we will have an image of three white dots, all equally exposed. There is no real limit to the number of 'passes' through the camera that can be made in this way, however practical limits do exist, based on the mechanical strength of the film (the perforations will eventually give up) and the 'fog level' of the emulsion.

Fog level is the limit at which background exposure becomes visible. Photons of light are assimilated by the emulsion, but must reach a certain minimum density threshold (D-min) before there is a visible effect. To use an analogy, imagine a glass beaker with black tape around the bottom 30 per cent. We can put in 5 per cent of liquid but it will have no visible effect. This can be repeated with an even larger 10 per cent and still it will have no effect. Two more measures of

10 per cent would be necessary before a visible result is evident but any additions thereafter would show. This is how a latent exposure builds up. If we now keep adding liquid the beaker will gradually fill up, until it reaches 100 per cent, after which no amount of further additions will have any effect. This is equivalent to film negative where, once maximum density (peak white) is reached, further exposure will make no difference. Returning to the white dots, this is why it is important to make sure that the black background is as dark as possible. With even a small amount of luminance this will slowly build up on our multiple exposures until in the end the background might be murky grey rather than the pure black we require. This is why 'black outs' in VFX processes must be as dark as possible.

Multiple passes of film require an extremely steady camera. It should be mounted on a suitably stable support which is weighted down and not subject to movement. The camera mechanism should be very steady with neither vertical (float) nor horizontal (weave) movement and preferably pin registered. For this type of shot the camera should be steady-tested in advance by shooting a white grid on a black background as two slightly displaced passes on the same length of film. The resultant image will show up any errors in the form of relative movement between the lines (see figure below).

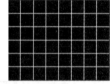 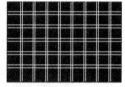

1st pass of grid white on black

2nd pass with grid slightly moved

Combined latent image will show any weave

For anything but static double exposures, the film must start on exactly the same frame for each pass and the actions be cued after the same interval. On computer-controlled cameras this can easily be achieved by specifying a particular start frame, although it should be ascertained whether the camera has a facility to cap the shutter when running backwards. On conventional cameras it will be necessary to make some physical mark on the film and align it to a common point. Most usually a hole is punched in a frame and, with the lens removed, centralized in the gate. Alternatively it can be aligned with some point in the film path with the door open. A nick in the film, a scratch, indelible ink mark or small piece of thread tied round a sprocket hole are all alternative methods of marking, but it is essential that no confetti is left inside the camera.

Having set the marker it is then necessary to move beyond the fogged section of film prior to recording the action. This can be done by stop watch or using the camera's footage counter. Loops and take-up spool tension should be checked before each pass to guarantee that the run up time will remain the same. When finished it is best to remove the film and rewind it in a changing bag to avoid undue wear and tear, but if a backward-running camera function is used then be sure to cap the lens whilst doing so.

Use of this technique requires careful planning, particularly since the elements may be shot at various times during a long schedule. Considerations should include the relative exposures of the different elements of the shot. In a ghost effect, for example, it may be that the background setting wants to be quite dark to make the shot eerie, but also the ghost pass needs to be kept down in exposure to make the figure look quite transparent. With the background dark and the ghost figure bright with a light costume he might actually appear completely solid and therefore real, destroying the effect.

This technique gains us a first generation result on an original negative without any post-production work necessary. However, it does suffer from the big disadvantage that if a mistake is made on any element, then it will be necessary to start all over again. To avoid this it is often expedient to record two or three takes of each exposure and build up a range of versions, so that if any one is spoilt the others provide a back-up.

Film's ability to build multiple exposures on top of one another results in a number of applications, the simplest of which is the mix or cross-dissolve. This is made by recording an entire scene and then, at a known point, reducing its exposure to zero. This is rewound and, starting at the beginning of the previous scene's fade out, the next scene is faded up in the same number of frames and then played as normal. Once processed the result will be a mix between scenes. The actual fading in and out can be created by use of a variable shutter which closes down entirely (e.g., on Mitchell cameras), by sliding across a variable neutral density shutter which goes from fully opaque to transparent or by using an external large black diaphragm (similar to that in the lens) mounted close enough to the lens to be soft. Some older lenses stop down far enough to accomplish the necessary reduction in exposure, but this method is not recommended since it changes the DoF and can alter other visible characteristics of the image.

Rarely contemplated these days, even though computer-controlled cameras make it much easier to achieve, this was the method used for almost all mixes during the silent film era. Although it can achieve a normal production mix (e.g., the passing of time) this effect is also an important tool in the creation of VFX and many of the great classics were produced using it.

A simple dissolve will enable an object to appear or disappear very smoothly. It could be used to make a transporter effect, an imagined character fade from thought or a magician vanish. In all cases the setting and actor would be faded out and then without the actor the empty set would be faded in.

But, expanding on the idea, one object can be replaced with another and so we can do substitution effects, just like stop/start but with the added subtlety of a gradual transformation rather than a jump. Thus the robot can slowly be cross-faded to the living actor playing its android alter ego. But be careful that nothing in the setting changes from one take to the next, since even an altered shadow will be very obvious if it moves over the mix. Given the time required to wind back film and set up the second pass it will be best to keep all unnecessary personnel well away from the area seen by the lens.

Multiple mixes further increase the sophistication possible with, for example, the change from Dr Jekyll to Mr Hyde in which the make-up is added in a series

5 Composite photography

of layers combined with a series of mixes. When doing this, very careful alignment of the moving parts of the frame are needed. In a Jekyll and Hyde shot for instance, the artiste's head should be held in some way so that the actor can comfortably keep it still. A drawing on a picture monitor and replay facility from the video assist are almost essential when doing this and the difficulty for the artiste should not be underestimated. Where complex make-up is involved, for instance in a man-into-'wolfman' type effect, it is usually best to start with the heavy make-up in place and then to remove it piece by piece – even if this requires the effect to be done backwards and reversed in post-production. This same effect can be applied on an ever-larger scale by, for instance, altering an entire set to show the passing of time. Again it is best to work from whichever is the more complex end of the process. If it is a house deteriorating and falling apart, then it should start from the present and gradually be dulled down with paint, start to have pieces removed, burnt and corroded until the necessary degeneration has been achieved.

The next stage of complexity is of course to leave the double exposure going for the whole of the shot. With this technique it is possible to create the same effects as Pepper's ghost, but with all the advantages of shooting the elements separately with totally independent control of exposure, scale and so on. The easiest way to create a ghost effect is to do a double pass, the first on the empty set and the second without moving the camera, on the same set with full action. The usual rules about nothing being moved apply but, additionally, it is necessary to calculate carefully the exposures. If we want the 'ghost' to be at 50 per cent density then both passes should be shot at 50 per cent of exposure (i.e., one stop down). On replay any area where the action does not cross will be made up of 50 per cent from the first and 50 per cent from the second runs, adding up to a full 100 per cent. Where the artiste is, we will get 50 per cent setting from the first run, and 50 per cent of the artiste from the second. The result will show the setting seen through the partially transparent actor. The great advantage is that the character will automatically be hidden behind any objects in the set such as tables or chairs when he goes behind them, but will transparently go in front of them when he is in the foreground (see figure below).

1st pass shows empty set on it s own

2nd pass with actor playing out his role

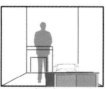

composite shows actor transparent but with foreground objects solid

This is quick and simple to achieve, particularly compared with the 50/50 mirror technique where two sets are required.

However, if the ghostly figure is to be scaled (shot at a differing size), made to float (on a rig) or to cohabit the frame with a solid 'real' character then he must be shot on a separate all-black set, as with Pepper's ghost. Much more complex to plan and execute, consider the example of a ghost interacting with a solid, live character in the set.

First of all, to get full exposure on the setting and real person, it will have to be shot as a normal 100 per cent exposure and the ghost added in a separate 50 per cent recording over the first pass. In reality they can be shot in any order that is convenient, with the relative stops subject to testing. The second pass, on the ghost, will have to be photographed on a set which is identically proportioned to the first, but all black with blacked replicas of any furniture or fittings with which he might interact – such as sit on or pass behind. This will all have to be very accurately built and positioned, with the camera matching exactly its lens height, tilt, pan, focus and distance relative to the set, assuming of course the same camera and lens. This will require very careful measuring and logging of all these variables. Once the scene is set up, it will require careful timing on the part of the actors to ensure that their interactions work. If there are not many objects in the black set, then it is best to have black markers such as posts to give the actor an idea of geography and eyelines. Better still is the idea of having the actor from the main set dressed in black repeating his lines and movements in the dark set.

A popular variation on this is where the same actor plays both parts, as for example where a person imagines talking to themselves. Here a stand-in wearing black can assist in the dark set, but sadly when working in the main set the actor will have to rely on his own imagination – although obviously somebody can read his lines off-camera. In this type of shot a video assist is essential, and obviously on replay the actor can learn his movements. During the take, a replay will offer the opportunity to hear the original sound and any directions called out by the director as a guide.

One final variation is where the ghost might be of a different scale to, or even float around, the set. For making the figure bigger or smaller the camera will need to be moved in or out on the black set and any objects in that set will need to be scaled up accordingly. Of course, except for items such as a chair with which the character interacts, card, plywood or poly (foamcore) cut-outs may be used. Since the elements will all be shot on the original negative there is no second chance. Unless the shots are done consecutively on the same stage, with the same equipment, and it has not been adjusted or turned off and on, the video monitor is not a trustworthy method since the video tap may not be identically aligned for both takes. For post-production methods this does not matter since if there is a misalignment the entire frame can be shifted afterward, but with double exposure this adjustment is not possible and therefore it is too chancy. Grids or the viewfinder graticule are the most accurate way of achieving such a line up.

To have the actor float about he will have to be moved on a blacked-out rig such as a harness and wires, or fork-lift truck. If there are no interactive elements such as tables, then the movement may be made by the camera, but where set elements exist these would obviously float too.

Double exposures can also be used to insert live action into miniatures since another element may be dropped into any area where there is black unexposed negative. For example, a castle entrance or window in a large modern building could be blacked out and then an interior complete with people shot as a subsequent re-exposure on the live action stage. As always, scale, size and positioning have to be worked out carefully and matching of light direction and all the usual parameters. It is in shots such as this, with architectural elements close together, that float must be avoided at all costs if the effect is not going to be given away. Similarly the black out on both elements must be absolute or one element will stand out (see figure below).

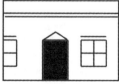  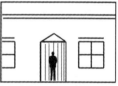

miniature shot with doorway blacked out

live action shot with door to match miniature

latent image combines both elements

Double exposure may also be used to 'print in' lighting effects such as beams of light from a high window. In miniatures work multiple exposures are frequently used to produce creative lighting. Imagine a shot of a town at night. Lighting is required inside the houses, but can only be at quite a low level because of heat problems. Thus a pass is made on the miniature at 5 fps. Then the small lights are turned off, the film rewound and another pass made at 25 fps with the normal theatrical lighting of the scene.

This same technique can be used for shooting live action scenes (such as background plates) in difficult locations where the ideal lighting is not possible. Light fittings are often not permitted in a cathedral for instance. The location is renowned for its beautiful stained glass windows, but our wide shot 'plate' is on a sunny day where the windows are very bright, with burnt out pools of light on the flagstones, but the walls are about ten stops down. The solution is to do one pass exposed for the stained glass and the pools of light below. If desired, smoke can be added to show up the beams of light. A second pass is then made with the windows covered over with tarpaulins (usually done on the outside) or some other suitable method and the interior lit, however dimly, as permitted by the management. This can be shot at a slow frame rate if necessary. Finally if there are some figures in the shot these can be lit as a third pass, if there are not enough lamps, or captured in the second pass, if there are. Where stills of a very dark building are required for a process background it is possible to leave the shutter open and literally paint in exposure using a small hand-held spot (see figure below).

exposed for windows

with smoke added exposed for lightbeams

windows covered, action area lit and exposed for drama

latent image combines all of the elements on one piece of film

This same technique can be used to burn stars into a night exterior – the stars being the pinholes discussed earlier or sugar on black velvet. In either case the black must be zero exposure or its texture may show up and, if there is action in the foreground, either it must be kept clear of the stars or *vice versa*.

Finally double exposure can be used to 'burn in' titles. The effect of an over-exposed white out of black title superimposed by double exposure is much 'softer' in the minds of some graphic designers (a bit like vinyl versus CD audio) and obviously if desired the exposure can be reduced to give a semi-transparent look. The titles can be brought into focus by adjusting the lens and moved by panning, zooming or tilting the camera. The best method is to use backlit transparencies or cutouts, whereas photo-prints or photo-mechanical transfers (pmt's) are best avoided since their blacks are not usually dense enough. With backlit artwork it is possible to do a second pass with a suitable diffusion filter so as to create a glow. This may be filtered in a different colour to the main exposure. Very popular with art directors, this technique works well so long as there are not areas which are very bright. A glow pass can of course be applied to other subjects such as the flying models as in *Close Encounters of the Third Kind* (1977) where the craft were almost entirely made up from glow passes.

Video superimposition

Once a video image is recorded on to tape it cannot be added to. Another recording will erase what is already on the tape. Nor would switching off the erase head allow a second signal to be superimposed on the first, because there is no simple way of aligning the synchronizing pulses of the two signals. The same principles apply to digital cameras, whether recorded on analogue or digital tape systems, both of which still work on the once-only magnetic recording model.

However, there is a way of creating first generation recordings on tape which allow superimpositions to be made using multiple cameras. Because video is a continuous analogue electrical signal it is possible to combine, within certain technical constraints, two or more shots together. Video signals contain a series of synchronizing pulses to establish the starts of fields and lines and these must be aligned if two signals are going to be combined. A video signal cannot exceed one volt and therefore it must be gated/filtered in some way to stay 'legal'. The special electronics necessary to achieve these actions are built in to vision mixers (video switchers) and, with these, mixes and superimpositions can easily be achieved between any video sources feeding the system so long as they are synchronized.

There are three techniques for adding signals together without exceeding the 1 V maximum: mix, add mix and NAM (non-additive mix). To mix between two video signals they are fed into a combining circuit, with one feed being reduced from full signal to black whilst the other is synchronously increased from zero to full level. On most machines, a so-called ganged fader controls this process. This mechanically links together the levers respectively increasing and decreasing the two signals. Using a ganged control, as you increase one lever you simultaneously reduce the other. With such a control you will have 50%/50% or 75%/25% or 10%/90% and so on with no alternatives. On some machines the faders can be split but a limiter is connected to stop the signal from going above the max. An 'additive mix' has controls which permit both signals to be faded independently anywhere between full and zero. Since such a device would permit a signal of 200 per cent (2 V) they are followed by a 'stab amp' (stabilizing amplifier) which limits the signal to broadcast specs. The additive mix gives the same general effect as the film double exposure complete with the transparency effects. Finally there is a so-called 'non-additive' mix or NAM, and this is where the signal is filtered such that at any point when added together the highest of the two voltages will be passed. Thus the brighter image will appear to be laid over the darker one and there will be no transparency effect.

With the exception of effects requiring the same actor in two or more elements at the same time, all of the effects produced by an in-camera film super or mix can be created live in video. These effects will require two or more cameras, depending on the number of layers, with the combination taking place electronically and live. For instance, ghost effects would require the main setting and either an identical replica or a black set, with a camera looking at each. These would have to be carefully aligned – easy on a monitor. The main set would have any live action on it and the black set would, as before, show the ghost.

These two images would be combined live in the switcher (mixer) offering the convenience of adjusting levels whilst looking at the composite (figure below).

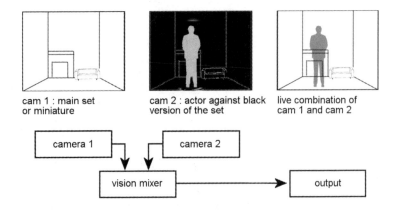

cam 1 : main set
or miniature

cam 2 : actor against black
version of the set

live combination of
cam 1 and cam 2

On many modern mixer/switchers this combination might have to be done in a more complex fashion since a straight additive mix is not always available. All of the techniques described for a film super can be used with the same considerations, except that they will be shot simultaneously with multiple cameras, rather than separately on the same camera and strip of film.

Combinations with miniatures are particularly convenient by this method, since the model can be pictured by one camera, and the live element by another. Since the combination appears live on the monitor it is very easy to align lighting and other elements to exactly match. A NAM would most conveniently make the combination since it would ensure that both elements were combined at full levels. Light beams, stars and titles would also be best served by a NAM, ensuring that they had no transparency. Graphical and still images could come from other sources such as a slide machine or rostrum. The technique is the same irrespective of the video signal's origin. However, multiple pass techniques involving making changes between passes will not be possible since there is effectively just one live pass here.

One effect which is unique to video is the 'howlaround' – an additional way of creating unreal stylized images. This depends on the ability to feed a picture monitor with the output of a camera looking at a monitor. Let's say the monitor is fed with an image of the letter X mixed with the output of a camera and that camera is itself framed up on that same monitor (see figure below). If the camera is panned slightly to one side then the monitor will, on the next frame, receive an image of the X, plus the image from the camera with it slightly to the side. This means that on frame 2 there will be two Xs, slightly displaced. When shot by the monitor these two Xs will now be shifted slightly to the side and on frame 3 will be added to the original. At 25 fps this will almost instantly result in a hall of mirrors effect which will vary in the most intriguing way if the camera position is interactively altered by zooming, panning or tilting.

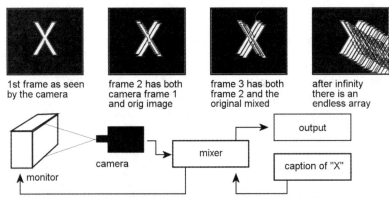

1st frame as seen by the camera

frame 2 has both camera frame 1 and orig image

frame 3 has both frame 2 and the original mixed

after infinity there is an endless array

output

mixer

camera

caption of "X"

monitor

the vision mixer has a 50/50 mix between caption and camera fed to the monitor

Matte and split-screen

The 'matte' process combines the concepts of mask and re-recording over a latent image (or superimposing two video sources). With this technique an area of the image is 'held back' (masked or matted out) so that it remains unexposed during photography of the scene. Then, with a complementary mask (countermatte) in place, a second pass is made to fill in the missing area whilst adding no further exposure to the already existing latent image.

To show a character talking to his identical twin, a camera could be set up to frame the 2-shot with the actor and a stand-in. Everything would be tied down and locked off and a black mask would be set up to cover the stand-in side of frame. The mask should be arranged so that it is totally black and such that it could easily be replaced by a precisely aligned complementary mask (see figure below).

cam 1 : left of
lens covered
by black mask

cam 2 : right of
lens covered
by black mask

camera 2 image
with frame left
matted black

camera 1 image
with frame right
matted black

latent image
is a composite
of both scenes

matte covering
frame right

artiste frame right

cam 1

artiste frame left

cam 2

matte covering
frame left

CREATING AN
IN-CAMERA
MATTE SHOT/
SPLIT-SCREEN

The actor and stand-in would now be filmed playing their roles. Once a satisfactory take was recorded the film would be wound back to the start point and the mask replaced with one which exactly aligned with its inner edge and covered the opposite half of the frame. The actor would change into his other character's costume, swap positions with the stand-in and the scene would now be re-filmed. The result would show the left and right parts of the picture combined with a soft demarcation line and a perfectly exposed first generation image of one actor playing two roles in a single setting. These masks are known as 'matte' and 'countermatte', the join as a 'matte line' and the whole as a 'matte shot'. Where two images are combined in this way the composite is generally referred to as a split-screen. As with other double-exposure techniques it depends on the camera being absolutely steady, nothing moving between takes and none of the action crossing the split.

For the easy creation of mattes early cameras had a set of precise metal shutters positioned at the gate where they would be sharp, but most matte shots are done with the mask positioned in front of the lens. The so-called 'matte-box' was originally designed to make placement and shading of these masks quick and easy. This is an incredible capability of film since it permits first generation composites to be made in-camera with extreme precision. When there is a long period of time between shooting two elements the first can be recorded for an extended time enabling the end to be cut off and processed. This can then be used to precisely align the countermatte whilst shooting the second element. The clipped frame can be put into the gate on some cameras so that the scene can be viewed through it, or better still, it can be telecined and put onto tape to be played into the video tap. Where this is done it will be necessary to specially align the assist system since these are not always set up in the same way nor is the film always telecined with the same framing.

The only foolproof method of aligning a video assist for coincident replay is to shoot a chart indicating graticule alignment in the viewfinder (see figure below).

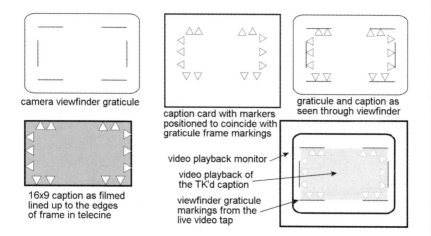

camera viewfinder graticule

caption card with markers positioned to coincide with graticule frame markings

graticule and caption as seen through viewfinder

16x9 caption as filmed lined up to the edges of frame in telecine

video playback monitor

video playback of the TK'd caption

viewfinder graticule markings from the live video tap

For instance, if shooting in a 16 × 9 aspect ratio then a chart with a clearly marked 16 × 9 grid on it would, through the viewfinder, be positioned to exactly sit under the viewfinder markings. In telecine (TK) the scanned area would be aligned with the chart and it would be TK'd at the start of the scene. When the replay footage is made up this chart would be at the head. The chart would now be played in a mix with the video tape and the camera graticule and the off-tape chart would be aligned, with the resultant new chart recorded onto the front of the shot (this is more important in doing multiple passes recorded on separate rolls of film – dealt with later). Adjustment of the two pictures to coincide is best done via the video assist system, but does require a device to move the picture (e.g., DVE – Digital Video Effects) to enlarge the camera graticule to positionally match the off-tape recording.

This technique of making split-screens can be used to combine any two or more pictures, be they live action, miniatures or graphical elements. However, combining the techniques of glass paintings and mattes, we get the 'glass matte' process which is much more flexible and allows the mask to be made in any conceivable shape. Imagine that we want to do a glass painting, but it is not practical to paint it at the location. So we take the panel of glass out to the set and place it as normal in front of the camera but, instead of painting the set extension, we actually just paint in matte black where the extensions will be required. This can be done easily and quickly. Now the scene is shot through the matte which leaves unexposed those areas of the negative where the painting is required. When the shot has been finished the actors can all be cleared and then the film is run on for a minute or so to provide test footage for fine-tuning the matte.

On returning to base a small section of the test material is cut off and processed. The glass is set up in front of a camera and the processed clip can either be printed at the correct scale to fit on to the glass or tracing paper can be fixed on the opposite side of the glass from the painting and the test frame projected on to it. Other alternatives include placing a frame in the gate and viewing through it or mixing a video transfer of it with the video tape but, whichever is used, the blacked-out area can now be painted in (see figure below).

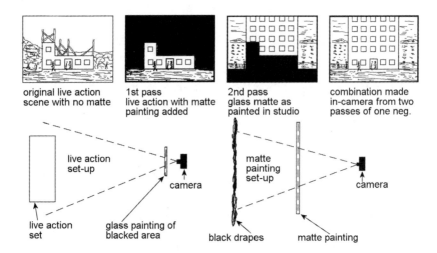

original live action scene with no matte

1st pass live action with matte painting added

2nd pass glass matte as painted in studio

combination made in-camera from two passes of one neg.

live action set-up

camera

glass painting of blacked area

live action set

matte painting set-up

camera

black drapes

matte painting

Black drapes are hung well behind the painting, which is front illuminated. A small section of the unprocessed film is run through the camera to double expose the matte painting with the latent live action image. This can then be processed and viewed to decide whether the combination is working, particularly in its colour matching. Necessary adjustments can then be made to either/both the painting and exposure, and another test produced. This process can be repeated until a perfect result is achieved, but with the obvious nervousness caused by the slowly dwindling supply of unprocessed clips which gradually eat their way towards the section of negative which bears the action takes. If this sounds scary, think of *Gone with the Wind* (1939) where the technique was used but, with no three-strip Technicolor camera available to the matte artistes, they had to use a normal camera and run each of the three colour negatives through it with the appropriate coloured filter!

In reality a smaller pane of glass is often used in the field to simply black out the areas to be matted and then, in post-production, a countermatte can be derived from the processed test strip. This technique can also be used to matte an image in order to have miniatures or live action elements added later. Indeed complex glass mattes might even be used to combine two live action elements as in the first example, but in such a case all of the parameters concerned with matching camera viewpoint and exposure would have to be exercised.

The 'garbage' matte is where a matte is used to screen out unwanted elements in shot such as lights or ladders (i.e., garbage – unwanted junk), and which would interfere with the successful operation of a process. Consider the example of a ghost shot against black and superimposed on to the main action set. If it were required to be small in frame, quite a wide shot might be needed and there could be considerable shoot-off with various pieces of equipment such as lights or the sound boom in the shot. Placing black mattes up close to the lens would cover these and eliminate the need for large set pieces and can also be used to shade the lens from strong backlights (see figure below).

  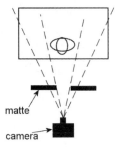

live action without
garbage matte

live action masked
by garbage matte

matte

camera

Generally garbage mattes do not need to be precise.

Video/digital switch and wipes

Obviously the inability of video to be double exposed means that, like superimposition, matte work cannot be achieved by multipass techniques. Once again, it is the live multicamera style of technique that allows this type of shot to be made. With two cameras being non-additive-mixed together it is easy to place a matte and corresponding countermatte such that the two cameras can be combined (see figure below).

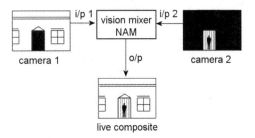

camera 1   i/p 1 → vision mixer NAM ← i/p 2   camera 2

o/p

live composite

This can be a straight split-screen or a more complex matte painted on glass. This technique works extremely well and is simple to set up accurately, since the result is available live on a picture monitor and, of course, there is no weave or grain to contend with.

Where video (and this includes digital video) really excels is in the use of special electronic tools including the 'switch' or 'add-circuit' and shape generator. The switch is like any two-way electrical switch except that it is incredibly

5 Composite photography

fast. It can have two synchronous signals fed to its inputs and switch between them as determined by a third signal (see figure below).

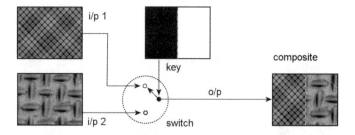

The control (or key) takes the form of a special signal derived from conventional video and can therefore be from any source. In the early days of television this process was called 'inlay' with the main picture called the background and the other image the infill. Vision mixers (video switchers) have built-in shape (or wipe) generators designed specifically for this purpose, but an external key can be fed from a camera, slide machine or any other video source.

Most modern equipment has a fast mixer rather than switch – it is in reality two variable attenuaters back to back. Therefore instead of choosing just one video stream it will output variable densities of the two inputs according to the greyscale of the control (see figure below). This means that the demarcation line between the images can be soft as well as hard.

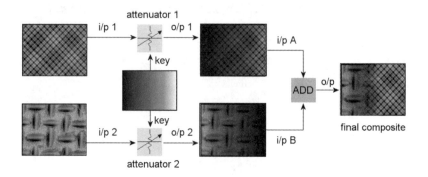

The standard vision mixer will permit wipes between the two chosen pictures and, with these at a static position, also provides split-screens. Most equipment offers a substantial range of shapes but there will always be at least horizontal and vertical lines, square and circle expanding from centre to off-screen and usually diagonal and corner box wipes (see top figure opposite).

These basic shapes can also be modified for positioning anywhere in frame and to be hard, soft or bordered, with a selectable colour and variable width. All of the techniques described for film mattes can be applied to video split-screens

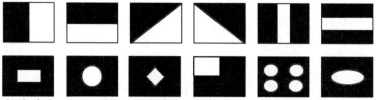

standard wipe shapes which can also be centred in the corners, multiplied or squeezed

by using one or more cameras live. The advantage is instant matching and matte accuracy assessment, but with the disadvantage of not being able to do effects involving multirole acting. On live productions this allows miniatures and other image-enhancement effects to be achieved but also provides the facility to use wipes as transitions.

The built-in controls will be suitable for wipes and split-screens of the more obvious types (such as two people talking on the phone – see figure below).

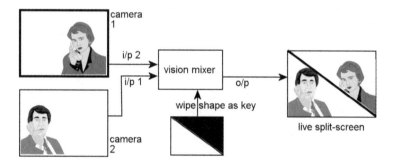

But for complex shapes it is necessary to draw mattes just as they are painted on glass for film. The best set-up for this is to have a camera looking at a light box (or use a digital paint system, discussed on page 229). Here a silhouette mask can be drawn and fed as a key to the switch. This hand-drawn matte can then be used exactly as a film matte to determine the demarcation join between two elements being combined, such as a miniature and live action set. The technique can also be used to generate wipe shapes too complex and specific to be available on standard shape generators. For example, in a drama about the stock market, a dollar sign wipe might be required and, with a white symbol on black ground made big enough for the camera to zoom right through it, a $ wipe could easily be achieved.

Finally, the video matte is perfect for graphics purposes. With white out of black artwork a hole can be cut in one picture and replaced with an image from another. For example, a title reading 'THE END' might be fed as the key combining two images, one of the final scene of the drama and the other of a suitable pattern on camera, or simply a colour from within the vision mixer. The great advantage of this is that it will be cut into the picture and not be slightly transparent as it would be with a superimposition (see figure below).

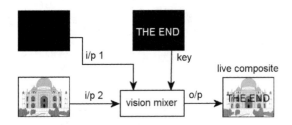

Rephotography/re-recording

All the techniques discussed so far have delivered a first generation film or tape, but allow for no failures at any stage. They are time-consuming to set up, although, in most cases, involve no post-production. In the modern world of tight budgets and even tighter schedules, minimizing studio time is a priority for most producers, but time spent in post-production is often not such an issue. Although the equipment can be expensive to hire (but is getting cheaper daily) the comparison between 50 people on the stage and two in an effects suite says it all! Since the development of digital techniques the move of effects creation from studio floor to edit suite has been rapid and, nowadays, most of the work is done there. The basic principles of this modern approach were developed in the early days of film and television but their use was restricted due to the limitations of copying analogue media.

All of the stress, heartache and chance involved in combining elements by live (video) or multipass (film) techniques can be swept away with the use of rephotography or re-recording techniques. Unlike all of the earlier film techniques, these methods do not rely on the latent image but require the film to be processed before the combination is made. Similarly in video the image must be recorded before a combination is possible.

Film rephotography
Apart from reversal stock, all current film systems involve the use of a negative/positive process. For simplicity let's consider black and white. The film emulsion is sensitive to light and, when processed, gets darker according to the amount of light absorbed. The result is a negative image of the scene. To create a viewable result the negative has to be copied on to another roll of film – the print. Since the print material acts in exactly the same way as the camera negative (original or o-neg) it will reverse all the tones again and produce a positive. In the normal way of things the print is produced on a contact printer where the positive and negative traverse a light source, in emulsion-to-emulsion contact. This process takes place at high speeds, since accurate steady registration is not a priority for release prints.

Now consider the multirun technique for the creation of a split-screen using front-of-camera mattes. If, instead of rewinding the film, we shoot the two elements one after the other (sequentially), not coincidentally, the result will be two sequences, one with the right element and an unexposed left of frame and the other with the left element and a blanked right side.

After developing and printing, one of these can be put through a printer and exposed on to a negative stock. The result will be a new negative with a latent image of only one side of frame with the other half still unexposed. If this unprocessed negative is now put back in the printer, but this time with the print of the other side of frame and run through, we will create a combined negative, just as we did in-camera using the earlier process. Once developed, a composite will exist on the negative just as before. This is the principle on which film 'optical' effects are based.

Sadly things are not so simple and this method of making combined prints would never be used. Print film uses KS perforations (see page 19) which are not accurate enough for effects purposes. Image quality deteriorates rapidly with analogue copying and therefore special media must be used. Each duplication of an image will increase contrast, grain, colour inaccuracy and will lower resolution. To compensate, special low-contrast, linear-gamma, fine-grain neg. perf. 'intermediate' stocks have been designed. Because there is an almost infinite amount of light available, these stocks are incredibly slow (normally less than ISO/ASA 1). In the black and white days intermediate stocks were known as fine-grains or lavenders (because of the emulsion colour) and in colour they can be used as an inter-positive (inter-pos, IP) made from camera original, or inter-negative (inter-neg, IN) made from the inter-pos. These techniques were not fully developed in the black and white era until fine-grain duplicating stocks were established and in colour until faster stocks were available. The usual method to make the optical described above would be to print the two elements on to an intermediate film (see figure below).

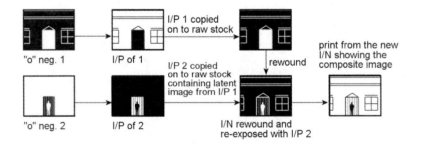

"o" neg. 1 — I/P of 1 — I/P 1 copied on to raw stock — rewound — print from the new I/N showing the composite image

I/P 2 copied on to raw stock containing latent image from I/P 1

"o" neg. 2 — I/P of 2 — I/N rewound and re-exposed with I/P 2

The benefits of this procedure are immediately obvious. All rewinding and aligning of raw stock are removed from the shoot environment, as are the problems of cueing precisely and timing the action. Furthermore, tests can be done without eroding the studio recordings, and composites can be remade over and over again without damaging the original footage. Most importantly, it is possible to make a version and, after processing, view it and assess whether it works. If it does not, then the relative start points of the elements can be adjusted and an improved version made.

A duplicate made on a contact printer would be neither of sufficient quality nor steadiness to make a good composite shot. To create a steady, well registered print the negative and raw stock must pass through a system with an intermittent pulldown mechanism and register pin so that they are both stationary when exposed. Such a device would have tight-fitting pins and so the raw stock would require B&H perforations. There are three machines which meet this specification, a bi-pack camera, a step printer and an optical printer.

Bi-pack (process) camera

This is a special camera with a gate capable of passing through two films in contact (see figure below). Special magazines allow two rolls of film to be loaded in separate compartments, but combined in their passage through the camera. In other respects this is a normal camera with a lens and other standard features.

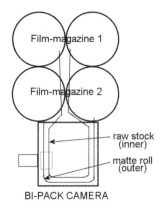

Film-magazine 1

Film-magazine 2

raw stock (inner)

matte roll (outer)

BI-PACK CAMERA

To combine two pre-matted elements, low-con prints would be made from the camera negatives to ensure their safety and also to make the masked side of frame opaque (in the negative it is clear). This inter-pos is loaded in emulsion-to-emulsion contact with raw stock and on the top (lens) side of the bi-pack. The camera is then pointed at a source of even white light (a front-lit board or light box) which is illuminated at a level sufficient to correctly expose the raw stock. Since this is a fully featured camera, two or more passes can be accurately made using standard matte techniques and therefore pre-matted elements can be combined to make a single inter-neg.

However, the exciting thing about this arrangement is that if the light box on which the camera is focused has an area masked out (see top figure opposite) then the corresponding area on the negative will be unexposed.

Using this technique, very accurately drawn and detailed mattes can be created and used during the post-production compositing process. This further

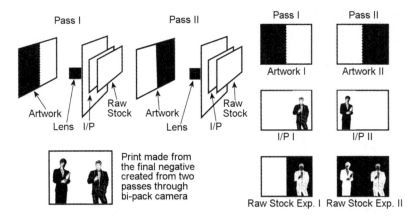

frees up the shooting end of production, permitting the various elements to be shot full-frame without recourse to masking out areas during action photography. This not only simplifies shooting but also allows the matte line, and its blend, to be decided in the relative peace of post-production. Furthermore these 'process' cameras can have a special 'rotoscope' attachment added to aid in drawing the matte. This is a mechanism that enables a light to be shone through the film gate from the rear and therefore turns the camera into a projector. The shot to be matted is placed in the gate (obviously without the raw stock loaded) and this is projected on to the white exposure surface where the matte area can be blocked in (see figure below).

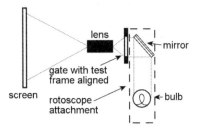

The rotoscope attachment is also the very best way of creating post-production glass paintings, since the image can be accurately projected on to the glass painted with a suitable white surface, or with white card on the reverse side. The process camera also provides the ultimate steady image quality necessary for such processes. To combine the glass shot in a bi-pack camera, a low-con inter-pos would be made of the live action (no holdback matte necessary) and this would be rotoscoped and then extended on the glass.

The painting would be on an opaque undercoat. A large white surface would be positioned some way behind the glass. The inter-pos would be loaded in contact with raw stock and they would be exposed by shooting the white surface evenly illuminated and with no light on the matte painting so that it would be

5 Composite photography

111

unexposed. The raw footage would be rewound and the inter-pos removed. With blackness behind the glass and the painting now illuminated, a second pass would be made, thus laying down both images on the negative. No damage is done to the original negative and therefore multiple tries can be made with corrective adjustments between each (see figure below).

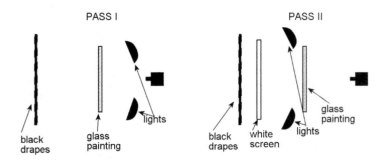

PASS I

black drapes   glass painting   lights

PASS II

black drapes   white screen   lights   glass painting

The bi-pack camera can be used to create some very sophisticated effects including titles and even wipes, in addition to post-production matting. However, along with other mechanical systems, it has been replaced in recent years by digital methods which are much more flexible.

Step printer

This is effectively a contact printer which uses an intermittent movement and register (full-fitting) pin gate. It should be remembered that to gain full benefit of this system B&H perforated stock must be used – print stock of this specification is a special order item. A lens focuses the light source but, unlike the bi-pack camera, it is designed for long runs of film. With digital post-production the preference is usually to run negative through the telecine or scanner so there is not much need for step prints these days – but if the 'print' look is required (as on some commercials) then a step print should be ordered to provide the steadiness necessary for effect work.

Optical printer

For more complex work the bi-pack contact printing method is not enough. There is too much wear and tear on the raw stock where it is physically in contact with the various inter-pos elements as they are exposed, rewound and reloaded. Additionally, contact printing disallows any adjustments to the frame such as enlarging, repositioning, rotating or otherwise manipulating the image visually or temporally.

An optical printer is actually built up from one or more projectors (printer heads) and a camera which can rephotograph their image. The basic configuration has a camera and projector separated by a lens adjusted for 1:1 reproduction since the film is being rephotographed at actual size (see figure opposite).

With this arrangement the raw stock and positive elements can be controlled independently. By altering the relative frame rates of the two systems, for

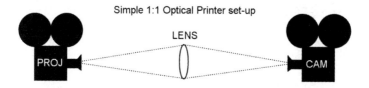

Simple 1:1 Optical Printer set-up

instance (step printing), the new negative can be temporally altered (e.g., if the projector winds on two frames for each frame of raw stock the new negative will show events at double the speed). Filters and other optical effects can be introduced into the light path to alter colour balance or add diffusion, etc. By alteration of focal length and/or the relative distances of camera and projector, the image can be resized. By addition of bi-pack magazines to the projector, mattes which have been pre-filmed can be introduced. These mattes are not confined to static masks but can be animated too, thus creating 'travelling' mattes.

Standard film rolls of animating mattes and countermattes (see figure below) can provide wipe shapes such as a horizontal line which travels across screen

covering up one image and on the second pass revealing the second. Timing of these films relative to the action elements can create and permit adjustment of a black bar (border) between the two. Using an animation camera or bi-pack camera with rotoscope attachment a hand-drawn travelling matte can be created to follow a particular object as it moves across frame.

Double- and even triple-head optical printers were used at one stage to permit effects such as wipes to be created in a single pass. The precision required of the physical and optical elements in an optical printer were phenomenal, given the huge magnifications involved, and so results were often variable. Larger formats such as vistaVision and 65 mm were once used to overcome these limitations. However, compared with the capabilities of digital effects, the optical printer is restricted in its flexibility, operationally fiddly and time-consuming to use. Additionally the system's dependence on 'duping' elements meant that it was very difficult to match them into surrounding shots.

There are two approaches to matching an effect into a sequence of shots. In the early days these effects were relatively costly to do and so budget-conscious studios wished to minimize the duration of dupe material, not to mention the inferior picture quality that came with it. This approach resulted in the 'optical' being cut in to the shot for just that section where the effect occurred. For example, if a character walked across shot, stopped, said the magic word and then faded out, the dupe negative would only be used for the few frames in which the actor was fading. To do this the original negative would be cut in up to the first frame of fade, then the dupe negative and, following the last frame in which the character was faintly visible, there would be a cut to the negative of

5 Composite photography

113

the empty set. The effect on-screen would be a nasty visual 'jump' in quality just before the effect and then again after it. In many 1930s movies and 1970s television one could always tell when a mix was about to happen as the picture suddenly turned grainy and contrasty (see figure below).

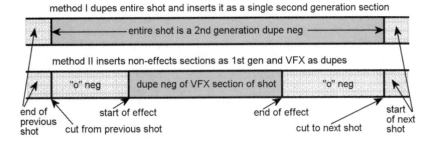

method I dupes entire shot and inserts it as a single second generation section

entire shot is a 2nd generation dupe neg

method II inserts non-effects sections as 1st gen and VFX as dupes

"o" neg   dupe neg of VFX section of shot   "o" neg

end of previous shot   start of effect   end of effect   start of next shot

cut from previous shot   cut to next shot

The alternative arrangement was to put the entire shot through the optical process from the cut-to-the-shot until the cut-away-from-it again. The theory was that with the change in picture content the jump in quality would be less noticeable. This was obviously a lot more expensive and time-consuming to do but generally was the better option. These two philosophies apply equally to inserting digital or CGI material into sequences and their relative merits are still hotly debated.

For these and other reasons the optical printer has been almost totally replaced by digital techniques and, unlike glass paintings, multirun and mirror techniques for example, its complexity makes it impractical for low-budget or student projects where many old techniques can still prove useful.

Video re-recording

Just as film can be rephotographed, so video can be re-recorded. The same problems occur in regard to analogue copying of video as with film. Each playback of a videotape is called a 'pass' and each additional copy or recording of a video signal is called a 'generation'. Seven analogue generations is the limit, after which the picture becomes unacceptable for broadcast use. The symptoms of too many generations start to show up after only about four. Copying videotape images results in an increase in noise, contrast and colour saturation, in an artificial-looking over-sharpness and in ever more obvious lines around edges known as 'ringing'.

The original Quad 2″ recording format permitted physical editing of the tape but this became impossible with the advent of helical scan recorders (e.g., 1″ and the Betacam family) and so the copying principle became the basis of all 'online' editing. 'Offline editing' is where copies are made, edited and then the original (master) tapes 'conformed' to exactly match the offline edit decision list (EDL) using timecode (see opposite).

In linear editing an edit is made by copying from a play machine to a record machine. When the first shot has been laid down, a frame (called the in-point) is chosen where the edit to the next shot should happen and, on the replay machine, a point is chosen where that next shot should start. The two tapes are electronically aligned so that these two chosen frames will coincide when both are played back. When this point is reached the recorder switches from play to record. The resulting tape will show a cut between the shots (see figure below).

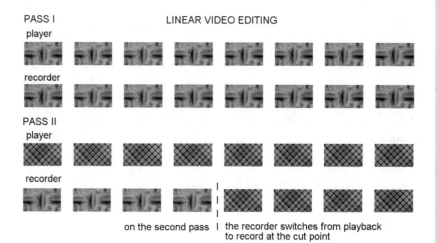

LINEAR VIDEO EDITING

on the second pass | the recorder switches from playback to record at the cut point

At first the synching of the two tapes was done by counting the control pulses representing the start of each frame, but this method was rapidly replaced on professional equipment by 'timecode', which allocates a specific code to each frame in the format HOURS:MINUTES:SECONDS:FRAMES. An international standard called SMPTE Timecode is universally used and recorded either as a linear signal on a sound or cue track (Longitudinal TimeCode – LTC) or within the actual picture signal (Vertical Interval TimeCode – VITC). To do a dissolve (or more complex effect) two play-in machines and one recorder are used (see figure below).

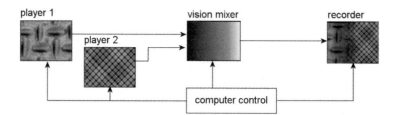

Each play-in VTR shows one of the two shots being mixed and the third records the output from the switcher. Many transitional effects can also be activated by timecode, as can most switchers (vision mixers). Computer control is

used to memorize the nominated frames where various specified events (cuts, dissolves, etc.) will take place and the list detailing all of the resultant timecodes is called the Edit Decision List (EDL).

The problem with linear editing is that each shot is laid down in sequence and therefore the length of a given shot cannot be altered without re-recording everything following that change. Most modern editing therefore uses non-linear editing (NLE) systems which may be either 'online' or 'offline'. In NLE the images are held on a computer hard disk and are therefore accessible in any order chosen irrespective of their actual position on the disk. The viewing order is determined by a list held in a database and when editing it is this list which is manipulated and not the actual frames. Thus sequences of shots can be almost infinitely re-ordered and 'tweaked' until the desired result is achieved. Editing software such as 'Avid' and 'Final Cut Pro' also permit a vast array of effects, sound and titling tasks to be executed within the program. Whilst complex VFX compositing is in progress effects editors will often create rough temporary versions (temps) of effects shots as placeholders until the 'finals' have been approved and can be inserted. Large projects often adopt a 'versioning' strategy wherein the latest versions of VFX are inserted daily so that producers and supervisors can precisely monitor the status of any given sequence.

The basic principle of re-recording is that in addition to, or in place of cameras, pre-recorded videotapes would also be used. Thus for the actor playing two parts, a locked-off camera could photograph him on one side of screen playing his first role. The tape would be rewound and replayed synchronously to the vision mixer (switcher) where a split-screen would be set up between live camera and off-tape image. It is most important to set up this VTR very carefully since differences in gain, timing or colour phase would instantly draw attention to the matte line. If required, a sound or picture cue can be recorded on the replay tape to help synchronize the action. A second video recorder can then record the combined output (figure below).

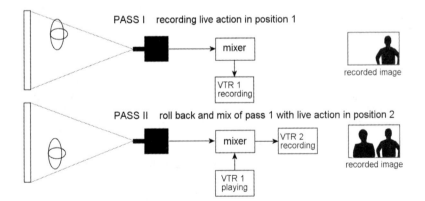

This technique is often called 'roll back and mix' from the early days of editing when it was used to provide dissolves between sequences shot as live. In the early days of video recording, such shots would usually be done as described above, but nowadays it is not necessary. However, the technique is still frequently used (even if the composite is not recorded) because replaying the earlier action 'feeds' the actor with the timing and previous lines and therefore aids the performance.

This same technique would also be used for combining a glass painting with a pre-recorded action sequence shot on location. The tape can be replayed onto a monitor with a NAM between the off-tape image and that of the camera shooting the glass (see figure below).

The painting can then be done whilst looking at the monitor (an easy skill to develop) and filling in the black hole left by the matte.

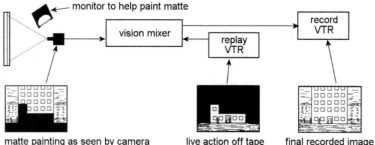

matte painting as seen by camera   live action off tape   final recorded image

If the action was shot without a matte then a video switch (keyer) can be fed from a video rostrum camera (camera looking at light box). The mixer can be set up so that under the camera anything white is replaced by the output of the VTR and anything black by the camera viewing the glass. Thus if under the camera a silhouette is drawn on tracing paper it can determine how the two video images are combined. By putting the output of the switcher on a monitor beside the rostrum a matte can be drawn to determine where the glass painting will appear over the original action shot (see figure below).

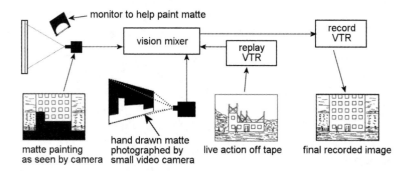

matte painting   hand drawn matte
as seen by camera photographed by   live action off tape   final recorded image
              small video camera

To make it easy to draw the outline the 'infill' (i.e., the image replacing the black) can initially be a bright saturated colour, which will show up well against the background image it is being drawn over. Once the matte is drawn the

5 Composite photography

117

intended video source can be switched back in again. To check the accuracy of the matte line, mixes or wipes (usually horizontal or vertical) can be run to and fro between the composite and any of the raw elements. This same technique can be applied to miniatures, photographs, graphics or even to small sections of set to be added in to location shots or pre-shot models.

The most usual method of compositing on video is (just like with film) to record the various elements separately and then combine them in post-production by feeding two or more video players into a mixer (switcher), combining them, and then feeding the result to an additional recorder. Thus, for example, the double role gag could be accomplished with a single camcorder on a location where the actor would play first one role and then the other. In post-production these two could be composited together and, if the demarcation was complex, it could be hand-drawn as described above. As with all the previously described film effects it is important to ensure that the effects elements are suitably shot, for example with rigidly locked-off stable cameras, and backgrounds with helpful architectural lines or heavy textures in which the matte line can easily be concealed.

In the early days of post-production effects and when tape systems were much less sophisticated, the main objective was to try to minimize the number of generations at almost any cost. Frequently commercials' editing sessions would use six play-in and one record machine in an attempt to cut down on the number of re-recordings necessary. As with film opticals, video multigeneration effects can be either cut in to a shot, or the entire shot may be put through the process.

To keep the generation count low it is often expedient to use the so-called 'invisible edit'. Let's say that our double role piece is altered to have the actor play five parts, with the first character being confronted by each of the others in turn. The first person enters frame from the right and then the subsequent characters come in from the left. All five pieces of action are recorded on a locked-off camera with stand-ins playing the various roles in each element, to feed the actor his lines and guarantee any shadows or reflections correctly reproduced. In post these could simply be matted one after the other by adding each in turn (see top figure opposite).

Pass one would combine the first (right) element and the second (left) element, creating a second generation tape. On the second pass this new tape would be replayed and have the third element added; on the third pass, the fourth character would be added and finally the fifth on the fourth pass, thus making the composite fifth generation. Given that the entire production would be dubbed to make a transmission copy this shot would be a sixth generation – not great in analogue.

Using invisible edits this generation count could be cut down to two. As before, the second element is added to the first by a split screen, and the composite recorded. Now the third element is set up alongside the original tape of the right-hand character – in other words the record tape remains the same. An edit is set up to the next frame just after the second character has exited on the

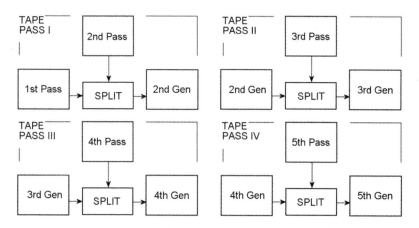

master of the first character, and the third character is added by a split screen (see figure below). The result is that the entrance of the third character is still only a second generation and, by using the same technique, an infinite number of additional visitors could all be added without any further generational loss.

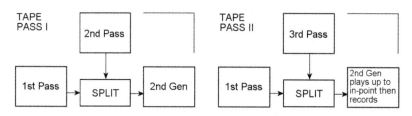

Digital video systems do not suffer from any generational losses at all and therefore avoid this complexity – they will be dealt with in Chapter 8.

Where a number of totally different elements are to be combined, other methods may need to be used to minimize generations. In a four-way multiscreen for instance, where four distinct shots are being added together, the invisible edit system could not be used. But careful planning can still reduce the generation count (see top figure on page 120). On pass I, images 1 and 2 can be combined to produce one master and, on pass II, images 3 and 4 can be combined to produce a second master.

On pass III the two masters are combined and the four-way split has been created in three rather than four generations. This example underlines the fact that very careful planning (best achieved by using technical storyboards) is needed, particularly to make sure that the various elements go on to the correct tapes. If two master elements which need to be combined end up on the same tape then one of them will have to be duped and thus unnecessarily drop a generation.

5 Composite photography

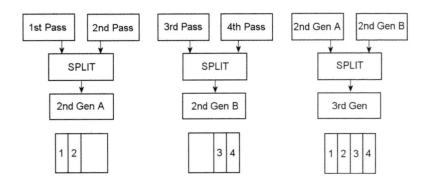

1st Pass	2nd Pass		3rd Pass	4th Pass		2nd Gen A	2nd Gen B

With machines capable of freeze frames and recorders capable of single-frame recording it is even possible to do travelling mattes frame by frame. In the double role example, a rushed location shoot with a single camera and no replay might result in the actors 'breaking the matte' by crossing the demarcation line or indeed this might be designed-in to make the effect more believable. For example one character might walk across frame to her stop position (see figure below) and then the other character enter frame and walk up to her. Astounded by their likeness, the first person might step back and then the second again step towards her. To keep this action all very close, a hand-drawn matte line might be animated to follow the action as it moves to and fro across the screen.

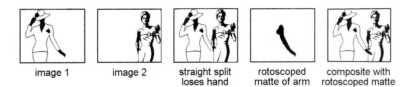

image 1   image 2   straight split   rotoscoped   composite with
                                  loses hand   matte of arm   rotoscoped matte

Such hand-drawn mattes are much easier to accomplish on video than in film opticals, since the frames are drawn and combined at one time as opposed to having to be photographed and processed as a sequence before compositing can begin. This type of work is even easier to deal with in digital. On the other hand these video processes are much simpler to deal with when using film-originated scenes. Remember that film only has 25 (Europe) or 24 (USA with 3/2 pulldown, see page 13) temporal frames per second, whereas video has 50 or 59.94 temporal fields – in short, it has twice as many mattes needed to composite the same duration. However, when transferring film for such purposes it must be done so, using a very steady telecine system and, if transferring from a print, it should be neg perf (see page 19).

6 Combined action with pre-shot backgrounds

The problem with techniques such as glass painting or matte shots is that they do not permit the foreground action to overlap the background. In the real world everything overlaps and for believability it should do so in VFX too. Fully integrating actors in synthesized scenes is one of visual effect's main tasks and the principal techniques for achieving it are so common that they tend to be used for all composite shots, even where a more basic system might do just as well. The simplest methods require that the background is pre-shot so that it can be placed behind the live action element as that is photographed. This is a disadvantage both organizationally and creatively because it requires pre-visualizing the shot and deciding up-front where and when it will be photographed. It also has technical consequences in that the background will be one generation greater than its foreground. This can result in the subject having a slightly stuck-on or cut-out appearance if the qualities of the two elements are not carefully matched.

Live action foregrounds may need to be pre-photographed because actors are unable to attend locations. This may be because of high costs where the locations are distant, inaccessible or too dangerous for the insurance company's tastes. Alternatively, the background may be totally imaginary and has to be created as a computer or physical model. Finally, a real background may need to be modified to fit the script's requirements properly, for example, where modern elements such as signage have been added to historic buildings.

Physical backgrounds

The easiest way of putting a subject, such as an actor, in front of a simple scenic background (e.g., one that does not move) is to stand him in front of a 'backdrop'. This is an extension of the glass painting principle where the background is painted in its entirety and at a scale appropriate for it to be placed behind the subject. The basis of most scenery used in the theatre, this would not be classified by most people as an 'effect' at all. It does, however, form the basis for many of the more complex effects systems.

For a painted back-drop to succeed, it must have the perspective of the taking lens and have correctly aligned vanishing points. In other words, it should have the same viewpoint as the camera. If the painting is looking down slightly then the camera should look down too; an upward tilt would be totally unacceptable. The lighting shown in the painting should be directionally and qualitatively the same as that on the live action. The foreground elements should be positioned far enough in front of the backing to ensure that they can be independently illuminated without affecting one another, and to give suitable separation. For example, if a close shot is being made then the background should be far enough away to be thrown out of focus, if that is what would be expected were the shot real.

One major problem with this arrangement is that the background is at a uniform distance and therefore focus. If the background is supposed to be distant then it may be too clear, and, although it can be painted to suggest atmospheric perspective, this is not controllable during the photography.

Large scrims or nets can be used here to introduce a variable diffusion controlled by how much frontal light is applied (see figure below).

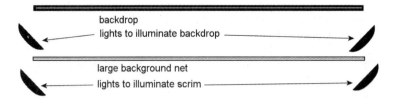

For instance, if the foreground net curtain is totally lit and the back-drop unlit, then there will be a pure white background. If the net is kept shaded and the back-drop is fully illuminated, then it will be only slightly diffused but fully visible. Any adjustment between these two extremes will determine the clarity and visibility of the backing. Excellent transitions between backgrounds can be made by painting a different background image on the net and then cross-fading the lights between the two – this has been used to great effect on many movies, most famously by Vittorio Storaro on *One from the Heart* (1982).

The style of the painting is down to the individual shot but, in general, scenic painters are able to produce extraordinarily realistic back-drops (cycloramas, cycs) in a very impressionistic way and with a frighteningly small amount of detail. For an individual pick-up shot, say an extra close up deemed necessary during editing, the first thought is often to send out a crew to shoot a suitable background and then composite it behind the actor. All too often this expense and delay could be avoided by having an artist view a pertinent shot from the sequence and then simply paint the necessary background. In most cases, it hardly matters that on a close-up the background is not moving, given that it will be out of focus.

The theatrical back-drop becomes a visual effect by the simple act of painting it around the circumference of a large drum (see figure below).

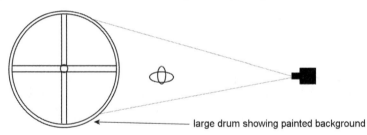

large drum showing painted background

123

This can be used to provide moving backgrounds behind characters, for example whilst horse riding or travelling in a vehicle. As long as it is required that the background be blurred and indistinct, this arrangement can work extremely well. If the repetition is too frequent with even a wide diameter drum, then a large loop stretched across two drums can be used to provide a longer continuously changing background.

The final refinement to this technique is to replace the painting with a photograph. Taking into consideration all of the factors including lighting, perspective, lens and angle involved in a painted backing, a large photograph can be placed behind the live action to excellent effect. The image can be in the form of a front-lit print (photo blow-up, PBU) or a backlit transparency (translite). When using a photo backing, special care has to be taken in controlling its contrast, colour and gamma, so as to match that of the live action in front of it (not to mention the film or video system being used). Where very contrasty backings are requisite, or where light from the background should appear to fall on the live action, then translites are to be recommended, although they are relatively expensive to have made and require care in lighting.

If a very small stage is being used it is possible to make extremely wide shots using a combination of PBU and glass shot. The photo of the entire image is mounted on glass and just the small section where the artiste will appear is cut out. A full-scale PBU is made of just this section and placed behind the artiste to align with the clear section in the glass foreground. With careful control of the light levels and chosen demarcation line, an excellent composite can be made very economically (see figure below).

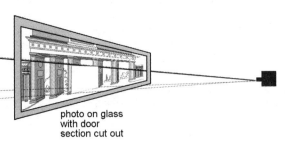

photo blow up
of doorway section

photo on glass
with door
section cut out

Shooting backplates

No matter what system is used for laying a foreground subject over a background, somewhere along the line that background will need to be shot. In most cases the foreground element will not be available to the crew shooting the background and, often, information concerning what needs to be shot will be scant! Moving material shot to go behind a foreground is often called a backplate, or simply 'plate' (from early systems which used a 'plate'-sized transparency). A still image used as a backplate is called a 'stereo' in the USA (after stereoptican – an early projection device).

Irrespective of the compositing system used the quality of the 'plate' will influence the success of the finished product, whether it is photographed before or after the foreground element. The keyword here is 'matching'. If the foreground and background match one another in technical and aesthetic terms, then they will invisibly combine and fool the audience. But any number of subtle differences can contribute to the 'stuck-on' or otherwise inexplicably unconvincing look that composites can so often display. For this reason it is important to understand what the shot is to be used for and to get as much information as possible. If only a verbal description is given, then it is often worth drawing up what you deduce the shot might be and getting the director to OK it before setting off for some distant land.

The objective is to suggest that the foreground and background are simultaneously shot, by the same camera, from the same position. Thus, the angle of view, lens characteristics and all other camera variables, as well as its physical position relative to the scene, must be identical during both recordings. Ideally the two elements would be shot with the same camera and lens, with the same

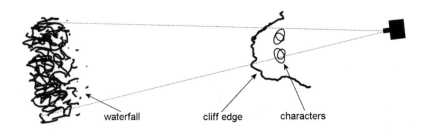

waterfall   cliff edge   characters

recording medium (film stock or tape format) and with the same physical attributes (e.g., camera height, inclination and subject distance).

Imagine that we are providing the background for a 2-shot – a man and woman arguing at the edge of a large waterfall (see figure above). The shot is from the cliff edge opposite the waterfall and it is too dangerous, too moist and too noisy for the scene to be normally captured. The whole point is for the waterfall to appear between the two actors, so the background part of the shot must be photographed first, to ensure a correctly framed line up. Even if this forces the shot to be on a rather wide lens, this would still be acceptable since the whole idea is to achieve a realistic effect – if the shot were done for real then this is the lens that would have to be used. On the other hand it is preferable to use a 'normal' lens to avoid directing the audience's attention to the shot!

To frame-in the waterfall the inclination of the camera and its height, which are interdependent, must also be related to the framing of the actors. The most elegant method of achieving this is to have two stand-ins whose heights match the actual performers. The stand-ins are placed and framed for the final composition and the camera locked off. Now the inclination, camera height and its distance from the performers can be measured, the exposure and focus set, and a short run made of the complete composition (i.e., including the actors) for use as a reference to show how the final image should look.

Next, the stand-ins exit frame and the empty background is recorded with nothing altered. The great advantage of this approach is that the focus is correctly adjusted and therefore the waterfall will be appropriately out of focus. This is a point of some controversy – should the plate be shot 'in focus' or 'out of focus'? The theory goes that you can defocus in post in a variety of ways, but you can't put back focus once it is lost and, therefore, there is no going back on an 'out of focus' decision made at the shoot. However, post softening is not always able to match the look of a defocused lens (the whole field is equally softened rather than varying across a number of planes) so many would always argue for defocusing the camera. If the effect is liked then it saves time in post and automatically gives the correct look. On the other hand, flexibility is essential and the fact is that the waterfall, viewed as OK through a viewfinder enveloped by atomized water, may suddenly look too out of focus when seen in the clarity of a viewing room. Given the small cost involved, the only choice would be to shoot both, once out of focus and then with the lens focused on the waterfall. In addition it is also worth swinging to a wider lens (e.g., if you are using a 50 mm swap to a 35 mm) so as to provide an additional version which can be zoomed and otherwise reframed in post.

There is no room for artistic embellishment in these shots, they must first and foremost service the foreground element to which they belong. Thus for instance, in shooting a wide landscape (such as the waterfall), a foreground branch to 'compose' the shot is a no-go – when the 2-shot is laid over it, the branch, which is closer than the actors, would mysteriously appear behind them! If a foreground branch is required then it should be shot along with the actors as part of the foreground pass.

When it comes to shooting the foreground the same focal length lens (preferably the actual lens) camera height, inclination and subject distance should be set up. Ideally the same DoF should also be adopted, otherwise there might be inconsistencies between planes of focus. In this example, the only 'cheat' might be to over-crank slightly so as to slow down the waterfall just a fraction – to make it look more powerful. But in most cases it is important to have the same shutter speed in order to guarantee similar motion blur.

If the camera position necessary to get the shot was 'right on the edge' and it was therefore impossible to shoot the reference 2-shot, the easiest solution would be to pull back a few feet or pan the camera to the side and frame the stand-ins at the correct distance. Then, with the camera locked off, move forward to the correct position (or pan back) maintaining the inclination and camera height – the small difference in parallax will not be an issue. This example describes a very simple shot, but shows just how complicated the issue of pre-photographing 'plates' can be. This work can also prove very time-consuming, so be prepared to get up at 4 a.m. every day for a month whilst trying to capture the perfect sunrise.

The human vision system assumes that 'the Earth' is solid and therefore that any movement must be in the foreground irrespective of which element is actually moving. In our 2-shot example, if the background shot were jiggling about, the audience would see it as the couple in the foreground shaking inexplicably. Thus the camera should be as physically steady as possible and, in the waterfall example, it should be anchored with sandbags, rocks or whatever to ensure the maximum steadiness. When attached to objects this should be done both safely and to ensure the steadiest shot. In many cases this may require special rigs to be made up, or the use of special stabilizing equipment such as gyroscopic heads (on boats or helicopters) or rigid mounting plates with retaining straps in such inhospitable places as rollercoasters!

Since in many compositing systems the background will be processed in some manner and therefore undergo a hit in quality, it is absolutely essential that the 'plate' is of the very best quality. The camera mechanism itself should be internally stable, preferably with register pins (e.g., Panaflex, Moviecam or later Arri models) and should be steady-tested before taking out in the field. The very best quality should be pursued and, if possible, a higher standard format than that used for the rest of the production. With 35 mm, for instance, fine-grained (i.e., slow) stocks and an open gate should be used to allow for later adjustment and minimal grain whilst, if large-screen projection is to be used, then a larger format such as vistaVision (8-perf) or 65 mm may be contemplated. Another way of utilizing the full 35 mm frame is to use anamorphic ('Scope) lenses. For video, no gain, component and digital but with minimal compression, will give the best results and it may be worth considering higher resolution systems for complex effects shots. Processing usually affects contrast as well as grain, so it is recommended that steps are taken to keep it in line, such as avoiding contrasty lighting and over- or under-exposure which will need correction at the lab or colour grading stages. If, in the case of film, a print will be required (e.g., for projection systems), then it should be made on a step printer using neg. perf print stock to ensure maximum steadiness and may be worth printing on low-contrast material.

Where movement is concerned there are three approaches. One is to provide a large static frame, which contains all of the information over which the move will take place. The second approach is to make sure that the shot contains information that can be 'tracked' by special computer software. The final method is to use a motion control system (or field head) and then do matched moves when shooting the foreground or use the data to drive software if the foreground will be CGI. In this last case it should be noted that the use of such equipment can be a major exercise on a location, particularly if it is in some distant or hazardous region. Setting up motion shots can also be very time-consuming and therefore the decision to use this method should be given extremely careful thought.

If the camera movements are confined to panning or tilting then it should be possible to use a static shot across which the action can be added in post. If it

6 Combined action with pre-shot backgrounds

is only a short pan and the final shot will be in 4 × 3 aspect ratio then it may be possible to contain the action in a 'Scope anamorphic frame (see figure below).

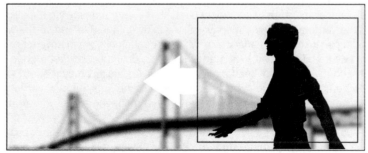

4 x 3 image can be added to and panned across the large 'scope frame

For a larger movement it may be necessary to 'tile' the shot. In this technique a number of overlapping frames are shot which will be joined in post-production to create a much bigger frame (see figure below).

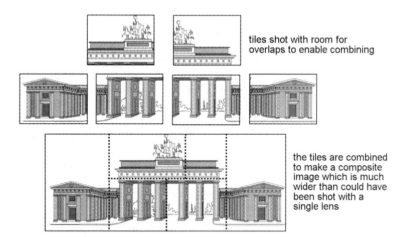

tiles shot with room for overlaps to enable combining

the tiles are combined to make a composite image which is much wider than could have been shot with a single lens

In this method there obviously cannot be anything moving across the overlapping edges of the tiles. Vertical, horizontal or even diagonal moves can be made using this technique and clever action can be choreographed to take place at various points within the composite frame.

When the camera will move through the background then it will be necessary to track any objects (actors included) into it. This is dealt with by placing some form of 'tracking markers' within the scene so that they can be accurately followed by 'tracking' software (see page 236). The shooting crew should bear in mind that any obvious markers that are not part of the scene will have to be removed in post. Consequently they should be minimized or, if possible, objects suitable for tracking but which are apparently part of the scene should be used. Ping pong balls or luminous tennis balls make excellent cheap and ready-made markers, whilst stones on a driveway or carefully positioned furniture and ornaments can make less obvious markers of equal usability.

In the case of moving shots with tracking markers, but also in all back-plates, it is essential to have good reference material (such as stills taken on the set) and detailed data. Everything that could possibly help the crew shooting the foreground (or CGI artistes creating it) should be provided. This should include information on the direction of light, weather conditions and any other details of the location shoot, not to mention all of the technical details already discussed. The distances between, and size of, tracking markers is very useful information and a plan including measurements between the set's main components, particularly the artistes, will save much time and money at later stages.

One of the most common types of moving back-plate, but one which can move freely, is the view from a travelling vehicle. Effectively the camera is fixed to the moving vehicle in these shots and therefore does not have to move in sympathy with the backplate. Shots of people in cars are very popular and a whole range of techniques have been developed for this specific category.

Consider what happens in a real car. Whether mounted on the frame or hand-held, the camera has a fixed view (apart from intentional camera movement) which is tied to the car interior. The entirety is moving along the road and therefore the view outside the car can be considered as independent of it. Two things will intrude on the interior – the external lighting (and therefore exposure) and big movements due to the forces of motion. Lighting can be extended into the foreground when it is shot, by moving/cross-fading lights. Whilst shooting the interior, sudden movements that would cause camera judder, lurches from the actors and an apparent movement with respect to the background, can be achieved by rocking the entire car (with or without the camera inside it) but there should be some restraint given that the whole idea of using composites is to avoid the excessive bumpiness of a real car ride!

If a bump occurs in the back-plate it is very difficult to time a corresponding bump to the studio mock-up, so it is important that the plate used for the scene be as smooth as possible. In the special circumstances where the shot must be timed to interior action, such as the car stopping and then starting again, a timed script must be provided and preferably the director should attend the shoot. However, matching shadows and highlights is easy, so anything goes.

Although possible and often done, it is not recommended that travelling vehicle 'plates' are photographed from a hand-held camera stuck out of a car or train window. For this purpose the camera should be properly mounted on a smooth vehicle and, if possible, with some form of stabilizing head (or lens). It should be locked off and under no circumstances should any attempt be made to compensate for large movements, such as when going over a hill. Throughout the world there are many grip-hire/transport companies who have vehicles designed specifically for shooting such material. These have various fixing points on their bodies to allow the most frequently used positions and boast a very smooth ride. Although the camera will need to move smoothly it will not have to be any steadier than for normal photography so neither steady testing nor a register-pinned camera will be required and, indeed, super 16 mm would be acceptable for many shots. Although far from ideal, If no stabilization is available and the camera does need to be hand-held (e.g., on a motorbike) then wide lenses will minimize vibrations and, in post, the shot can be tightened and stabilized using special software.

Cameras should be positioned at approximately the height and angle at which they would be inside the scripted car and should be equipped with the same focal length lens (or one notch wider to allow for adjustment in compositing). If in doubt, then the camera should be roughly level, with the horizon line just above centre and, for most purposes, have a 35–50 mm lens for 35 mm film or, for video, a lens with 25°–45° horizontal angle of view.

One pass is required for each different angle within a scene. Thus, for instance, if shooting a conversation between two people in the back seat of a car, two sideways shots and one back-facing shot would be needed to cover two close-ups and a 2-shot (see figure below).

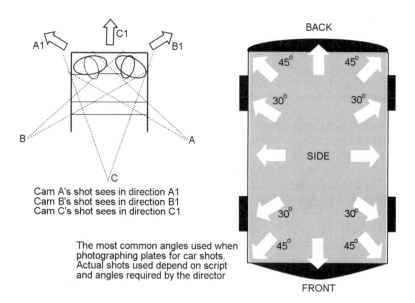

Cam A's shot sees in direction A1
Cam B's shot sees in direction B1
Cam C's shot sees in direction C1

The most common angles used when photographing plates for car shots. Actual shots used depend on script and angles required by the director

The most common angles are 45° or 30° towards the back and/or front, sideways, front- and back-facing. If practical it is usually best to shoot all the angles at once using multiple cameras. This absolutely guarantees consistent lighting and action. If a fairly wide shot is being made in the car, which sees out of two windows at once, then two plates can be shot as tiles to fill in the two views (see figure below).

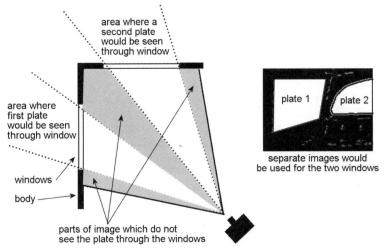

separate images would
be used for the two windows

If time is a major problem then it is sometimes possible to shoot only one direction and reverse it for the opposite direction but, of course, the direction of travel will change and in most cases (but not all) this might be obvious.

Shots facing directly forwards or backwards will tend to look as though the travel is slightly slower than in reality. This effect will be increased with wider, and decreased with narrower, lenses. Similarly, shots made at right angles to the direction of motion will appear to be faster than in reality, and this effect will be increased by tightening the focal length, or decreased with widening it. It is therefore usually worth adjusting the car's speed when shooting these angles – varying camera speed is not appropriate because it would cause pedestrians to move unnaturally.

As with all effects components, it is essential to get as much information as possible about the use for the plates. What sort of car, what time of day, what is the action, the mood, the car speed and weather? Is this a car chase or a romantic honeymoon, how should it look and where are the actors seated? Armed with all this information it will be possible to organize the shot – are police required, at what time of day are local traffic jams and is heavy traffic preferred or a clean run? All of these questions must be answered before hiring an expensive vehicle, equipment and personnel.

Background (scenic) projection

Instead of a large printed still-photograph or painting, a screen can be placed behind the foreground action and still or motion footage projected on to it. This is the basis of background or scenic projection. The screen can be either translucent, with images projected on its rear, or solid, with the images projected on its front. It can be either very large and fill the entire background or it can be very small and integrated into the setting. The projected image can be a film print or video, pre-recorded or live. The main advantage of the system is that, in all its forms, the composite can be seen through the camera viewfinder/video tap and, in the rear-projected systems, by everyone on the set. The camera is free to pan and tilt on all systems and to make certain limited moves in rear systems. With all of these processes a complete composite is created in-camera and can be seen in rushes – there is no lengthy delay waiting to know if the shot has worked. The disadvantage is that with all the methods apart from live video, the background image must be pre-recorded and therefore the shots have to be meticulously planned in advance so that crews can prepare them in time. Also, all systems share the need for complex and often heavy equipment, specialized knowledge and involve tricky optical and camera-projector synching issues.

Rear projection

Often incorrectly known as 'back' projection or BP (easily confused with the generic term of 'background' projection) and also known as transparency or process projection, rear projection (RP) was perfected in the 1930s using much of the new technology devised for sound. With the coming of colour, projection became the main effects tool for putting actors into separately shot backgrounds, because of the difficulty of using other compositing systems with early colour processes. In the 1940s and 50s scenic projection was overused and although the majority of rear projection shots go unnoticed to this day it got a bad name! In the late 1960s RP was eclipsed by a form of frontal projection but, with the arrival of digital compositing methods in which blue/green screen systems have been perfected, projection has largely fallen into disuse. However, with the coming of new digital projection systems and other large-screen display technologies, there will almost certainly be a revival of the technique, given its superiority from an actor's perspective. This is because, to date, uniquely, this system allows the artiste standing in front of it to see what it is showing. Much of the problem with blue/green screen shots comes from the inability of the actors to see or know what on Earth (or off the Earth) is happening. Timing of shots is an ordeal and so is cueing them – but not in RP, where the actors can see what is happening and take their own lead from the background image itself.

Unfortunately, mounting a rear projection shot is quite intricate and the system suffers from a lot of optical and synchronizing difficulties.

The basic set-up (see lower figure opposite) is to project a picture on to the back of a translucent screen with a camera shooting it from the front side. The action is played betwixt camera and screen. The projector and camera shutters or scanning must be exactly in synch to avoid a variety of defects.

For film, a special projector is required which has a camera-like movement with register pins and requires prints made on B&H perforated stock. Without this arrangement the film weave would be too great for the magnification involved and the solid-floor standing foreground would appear to jiggle about.

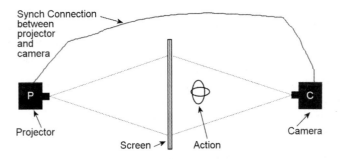

Synch Connection between projector and camera

P — Projector

Screen → | Action

C — Camera

Additionally low-contrast or flashed prints may be necessary since they are being rephotographed on to normal camera negative rather than the special fine-grained low-con intermediate stocks which are designed for this purpose.

Also in common with camera mechanisms, process projectors must have a single-bladed shutter rather than the standard two-bladed Maltese cross arrangement in normal theatrical projectors. This is because it is necessary to have the camera and projector shutters precisely in step so that exposure and pulldown phases coincide – otherwise maximum image transmission would not occur. This arrangement (see figure below) means that when a reflex camera is running, no screen image will be seen at all in the viewfinder because both shutters are simultaneously closed and, of course, a reflex viewfinder only sees through the lens when the shutter *is* closed.

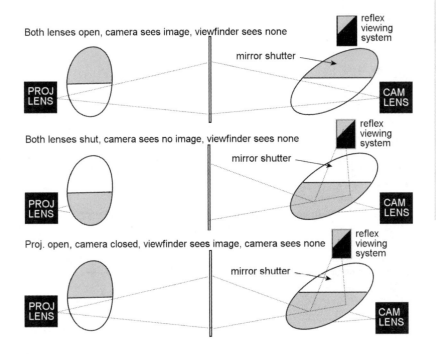

Both lenses open, camera sees image, viewfinder sees none

reflex viewing system

mirror shutter

PROJ LENS — CAM LENS

Both lenses shut, camera sees no image, viewfinder sees none

reflex viewing system

mirror shutter

PROJ LENS — CAM LENS

Proj. open, camera closed, viewfinder sees image, camera sees none

reflex viewing system

mirror shutter

PROJ LENS — CAM LENS

The single-bladed shutter means that the image flickers horribly to those watching it and also confuses both the eye and exposure meter when estimating the stop. Correct exposure is therefore subject to experience and careful testing.

A special interlock system is required to properly synchronize with the camera. The standard method is to use 'selsyn' slave motors on the camera and projector, both locked to a separate 'master'. If computer control is being used then stepper drives can be used on projector and camera. If a video camera is being used to shoot, then the projector should be locked to the camera synchs. These projectors have to be quite powerful since a lot of light is lost from one side of the screen to the other and therefore they may have cooling systems which can be very noisy and require soundproofing. Wide-angle lenses cause extensive distortion and add to 'hot-spot' problems so have to be avoided; therefore the projector-to-screen distance is quite large. This means that a lot of space on an RP stage is wasted on 'throw'. One solution is to use a large front-silvered (and optically very flat) mirror to fold back the projected beam of light and to flip the film to maintain orientation (see figure below).

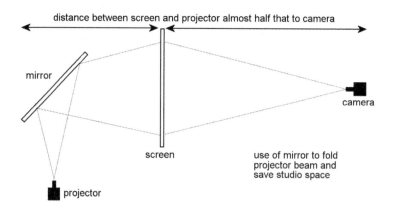

distance between screen and projector almost half that to camera

mirror

camera

screen

projector

use of mirror to fold
projector beam and
save studio space

Apart from being driven by a selsyn motor or a computer-controlled motor, which is able to lock to external pulses, there are no particularly special requirements for the camera. Since it is photographing both the live action image and the projected image together it does not need to be pin-registered and indeed can even be hand-held.

'Hot-spot' is the main defect in rear projection. The distance from the screen centre to the projector lens is less than it is to the edges and therefore, because of light's inverse square law, the image brightness at the edge of screen will be less than in the middle. The narrower the projection lens (and indeed camera lens too) then the less this effect, whereas the closer the projector to the screen the greater the effect. Vignetting also occurs because of the greater transmission in the centre of the screen (because the light is coming from directly behind it). Added together, these affect the image in the same way and can be very obvious and so must be minimized. The specially formulated translucent screen material used for rear projection is a compromise between letting through the maximum light (high gain) but therefore emphasizing the hot-spot, or by heavily diffusing the image which reduces light transmission, softens the image and cuts down on the hot-spot. Materials corresponding to these two extremes are made especially for the process.

The hot-spot can be lessened by adjusting the condensers in the projection system and by introducing a small disk of opaque or filter material within the optical system or in front of the lens. However, if these methods are used, camera movement will be impossible. Special screens have also been formulated which are less dense at the edges than the centre and similarly made filters can be placed between the projector and screen. Finally, the back-plate itself can be pre-processed to be more dense in the centre. However, the problem with all of these systems is that they depend on attenuating the light reaching the centre of the screen and therefore making worse the problem of insufficient light, which is itself a potential worry with RP. This is one of the areas wherein modern video projectors can offer great potential, because it is possible to apply the necessary corrections digitally whilst actually looking at the image through the camera viewfinder.

Alignment of the projector, screen, camera and action must be precise. Given that the projected image is two-dimensional (i.e., flat) the camera must look on to it relatively squarely or the image will be distorted, not to mention reducing the brightness of the displayed picture. As a rule of thumb, the optical axis of camera and projector should both line up at right angles to the screen. As narrow a lens as practical should be chosen for the camera to minimize the hot-spot and to allow the live action elements to be as far from the screen as possible. It is important to maintain this separation so that the screen can have the minimum of frontal light falling on it and also reflecting off the backs of the artistes in front of it, otherwise the image will be desaturated and have milky blacks. The camera can pan and tilt without any problem and can be off-axis by about 5° without unduly affecting performance. As long as it moves relatively straight along the optical axis, the camera can also track in or out from the screen, but closing in on the image will obviously increase its enlargement and therefore grain could become a problem. Only certain moves will work. Tracking in to a close-up, for instance, can look phoney when the projected background is meant to be distant, because it will be magnified equally with the artiste as the camera closes in, whereas, in reality, it would hardly change size. If a lot of movement is required then it might be worth considering using a larger format for projection than is being used for photography. Thus the camera may use 35 mm film and the projected image vistaVision. This arrangement would allow the camera to track in quite close to the screen without any visible loss in image quality.

To make one of these shots a success, the matching of foreground and background is of prime importance. Lighting, contrast and exposure should match with particular attention to direction and colour of light. The addition of interactive lighting really makes the illusion work. In a car shot, for instance, lights can be panned on and off the vehicle and branches passed over the key to match the scene shown in the plate. Sizes and angles should also match and, with suitable data from the shooting crew, this should be easy to set up. However, without precise notes it can be very difficult to guess correctly where the actors should be placed. If the screen is built into a larger setting then care should be taken to avoid shadows or reflections passing over it and the perspective of the set and projected image should match. Where projection is used to back a car, it is best to keep the screen as far away as possible, so as to keep it shaded.

If reflections are required on, say, a windshield, then a screen can be placed in front of it (see figure below) to create a very believable effect.

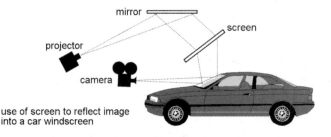

use of screen to reflect image
into a car windscreen

Once everything is set up, the shooting should be reasonably straightforward but, with film, either the projected scene will need to be repeated a number of times on one roll or, after each take, it will be necessary to stop and rewind it back to the start. The consequent wear and tear means that it will always be necessary to have multiple rolls of film available so that for the 'take' there is a clean roll available. Since the projector and camera will usually be so far apart, it is worth having an intercom system in place to coordinate the running up of scenes with the rolling of the camera. Of course, one of the great features of the system is that no such problems occur for the artistes, because they can see (and hear) the projected image for themselves. The intercom will also be necessary for focusing since the focus setting is slightly different between the front and back of the screen and therefore the projectionist cannot see correct focus from his side.

Rear projection is capable of some very sophisticated tricks including our favourite of the actor talking to him or herself. Getting the sizing correct for this is tricky, but on any shot apart from a side-on medium 2-shot, the live actor can see his pre-recorded alter-ego's performance and therefore judge his reactions to perfection. The camera can also pan, and one of the artistes can pass in front of the other. It is also possible to make composite camera moves with movement initially on the 'plate' and then continued on the live action camera, such as the famous crab around Valli in Hitchcock's *Paradine Case* (1947). The background camera pans around the courtroom whilst the actress, seated on a chair in front of the RP, is revolved. This complicated set-up was devised to gain an impossibly huge DoF. The use of treadmills and other similar aids permit all manner of apparently moving shots to be created.

Front projection

Front projection employs a reflective screen as used in a cinema and brings the projector around to the camera side. This immediately gets rid of the RP requirement for a huge amount of stage space, but suffers from the talent being unable to go between the projector and screen without being illuminated by its very bright light and consequently casting a dense shadow on the background image.

This is fine for backing newsreaders who are clear of the screen (see figure below), or on very large sets where the projector can be hidden and its beam kept clear of the talent, such as creating a high rose window in a church set.

in camera composite using foreground projection

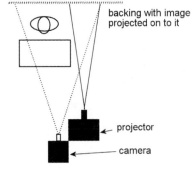

backing with image projected on to it

projector

camera

It can also be used in 'disco' style sequences where the artistes are intended to be overlaid by the projected image – a particularly popular effect in its own right and typified by innumerable *James Bond* title sequences. In all cases it is essential that the screen is shaded as much as possible from any stray light, since only the faintest amount of contamination will destroy the blacks and desaturate the image. With the exception of special situations such as mentioned, front projection is never used for shots where the combination should be undetectable.

However, a variation on front projection known as 'front axial projection' (FAP) went mainstream in the 1960s after being used to project stills on the dawn-of-man sequence of *2001: A Space Odyssey* (1968). Following this it was used extensively until blue-screen systems were perfected two decades later. FAP was made possible by the 3M company's 1949 invention of a retro-reflective material called 'Scotchlite', which was designed to cheaply replace the 'cats eyes' used to aid night driving. This material is constructed from tiny glass beads and has the amazing property of reflecting around 95 per cent of the incident light directly back towards the source (see figure below) with very little reflected in any other direction.

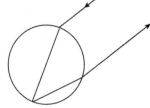

a single bead of Scotchlite light leaves along parallel path - so close as to be effectively along same line

ordinary materials reflect in many directions

Scotchlite reflects incoming light back along its original path

For background projection the screen is surfaced with Scotchlite and the camera positioned exactly as it would be for rear projection. The projector is set up at right angles to the camera (see figure below) with a beamsplitter set between the two lenses such that the projector will reflect its beam towards the screen and the camera will view it through the mirror's surface. The optical axes of both camera and projector are effectively superimposed and so the return beam of light will be directed straight into the camera lens. With a 50/50 split, one stop is lost from the projector's original intensity at the screen, and one stop is lost from the entire exposure at the camera.

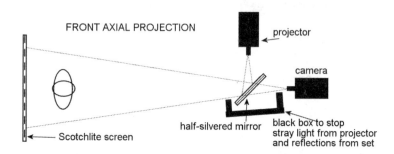

FRONT AXIAL PROJECTION — projector — camera — half-silvered mirror — black box to stop stray light from projector and reflections from set — Scotchlite screen

Since almost all of the light is returned, the projector can be of a much lower power than would be the case for any other system. An FAP projector might use a 2 kW quartz bulb in comparison with the 150 kW arc used in RP. Typically 1 ft/cdl at the screen would give the same exposure as 400 ft/cdl illumination on the artiste in front of it. Indeed, the intensity of the projected image is so low that when an actor stands in front of the screen under normal illumination, the projected image will be totally washed out and invisible.

Because of the projection system's efficiency it is possible to shift to 70 per cent transmission and 30 per cent reflection to increase the photographic exposure. However, against this, the screen material may add a slight green cast and this will have to be compensated for by filtration on the projector lens. Despite being much smaller, the projector will usually be much closer to the action than in RP and therefore may still require to be soundproofed. Because of the complexity of this optical arrangement, camera, projector and beamsplitter should be built into a special rig, which is vibration-free and rock-steady, yet reasonably easy to move around. Given that the projectors do not need to be very powerful, it is possible to construct them from an old register-pin camera such as a Mitchell NC. An extra precaution required in FAP is that reflections in the beamsplitter must be eliminated (see Schufftan process, page 89). It is also necessary to position a 'black box' to capture the stray projector light which goes straight through the beamsplitter (50 per cent or more of its power!). It will be necessary to flip the film in the projector to compensate for the mirror.

Normal studio lighting can be used on the setting and talent since any reaching the screen will be thrown back towards the luminaire causing it and not to the camera. With the normal high-gain Scotchlite, only lights within a 30° radius from the optical axis will start to reflect back towards the camera. If there seems to be too much ambient light then turn off everything else and, whilst viewing through the camera, have the various suspect lights flashed – the guilty party will become immediately obvious! Determining exposure is very difficult and can only be approximately worked out by using a spot meter from the camera lens position but through the beamsplitter. Getting the balance between foreground and background is difficult and best solved with a Polaroid or digital camera to visually test the settings.

One remaining problem is that there will be a shadow of the artiste standing between the projector and screen (see figure below) but, if the camera and projector are correctly aligned, that shadow will fall precisely behind the body causing it.

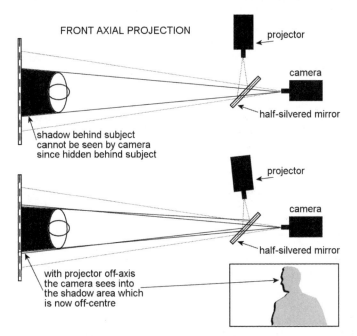

FRONT AXIAL PROJECTION

projector

camera

half-silvered mirror

shadow behind subject
cannot be seen by camera
since hidden behind subject

projector

camera

half-silvered mirror

with projector off-axis
the camera sees into
the shadow area which
is now off-centre

Looking through the camera viewfinder it is possible to see if a shadow exists – it takes the form of a fringe or 'matte-line' around the edge of the subject. The shadow is usually a product of optical axes misalignment. The easy way to align the system is to place three lighting stands with a square of 3M material to the left, middle and right of screen at the subject distance from camera. If there is a shadow to the left of all three then shift the camera to the right and *vice versa*. If there is a shadow on the inner edges pull back the camera and, if on the outer edges, push it in. If the subject will only be in the middle of frame then one stand in that position will suffice but the entire field of subject movement must be checked. Projector-bulb alignment and lenses of different width front-element, on camera and projector, can also affect the shadow. If the camera lens front surface is wider than the projector lens then it should be moved back slightly or, if narrower, moved in.

The camera and projector will both need to have the same focal length lens since they are in a 1:1 relationship and should be positioned with their respective nodal points equidistant from the beamsplitter. The easiest way to find the correct camera lens position is to set up the projector/beamsplitter and then find the focused virtual image from the projector with a small piece of tracing paper. Finally, the DoF of the projector lens must include both screen and subject. If the actor is outside this range then her shadow will be out of focus and will show as a halo at the screen. For this reason it is necessary to have an iris diaphragm on the projector lens and to make sure the DoF stretches at least to the subject. Consequently it is good to use wider lenses on FAP systems than on RP.

Synchronizing camera and projector, keeping the screen reasonably shaded and matching angles, lighting and so on, are all identical to their equivalents in rear projection. Since the camera and projector are optically bound together it will be necessary to nodally mount the camera if it is to pan or tilt whilst looking at an FAP screen, so as to maintain their relationship. It is not practical to track the camera independently since it must have a fixed relationship to the projector; however, certain motion tricks are discussed below.

Scotchlite is available in rolls of self-adhesive material or as a paint. The grade normally used is 7610 high gain, available in rolls of 24 ft × 50 yards. A high contrast version, 7615, is also available with a tighter return angle. It varies quite considerably in density from batch to batch and therefore applying the roll material as one would wallpaper can produce visible joins between sheets. It is therefore more usual to cut the material into smaller pieces and randomly cover the cyc with these in a patchwork manner. If it must be used as rolls then it should be applied horizontally, to minimize the number of strips. The join can be overlapped or, if butted together, can be covered with thin strips. To minimize this problem all the material used to build a screen should be from the same batch. The Scotchlite surface is very delicate and therefore should be handled with gloves and trims should be kept and numbered so that they can be used to patch up areas laid from the same section of a roll. The screen should be flat to prevent the angle of reflection and thus image density from varying. The paint is not as effective as the roll material and is very expensive.

FAP has many advantages over RP. Because it does not depend on diffusion it has no hot-spot and produces a very sharp image. Only with an enormous (80 ft-wide or bigger) screen does it suffer from vignetting and this can be minimized by using a curved screen. Stray light washing out the image is much less of a problem and a far cheaper and simpler projector will suffice. Disadvantages are that the artistes cannot see the image and camera movement is much more restricted.

Because of the optical nature of Scotchlite it is possible to create masks and foreground mattes using it. For instance let's imagine that we are putting a live actor into a photograph of an office (see top figure opposite).

This has two dramatic features, a door in the distance through which our character will emerge and a large desk in the foreground behind which he will sit. By aligning a flat covered with 3M material to the edge of the door, our actor can wait behind this and emerge on cue. Another flat, cut to the shape of the desk, can be placed in the foreground and, obviously, when the actor goes

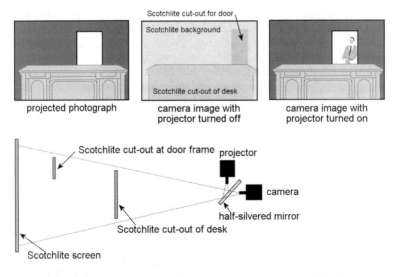

| projected photograph | camera image with projector turned off | camera image with projector turned on |

Scotchlite cut-out for door
Scotchlite background
Scotchlite cut-out of desk

Scotchlite cut-out at door frame   projector
camera
half-silvered mirror
Scotchlite cut-out of desk
Scotchlite screen

behind this he will be hidden by the flat over which is projected the desk image. This allows for some very sophisticated set-ups using artwork, stills or moving images. One last example is where a character is required to have a portion of his body missing – let's say the head! A mask covered in Scotchlite can be worn and will, like everything else, reflect back the projected image to source.

Along similar lines it can also be used to self-vignette or garbage matte. Where, for instance, lights and sound equipment are in the top of the shot, a card covered with 3M material can be lowered in to mask them out. Like a glass matte this needs to be within both camera and projector DoF.

Similarly, if a very wide angle is required it is only necessary to have suffi-cient Scotchlite behind the actor to back his movements and, closer to the camera, a vignette can replace all of the overshoot (figure below).

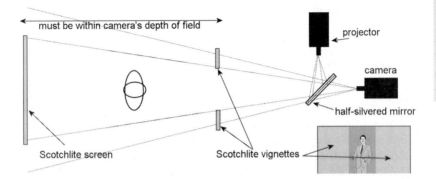

must be within camera's depth of field
projector
camera
half-silvered mirror
Scotchlite screen
Scotchlite vignettes

In situations where the mask is much closer to the rig than the main screen there may be a difference in image intensities. In this circumstance it may be necessary to apply a neutral density filter to the closer elements. This can be done with filter material or ND (neutral density) spray over a cell or glass placed just in front of the mask. The one scenic aspect of FAP, which is not possible to project, is the floor – the material is too delicate to walk on and would be at too acute an angle to the projector. It is therefore necessary to paint or otherwise dress any floor that the actors might visibly walk on.

Unlike rear projection, FAP allows special rigs and equipment to be positioned behind it and to be positioned in any plane. Combining these two faculties, a ceiling-mounted Scotchlite screen can have a hole cut in it from which a spaceman is suspended.

With the camera at floor level looking directly upwards (see figure below) the spaceman can be winched up or down and thus appear to float in front of whatever background might be projected.

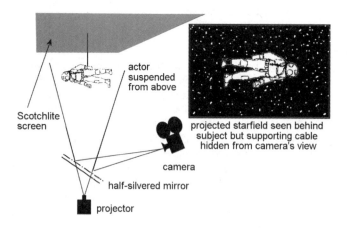

With a normal vertically mounted screen a crane arm can come through the screen to support foreground objects which can then be moved about whilst hiding the arm behind. Where rigs such as wires are required in front of the screen and are thus obvious (and, in the case of wires, their shadows are very obvious) the action can be recorded in front of the projected image. Then, with the rig and subject removed, a second pass of just the projected material can be made. This second pass will exactly match the density and look of the first combined take and can then be used in post to matte out the unwanted material.

A number of enhancements have been made to FAP too. Firstly it should be noted that if the entire rig were moved the projected image would remain the same size and fixed in frame (although if it got too close to the screen its texture would start to show up). This principle can be used to create moving subjects. For instance, if a spaceship is mounted from behind and the FAP rig is then slowly and smoothly moved towards it, the recorded image will picture the spaceship coming towards camera with the background remaining stationary. If this projected image were a planet, we have a standard space movie shot.

By mounting a zoom lens on the camera (nodally positioned) the camera can tighten or loosen on the entire composite. By using a zoom on the projector the background can be enlarged or reduced on shot while the foreground remains stationary. The 'zoptic' system invented by Zoran Peresic initially to make Superman fly, involves the complex mathematics of having a zoom on both projector and camera interlocked so that the foreground can be made to enlarge whilst the background remains stationary or drifts at a different speed. This cleverly achieves the effect of moving the entire rig without actually having to do so – a much more controllable and simpler arrangement if you have the optics to do it.

Advantage can also be taken of the unused side of the beamsplitter. Instead of the black box used to neutralize stray light from the projector, we can position a small set covered in black and, with a suitably attired actor, can create a Pepper's ghost effect since he will reflect directly into the camera lens. This can also be combined with masks to insert additional pictorial content, as in the Schufftan process (see figure below).

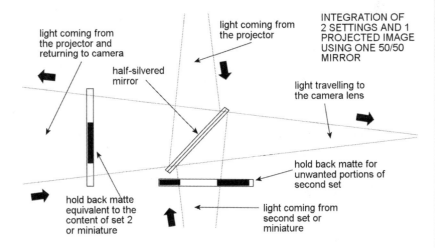

light coming from the projector and returning to camera

light coming from the projector

INTEGRATION OF 2 SETTINGS AND 1 PROJECTED IMAGE USING ONE 50/50 MIRROR

half-silvered mirror

light travelling to the camera lens

hold back matte for unwanted portions of second set

hold back matte equivalent to the content of set 2 or miniature

light coming from second set or miniature

But, even more ingeniously, a second 3M screen can be positioned to pick up this stray projected light. Obviously this would mean that any action would become a superimposed image. However, with suitable masks, it can be used to reinsert material from the projected image in front of the action without having to resort to full-scale cut-outs between camera and subject (see figure on page 144).

This 'dual screen' system was perfected as the proprietary process 'Introvision', most famously used to create the end sequence of *Outland* (1981).

Scotchlite can also be used for a large number of special purposes apart from FAP. Where mystical characters are required to have extremely bright clothing they can wear costumes fabricated from 3M material. Similarly for special objects or graphics within a set, or items such as glasses or dots against black to provide a star backing. In all these cases the complexity of a projector is not required, but a small low-powered lamp easily mounted on the camera will

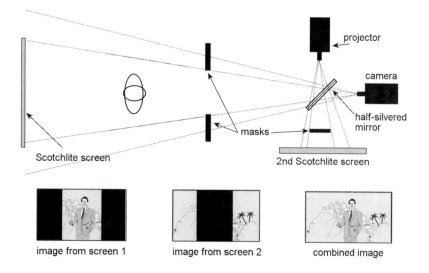

Scotchlite screen

projector

camera

half-silvered mirror

masks

2nd Scotchlite screen

image from screen 1   image from screen 2   combined image

usually suffice. Finally, Scotchlite screens can be used to create blue/green backings for other compositing processes, with the advantages of very pure colour and no light reflected back on to the artistes or setting.

Miniature projection

Where front and rear projection use big screens to enlarge pre-shot backgrounds such as miniatures behind live action, so miniature projection uses very small screens to reduce pre-shot live action into specially created settings such as miniatures. An incredible example of this technique is the last shot of *The Hunchback of Notre Dame* (1939). The shot starts close on Charles Laughton as Quasimodo. He is leaning against a gargoyle and flamboyantly looking around him. The camera pulls back, first to show him sitting high in the cathedral, but continues to track back all in one single smoothly operated shot to show the whole of Notre Dame and then medieval Paris surrounding it. Made in 1939, how can such a shot be done so flawlessly? A huge model of Paris dwarfed by its cathedral was built to quite a large scale and, high in the tower, bounded by a pillar, shadow, balustrade and the gargoyle, was an aperture in the model behind which was a very small rear projection screen. Laughton was pre-photographed against a dark masonry background and this was then projected into the tiny screen. With an interlocked camera and careful lighting it was possible to do any move the director might conceive of.

Small RP screens incorporated into miniatures were used in the original *King Kong* (1933) to place live action into stop frame sequences and, similarly, in the films of Ray Harryhausen. Miniature rear projection and stop frame animation is a very powerful combination. With a screen integrated into the stop motion set the projected live action image can be moved on one frame after each single frame exposure is made. Furthermore, the animated elements can be made to apparently interact with the projected action. For example, human characters can taunt a dinosaur with spears and even appear to prod it. The one potential visual problem is that the 'plate' will have motion blur and the animation will not. To correct this, various techniques are applied to blur the stop frame models, such as 'jiggling' them slightly just before exposure if on wires, recording multiple character positions on one frame or, if the models are computer-controlled, then moving them slightly during exposure (this technique is called Go-Motion). Alternatively modern post-production offers the possibility of adding computer-generated motion blur during post – but care has to be taken not to add it to the already blurred projected background.

Sometimes small, even super 8 mm projectors, are actually concealed inside the miniature or set. An example is where interiors were projected within some of the space vehicles in *2001: A Space Odyssey* (1968). In this instance it was to allow free movement of the model without having to worry about projectors trying to track it from behind. In countless sci-fi films, futuristic control panels are created by having projectors hidden inside them.

Miniature projection can use FAP, rear, front or video projection. All of these processes operate in exactly the same way and with the same advantages and disadvantages as they do in their full-scale live action counterparts. The only real difference is that in rear projection there is an almost unlimited quantity of light available and the camera may get so close to the screen that its texture starts to show. Modern screen material is extremely good, but if the shot is very tight, then it may be necessary to slightly move the screen between each frame to eliminate its granularity. FAP screens are very easy to install into miniatures and models but, of course, the shots will usually have to be static. RP installations have to be well-planned and involve quite a bit of preparation, but offer total flexibility for movement and shooting method.

Miniature projection can be easily added to glass paintings and gives them an added pinch of realism by introducing live action. This method makes assessment of the composite at the time of painting the image much easier and avoids the rigours of latent image combining or the complexities of post. Perhaps the most famous shot done this way was the final image from *Raiders of the Lost Ark* (1981) where the custodian pushes a trolley between all the crates containing who knows what secrets hidden by successive governments.

Where many images need to be added to a shot or the screen exposure is vastly different from the model containing it, multiple exposures can be made. For instance, imagine a shot containing a spacecraft which needs to be brightly and sharply exposed by a single source, but contains a miniature projection screen to show the crew looking out into space. The screen is initially left in darkness and the 'beauty' pass made with the necessary intense light of space. The film is rewound and all of the lights extinguished. Now the projector is turned on and the insert material recorded at the appropriate exposure level. This was the technique used for no less than 12 passes to create the 'Ewok's village' sequence in *Return of the Jedi* (1983).

Although not strictly projection systems, live action can also be inserted into miniatures and other similar small-scale set-ups by using video monitors, LCD screens or Plasma screens, as described in the next section.

Large-screen video (including video projection)

Large-screen video technologies are only now being perfected but, once they are, rear projection will again become a major player in the effects arena. As stressed earlier, the ability for the actors and indeed everybody else to see the picture they are supposed to be interacting with, is of inestimable value. Any of the projection systems discussed can have a video projector substituted for the film machine and pretty well everything else remains the same.

Differences include the fact that lens distortions, keystoning, hot-spot, vignetting and colour compensation problems can all be eliminated by computer pre-processing, which can compensate for a particular defect in real time. This immediately simplifies the process and improves its quality, as do new high-gain screen materials such as those being developed by 3M company using the principles on which Scotchlite was based. Digital projection systems based on digital light processing (DLP) and liquid crystal display (LCD) (see below) technologies have the added advantage of not needing to be synchronized with the camera since their method of updating the image does not result in the blacked out phases which characterize both film and video processes. Finally, the fact that high resolutions can be played off hard disk with the consequent benefits of instant cueing should not be underestimated.

CRT

This method uses what is essentially a high-gained conventional TV (Cathode Ray) tube. Usually three (typically 9″) overdriven monochrome tubes are used with additive filters (red, blue and green). There is a limit to the intensity these are capable of (maximum 350 ANSI Lumens), they are bulky and can only be focused within a very short range because the three lenses are at fixed angles. Precise alignment is nigh on impossible, so these systems are plagued by colour fringing and therefore are not recommended for FX use.

LCD

Liquid crystal displays involve a special liquid held between glass plates. Tiny crystals held in suspension can be orientated electronically and polarize light passing through them. The light also has to go through a fixed polarizing filter and therefore the combination of the two will pass or stop light according to the orientation of the suspended micro-filters. LCDs are the main screen technology used in laptop computers, calculators and watches, all of which use a uniform backlight or reflective mirror. Projectors use smaller (2″ or 3″) LCDs which have a powerful spot beam and lens system to project the image. Resolutions go up to 1280 × 1024 and high-powered models reaching up to 7500 ANSI Lumens are available at a price. This would be quite capable of illuminating a screen of 24 ft width. There is a huge range of LCD projectors suitable for every size of image and budget, too. The contrast is reasonable and because of lag in the system synchronization is not a problem with most shutter speeds. D-ILA projectors by JVC/Hughes use a proprietary reflective LCD and these have much better contrast and resolution than other types.

DLP

Digital light processing systems use Texas Instrument's micro-mirror (DMD) chips. Every pixel is represented by a tiny mirror which can be switched on or off by reflecting incident light to a light trap or the lens (and screen beyond). Light intensity is varied by the speed at which the mirrors are switched. Currently the favoured technology for Digital Cinema, DLP projectors are available all the way up to US$100 000-systems capable of over 17 000 ANSI Lumens and able to fill a 50-ft-wide screen! Much cheaper systems are also available in a wide range of resolutions currently to a maximum of 1280 × 1024. The newer 'black' chips offer quite good contrast and colorimetry and are eminently suitable for rear projection, among other uses.

Large-screen devices

All projection systems are inefficient. Front and rear projection systems lose a fantastic percentage of their signal through screen diffusion, whilst FAP loses 50 per cent of its light through the beamsplitter. A wide variety of large-screen video display systems have been developed in recent years for the exhibition and events industry. These need to be bright enough for viewing in open daylight, such as during a football match or pop concert and therefore have to use a much more efficient technology than projection. The Sony Jumbotron, for example, uses a small diameter CRT for each pixel and, being built up from programmable modules, is very flexible, with screens having been installed as large as 40 m × 25 m. The Panasonic AstroVision screen uses fluorescent discharge tubes in modules 6 ft × 4½ ft and the Mitsubishi Diamond Vision was the first to use LED technology.

LED is the most common technology in this field and special high-output units are available at 6, 10, 15 and 25 mm widths. These systems are very expensive but create outstandingly bright images at almost any size imaginable because they can be butted up together in any configuration. The first system of this type, known as Matrix Lamp Screens, used conventional bulbs which were coloured and, like all of the high-output systems mentioned, could then create pixels of any colour by varying the intensity of the bulbs within each cluster (see figure below). These are not capable of the same output levels as more recent technologies and suffer from short bulb life and inconsistent colorimetry. All of these systems have inherent persistence and therefore can be photographed without specific synchronization.

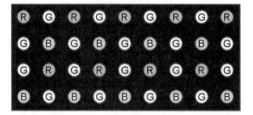

the image is made up from a matrix of lamps in groups of 4

any colour can be mixed by varying the brightness of the three primary colours

These screens are extremely large and, when viewed at all close to, the pixels are very obvious. For ordinary compositing they are not practical, but for special circumstances such as futuristic dramas requiring high-tech backgrounds, they will be the perfect choice – assuming the budget can absorb the large cost. On the other hand, it is important to realize that within the very near future LED screens, or other new systems still in development, will be able to produce superbly bright high-resolution images of exactly the size normally required for this type of work. Eventually these large-screen systems should totally replace the much more inefficient and space-hungry projection systems.

For miniatures and other close work it is possible to use all manner of conventional video displays. LCD and CRT video monitors and computer displays from inches across to the largest home cinema units can be built into models, sets or used as stand-alone devices. Where CRT screens are used the scanning method and speed are such that synchronization will require some special steps to be taken. If the camera (film or video) can be run off the same synch pulses as the monitor then they should lock together if they are both working on the same frequency (e.g., 25 fps or 29.94 fps). If other speeds are being used then, with film cameras, it will be necessary to use some form of synch box such as 'electronic cinematography' or the 24-frame video system. With the synch box connected and the correct shutter angle selected the camera is run without a mag and, looking through the gate, the frame bar rolled off the screen. Where video cameras are concerned the trick is to share synch pulses with the monitor and set it to a multiple of the camera speed.

For example if you are shooting at 25 fps then a computer monitor should be set to 75 Hz, or if 24 fps then at 72 Hz or 59.94 fps at 89.91 Hz. Many video cameras offer a 'clearscan' feature and this usually works a treat! Of course, as mentioned, the use of LCD and similar technologies which have lag may not require synchronization at all, depending on the shutter speed and particular screen.

Finally, between these two technologies there are gas plasma screens. These are the so-called flat screens which can be hung on a wall. They are bigger than most conventional TVs and monitors but smaller than large-screen devices. When new they give excellent pictures, they are bright and may not require synchronization with the camera depending on the model and specific speeds in use. These are currently the favourite for in-shot monitors on news and current affairs programmes, where they have almost totally replaced the inconvenience of blue screens for over shoulder image or for remote interviews. The downside is that their colour accuracy degenerates with time and they can easily burn (i.e., remember an image which has been left static for a long time).

7 Self-matting processes

Self-matting processes automatically derive travelling mattes of the foreground action without the necessity (and expense) of rotoscoping. They permit independent photography of *both* foreground and background; avoid the optical defects inherent in projection-style systems and the necessity of the background losing a generation relative to the foreground. Such systems give total flexibility and allow the creation of just about anything a director might think of. On the downside they are technically very complex and the background image will not be visible to the actors, nor indeed to anybody else, unless it is pre-shot and sophisticated monitoring equipment is used. The flexibility, convenience and superiority of digital systems have pretty well eliminated the use of optical methods for combining elements, but they will still be considered here for historical, contextual and explanatory reasons.

Brightness separation matte

The simplest way of automatically creating a matte from a foreground subject is to shoot it against a tonally different backing and by choosing an appropriate brightness or luminance level to isolate it. Imagine that we photograph a blonde, white-skinned female wearing a white dress and shoes against a black background. If she is evenly illuminated without dense shadows then it should be possible to combine her with a suitable background. If the area of the background where she was going to be placed was dark, then a superimposition might produce a relatively solid-looking combination. However, if the

live action
shot against
black

cam neg of live
action shot

contrasty print
(the matte) made
from cam neg

contrasty neg
(countermatte)
made from matte

original location
shot used for
the background

camera neg
of background

latent image
after pass of
bkgd and
countermatte

inter-pos created
after second pass
with cam neg and
the matte

inter-neg made
from the I/P

final print made
from the I/N

NOTE: in the above white represents
clear areas of the actual film material

background image was slightly lighter, then she might appear to be transparent. If, using film, we made a very contrasty print and then from this a very contrasty negative, we could create a matte and countermatte (see figure opposite). If a fine-grain interpositive (interpos, IP) was then produced by first running it with the background through a printer (or bipack camera) in contact with the matte, rewinding it and then re-exposing it, this time with the foreground negative (and a countermatte if necessary), the result would be a combined image (composite). From this interpos a new interneg could be made. This process would work equally well with a dark-skinned actor wearing a black suit and shoes photographed against a white background.

Exactly the same results can be achieved using a video switch (see page 105) with the foreground fed to its key input. This is known as a luminance key, foreground insertion, or overlay and, with the clipping, key or threshold level set such that everything below (or above) a certain level will be replaced by the background image, it will produce a composite (see figure below). On a digital system life becomes even simpler, where pixels above (or below) the chosen value in the foreground are replaced by the equivalent pixels from the background image.

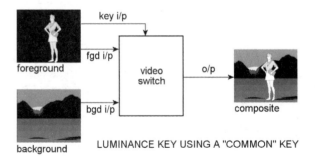

LUMINANCE KEY USING A "COMMON" KEY

Brightness separation has been around from the earliest days of film and television. Patented in 1918 by Frank Williams, it became known as The Williams' process and was used on many epics such as *The Thief of Baghdad* (1924) and *Ben Hur* (1925). Despite the development of blue screen and rear projection it was used for certain scenes in *King Kong* (1933) and *The Invisible Man* (1933) where it was considered more appropriate (the Invisible Man is wearing white bandages). In television the idea was patented in 1936 by J.L. Baird and A.V. Jones and first used in NBC's *Tom Corbett, Space Cadet*. The BBC patented a method using an electronic switch in 1950, calling the process 'inlay' and, where the foreground provided a 'common' key, 'overlay'. These early black and white processes were used extensively on light entertainment programmes, most notably *Ernie Kovacs* (USA) and *The Black and White Minstrel Show* (UK). With the coming of colour, luminance separation fell into disuse apart from titling, but became popular again when digital techniques provided a means of correcting its deficiencies.

Whether the combination is made live, in post-production, using film opticals, video or digital technology, the advantages, disadvantages and techniques remain the same. Where a shadow is required, white is the appropriate background, but with the exception of commercial's 'pack-shots' featuring dark packaging or models, it would rarely be used nowadays, with blue/green screen being a better option.

Black backgrounds, on the other hand, are used extensively if the compositing is to be digital. Black has the advantage of not requiring background lighting and thus can save complexity, time and therefore money during the shoot. Furthermore, rigs supporting the subject can easily be painted black and thus hidden. In all other techniques apart from luminance keying, masks, garbage mattes and vignettes all have to be balanced against the background brightness. For example in FAP, Scotchlite masks near the camera will need attenuation because of proximity to the projector, whilst blue screen foreground mattes will require careful matching of hue and luminance to the main blue backing. But black is black, so as long as it is shaded and kept below the chosen density it will match the background with minimal effort. For effects elements such as smoke and back-lit rain, black is far superior to colour processes such as blue screen, since it totally eliminates any blue spill and, in most digital recorders, luminance is sampled at a higher rate than colour components.

Brightness separation matting can be done live using video cameras and the built in luminance (luma) key of a standard switcher (vision mixer). This has the great advantage of allowing the final composite to be viewed as it is recorded, but the disadvantage of requiring a pre-shot or live background, and the performance being tied to any problems associated with that background. For instance, if both a model which is being manipulated and the actors being put in front of it are live, then a bad take on either set-up will spoil the composite and it will all have to be done again. If the separate elements were recorded independently and combined afterwards, then no good takes on either set-up would be lost due to an error in the other.

Post-production compositing is therefore to be recommended, particularly because luminance keys are frequently imperfect and may need sweetening. A speaking actor's mouth will be dark enough to show the background through it, as will shadows, for example, under his arms. In post-production it is quite easy to fix these errors and may be worth the effort and cost when compared with that of painting a studio blue and lighting it evenly. Not having to worry about the precise timing of the performance nor having to get a perfect key, will save quite a lot of time in the studio. Furthermore, technicians will not be under the same pressure to rapidly adjust levels when in the quiet of an effects suite rather than the crowded insanity of a sound stage full of impatient actors and other personnel. With the adoption of post-production compositing as the main method of combining separately shot elements, film has resurfaced as the dominant shooting medium for television as well as cinema because of the higher resolution, colour and contrast qualities produced in a telecine compared with the output of a video camera.

The use of foreground mattes to match elements behind which the actors may pass is very easy when using a black backing, but requires the background to be pre-shot and replayed on the stage to line it up. Again, such matte work is more easily dealt with in post-production where electronic paint systems can be used to quickly produce the necessary mattes and thus avoid slowing down the shoot. Even where the background does exist and complex movements by the artistes are required, it may be better to just approximate the mattes for line-up purposes and then to do them properly in post, thus saving precious shooting time.

If full-scale set pieces are not going to be used, the actors will still require some sort of visible markers to show where the features (e.g., furniture) they are supposed to be interacting with should be. Working in black this is very easy to do by using black posts representing, for example, doorways or windows – visible to the actors but not to the camera. Sometimes it may be convenient to place a monitor, showing the composite, on the actor's eye line so that they can see what they are doing without apparently gazing at something unseen out of shot. If the cast need to have dialogue fed to them then a double can either stand in the correct position and be removed in post, stand behind a black flat or, if they are going to move behind the main player, then dressed entirely in black (see figure below).

on stage a stand-in dressed in black

but on camera he cannot be seen

If the subject is a model of some sort which is being controlled from nearby then the rig operator becomes the 'artiste' and all of the same rules apply – usually they will be dressed in black so as not to show up. Two situations must be avoided. Firstly, where any such black control mechanism, be it a stand-in, operator or rig arm, causes an inexplicable shadow on the subject and, secondly, where it has to pass in front of the subject which would result in the obscured area vanishing in the composite. This is the one instance where post cannot help, unless at great expense and with extreme difficulty, by painting in the missing information frame by frame.

Technically, luminance keys require careful lining up since in the composite they are prone to dark areas becoming transparent and obvious black matte lines along edges. To avoid creating dark areas, lighting should be pretty frontal and, if from the side, then balanced by a higher fill level than would be usual. Having derived the matte in post, the brightness can always be reduced slightly to restore a more appropriate tonal range. Camera lift (in video) or over-exposure (in film) will not achieve the same effect since they will lift everything, including the backing. The key light will be more controllable if hard, but if soft is used, then the subject should be kept well away from the backing; a practice recommended even with hard light unless it is very steep. Kickers and backlights are good if the composite allows it, because they will reduce shading along the subject's edges.

7 Self-matting processes

Diffusion is bad since it will make a graduated demarcation line between the subject's edge and the black backing, thus eating it away. If necessary, diffusion should be added to the final composite thus concealing any matte edge. Matte lines can also be created by technical faults including timing errors caused by the foreground infill and key signal following electrical paths of different lengths or with different digital delays. 'Blanking' errors will also show up, if the widths or picture heights of foreground and background are different. This will result in a strip of pure background along one picture edge (see figure below).

matte line caused by timing error in key signal against foreground ——   blanking error resulting in background showing thru' along edge ←——

An easy way to check for these technical problems is to slowly slide a horizontal or vertical wipe across the picture looking at the subject's and picture's edges. To make sure that these adjustments are correctly set up, a monitor which has overscan (i.e., which shows the entire picture) must be used and should be slightly 'sat-up' (i.e., have the brightness turned up) since, if it is 'crushed' (i.e., has the brightness turned down), variations in black levels will be hidden. For example, imagine that we have a black flat aligned with a door in the background and from behind which our star will emerge. If this is not as black as the main backing, it may make keying difficult, and yet would not show up on a crushed floor monitor. This situation applies equally in a TV studio with live compositing or to a video tap on a film shoot. On a live key a white card held up against a black backing, with white keyed in as the background, will immediately show up any timing errors. Similarly, to show up areas of bad keying an obvious colour such as magenta can be keyed in as the background, where it will be immediately apparent if it cuts through the foreground.

For lining up content, the wipes as described can be very useful, but often a 50/50 mix can be more helpful. On video this would be between foreground and background and on film between the video tap and a replay machine. The mix rather than the composite will often make it much easier to see where masks and other live elements should be placed, particularly when marking, say, a black poly (foamcore) sheet with chalk ready to cut into a foreground vignette.

As with all compositing processes it is absolutely essential to match the foreground and background. Backgrounds should be shot in the same way as described for projection systems (page 124) but without necessarily being able to see the composite, camera positioning will have to be extremely well-planned and set. It will often be a good idea to mark the positions of elements in the original (background) shot on to the floor of the blacked out studio – this will help both the actors and the accurate positioning of the camera. It is often worthwhile to use aids to the matching process such as posts placed in particular positions relative to the camera. These can all be carefully noted and then having been reset identically in the studio, the live posts can be laid exactly on top of the pre-recorded ones in a 50/50 mix. With film the replay tape will have to be exactly sized and positioned to the video tap as described on page 103. A useful tool to make this process efficient is to have wireframe cubes in a colour which will show up and simply set them into shot – this is much quicker than placing individual posts or stands. Where miniatures are one of the elements, appropriately scaled cubes can be used (see figure below).

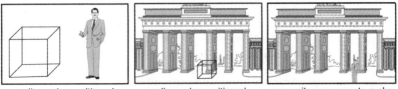

| scaling cube positioned beside the artiste | scaling cube positioned inside the miniature | composite very easy to make by aligning both cubes |

Despite the dominance of blue/green screen systems, luminance keying is still preferred in a lot of situations, even though it may need extensive retouching in post. At one extreme elements shot in very large environments may be more realistically shot against black. For instance, shots of cars, motorbikes or model planes which have to be photographed moving at high speed, but indoors under controlled lighting and for compositing with other elements, may have to be shot in very large spaces such as aircraft hangars. Merely blacking out the windows in such a structure can be a major task, let alone trying to evenly clothe it in blue. With walls maybe 300 ft long by 40 ft high, trying to evenly light a blue screen in this environment would involve a major military campaign not to mention trying to light the subject as well. To black out the interior, paint the floor black and then light only the subject would be a much simpler option – keying could be helped by selecting light-coloured subjects.

At the other extreme, luminance keying is an excellent method for shooting highly reflective and transparent subjects such as commercial pack shots of bottles or other glass and plastic fabrications. In between comes a vast array of specific situations, such as the ghost shots we have looked at before. To have our character talking to her own ghost we might, as always, shoot the first 'live' manifestation in the set. Normally the ghost re-incarnation would be shot against blue, but let's say that this set contains a huge amount of complicated furniture and ornaments. It could well work out much cheaper to drape the walls with black curtains and spray paint all of the interactive elements with black (this assumes a locked-off or computer-controlled camera). The character could have white make-up put on to appear more ghostly in addition to the accustomed white robe. Everything will fit perfectly, the elements will all self-matte and so will the ethereal version of the character. With luminance keying the simple rule is, where special circumstances suggest it, use a luminance key, otherwise use blue or green screen.

7 Self-matting processes

Multiple run mattes

Luminance keys work perfectly when applied to completely white objects washed by flat, even light. Sadly, in the real world, most subjects are highly detailed and look ever better as the light source moves to the side, introducing shading, texture and resulting in a chiaroscuro effect. Where static or repeatable subjects are involved, one solution employs multiple runs to optimize the image for each of its various uses. This means that in, say, a pack shot, which shows a multicoloured and sculpted cardboard box, we could make two passes. In the first (beauty) pass, the pack could be lit to look its best. If necessary there could even be small reflectors in the back of shot where they might create the perfect highlight. Once the shot is recorded, an additional (matte) pass can be made. This time the pack is sprayed with white paint, evenly lit with white light, and the background completely blacked out so as to give a perfect 'white out of black' matte. If more convenient or because the pack is, for example, an expensive oversized prop, it can be put in silhouette by switching off its key light and evenly lighting the surrounding background. For this purpose white cards can be placed around it (see figure below).

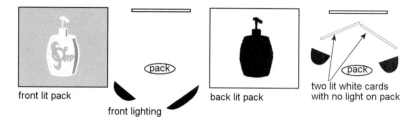

front lit pack

front lighting

pack

back lit pack

pack

two lit white cards
with no light on pack

The background into which the subject is matted might be something totally separate, such as a shot of countryside, clouds or a computer graphic. However, it may be that the purpose of the operation is to perfect the lighting of the pack and its 'actual background' which may be incompatible. In this case a third pass will be made with the pack removed and the background lit for its optimum effect – for example to achieve a perfect gradation perhaps between two colours (see figure below).

subtle graduated
lighting of background

lighting the backing

final composite over
separately lit
background

This technique is often known as front-light/back-light, since it was originally developed in rostrum animation work where an opaque 'cell' was first top lit and then, with the top light off, underlit by the light box incorporated in the stand. The technique came into its own with the development of computer-controlled camera rigs (e.g., motion control) which enabled multiple passes to be made on moving shots, and digital compositing which could sweeten the often imperfect mattes thus produced.

Where a model is supported by a rig it is usually better to try to use a black backing, with the arm also black, since this will simply merge into the background on the matte pass. However, it is not always possible to destroy the model by painting it white, nor to simply light it out if it has dark-coloured patches, so the support structure may need to be white. In this case it may be possible to support the model on pylons (plastic tubes which contain lighting elements) such as neon or fluorescent fittings.

Alternatively, the technique may be combined with another system such as FAP, wherein 3M paint can be applied to the armature and illuminated from camera, where a dimmer can adjust the brightness to match the background. Other special paints such as luminescent, green or blue can be used in association with the appropriate backgrounds. A transparent luminescent paint which fluoresces when illuminated with ultraviolet (black) light can be used to create a matte by doing one pass with normal lighting and one with UV light only. If the subject is painted with the special paint and shot against a black background then under UV light it will fluoresce, thus creating an inverted silhouette. This system is sometimes known as reverse blue screen because the matte will have the subject blue against a black background, unlike a blue screen which will produce the reverse. Since the rig is only a problem in the matte pass along with the subject it supports, it is usually quite a simple task to roto it out during post-production. Alternatively vignettes close to the camera may provide this service live.

Front-light/back-light is most frequently used in association with other techniques. Stop-frame animation, which needs to be composited with other elements, is often created using this method. After each normal exposure the key light is shaded off the subject (it must *not* be switched off during a stop motion effect where this might cause the bubble to fail) and a white card is held behind the subject. This does not have to be accurately positioned so long as it covers the whole of the active area (see figure below) and is not shadowed.

checkerboard recorded with alternating mattes and masters

A frame of this silhouetted mask is then exposed. The alternating mattes and masters are sequentially recorded down the tape or film, producing a 'checkerboard'. This has to be un-stitched during post to create a contiguous matte and master.

Rear projection is particularly suited to front-light/back-light matting. In this case it is generally used to permit the different lighting requirements of foreground and screen. Let's say that we are shooting a model spaceship which is floating above a large and colourful planet. The planet is pre-shot using either a physical or computer model and is projected on to a rear projection screen. The miniature is suspended in front of the screen and the camera set up to shoot both, as for a straightforward RP shot.

The problem is that the space model needs to be lit with a very bright single-source spot to emulate the sun in space. This will cause the model to be much overexposed compared with the typically dim projected image. Furthermore there are lights on the miniature which are dimmer even than the RP! The solution is to use multiple passes. The f/stop is set for DoF between screen and model and camera speed and/or shutter angle is used to set exposure. The first (beauty) pass has the screen covered over with black so that it is not exposed and the miniature illuminated as it will be seen. Next, the lights are switched off, speed is adjusted to expose the screen image and the RP is photographed. In this (background/matte) pass the f/stop must not be altered to ensure that the model is exactly the same sharpness as in the first pass. With synchronization between projector and camera the background plate is rephotographed with the miniature's silhouette hanging in front of it and, assuming nothing has moved, precisely aligned with its position on the beauty pass.

This procedure could use two runs over the same piece of film, resulting in an in-camera composite. However, it may be that full exposure is not possible with the same f/stop, or that the scene is being recorded on tape where the latent image technique is not available. In either case the second pass would involve the camera with precisely the same settings as the first but, this time, instead of the projected image, white light would be shone on the rear of the screen until it met the exposure requirements of the first pass. This would mean the miniature would have the same sharpness exactly as in the first pass but would now appear as a silhouette. With the model removed and a third pass made, this time with the camera focused on the screen and whatever f/stop required to expose it correctly. The three passes would be combined in post-production and, of course if required, the matte and master could be slowly moved during that stage. A final pass might be made to expose the windows of the spaceship, which if illuminated by fibre optics, would require a much greater exposure than any of the others. Having travelled this route it should be pointed out that the necessity of projecting the background shot becomes redundant and it might be better to digitize this as a separate element and combine it directly in post. If this were the case, then the model could be supported from behind since, without the projector, shadows would no longer be a problem.

The front-light/back-light process cannot be used on freely moving subject matter such as live actors since they would not be able to repeat their actions for the two (minimum) passes required. However, with suitable subjects such as models or packs, movement is possible by using a computer-controlled camera mounting or model mover: see motion control (page 205).

Colour separation matting

Film historic

By far the most common way of automatically generating mattes is by detecting a particular wavelength of light. This can be infra-red (IR), UV, sodium vapour (the yellow of street lights) or, most usually, blue, green or any other colour of the visible spectrum. The technique was initially developed for film and then later for television, but became the *de facto* standard for almost all such work when digital compositing took the lead.

The first system to use a blue screen was the Dunning process, patented in 1927. The system owed both its technology and success to the coming of sound. Uniquely for a colour separation technique the background had to be pre-shot. A print was made, bleached and dyed orange. This print was then loaded into a bi-pack camera with raw panchromatic film behind it. The camera was then set up in front of an orange-illuminated foreground behind which was a blue screen (see figure below).

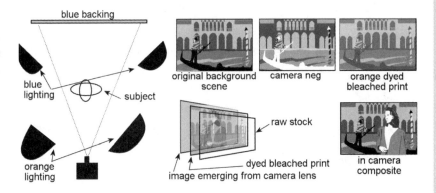

The orange-lit foreground passed through the orange-tinted background 'plate' pretty well unaffected, but the evenly lit blue screen acted as a printer light for it. When processed, the resulting negative showed a composite, which by definition could not have matte lines. However, the system did suffer from foreground transparency (or print-through) where the background plate was too dense, could not be used with colour film, required backgrounds to be pre-shot and, worst of all, if the system failed for some reason, the foreground would have to be re-shot. Made possible by the improvements in panchromatic film required to service sound film making, it was also the impossibility of shooting many location sound sequences that made the system a success. It permitted photography of actors in the quiet of a soundstage but backed by inhospitable noisy backgrounds. Even when RP came into use Dunning was still popular because, although early projection screens were of limited size, a Dunning screen could be as big as necessary.

The Williams' double matting system of 1932 solved many of the problems inherent in the Dunning process and became the model for most subsequent compositing systems right up to the present day. The Williams' process still required an ungainly bi-pack camera but needed neither orange light on the subject nor a pre-shot plate. In this system two panchromatic negatives ran through the camera which looked at a normally lit subject placed in front of a high-luminance blue screen. The film nearest the lens registered the image normally but was backed by a red filter so that, on the rear film, the blue became transparent and the subject relatively dark. This second film was then used to generate a matte and countermatte by the same successive printing techniques as in the original Williams' process. The double matting system was susceptible to transparent foregrounds and matte lines where the duping necessary to get a good matte caused the edges of the image to bleed. However, since it could be lit with ordinary white light (rather than orange) it was possible to deal with even larger scenes than with Dunning. It was first used in *King Kong* (1933) on the scenes where King Kong comes through the big village gates. To have lit this enormous set and its hundreds of extras with orange light would have been out of the question. When the patents ran out in 1940 the concepts used in the process were applied to the problem of colour matting.

Obviously the process could be operated using a single colour negative in place of the top pan film but the results would not be good, suffering particularly from grain in the rear negative. Better results could be obtained by deriving the mattes using colour filters in post-production. If a positive is printed onto pan film using first red and then blue filters, two new negatives will be created (see figure below).

| original camera neg of action against blue | inter-pos from camera neg | inter-neg made through blue filter | inter-neg made through red filter |

The red filtered one will have blue as pretty opaque and the artiste as relatively clear. The blue filtered neg will show clear blue and relatively opaque in the areas not blue. By making a print from the blue neg we would have a relatively clear artiste and once again an opaque blue area. The imperfections in the non-blue areas will be pretty well the opposite of those in the red filtered neg so, by making a matte from the combination of these, variations will mostly be annulled. Successive duplications on high-contrast stock will eventually lead to a good matte using the same techniques as in Williams'. Needless to say the same registration errors, image break-up and matte lines plague the process as in the earlier systems, because of image size changes. This description is somewhat simplified but demonstrates the technical principles.

Over the years much more advanced colour systems were developed most notably using the colour difference technique. This process utilized the three Technicolor B&W separations. Where a colour neg was used these had to be specially made. By printing various combinations of the seps it was possible to create a matte which would transmit blue where there was both blue and green but be opaque to blue on its own. Using this, it was possible to make a new action negative with little blue in the foreground and almost none in the background. This could then be combined to create a composite with much less colour spill in the foreground and better overall colour balance.

Finally there were a number of processes which used multi-film (double head or two-strip) systems to generate the matte during shooting. The idea was to have two film paths, one for the picture and one for the matte. Two cameras with a beamsplitter aligning their paths could produce a normal colour negative in one path and a B&W film in the other. For example, by having a blue filter and ortho film (film only sensitive to blue) in the secondary path you could instantly create a blue screen matte. With the emergence of monopack colour negative film in the early 1950s, all the beautifully engineered Technicolor cameras became available and, with their two film paths, they enabled a number of processes to be easily built.

The trick was to find a way of creating a normal negative for the live action and yet with a perfect matte. At its simplest you could have a colour neg in one 'clear' path and a filter of the screen colour or its complement in the other. Thus, for example, a blue screen matte would be recorded via a blue or orange filter producing a matte or countermatte. However, the quest was to find a system which did not suffer from foreground colour infection nor the problem of having to avoid certain colours, for example, having no blue in the costumes. Two alternatives were available: one was to use light outside the visible spectrum and the other was to choose a colour of such a precise wavelength that it would not matter.

An Ultra Violet system was developed and patented by Warner Bros. Light on the foreground had the UV content filtered out and then a rear projection screen was illuminated by UV lights or white light with UV filters. It was most important to avoid the light from either contaminating the other. The camera had a special mirror which reflected UV light to one film and passed the rest to the other. Since UV is not visible, the master neg had a black background, the foreground was not infected from the screen and there was no restriction on the foreground colours. But there are problems, since the wavelength of UV is shorter than visible light the lens will focus the image closer than it does the visible master image and, thus, the UV film plane has to be closer and so produces a slightly smaller image. The matte therefore requires slight magnification to precisely fit the master. Additionally the shorter wavelength means that UV light is easily diffused and so can spread when passing through glass, etc.

Another system perfected by the cinematographer Gerald Herschfield operated on similar principles using infra red (IR) light. This had the advantage that, being of a longer wavelength, the light did not disperse as did UV but it did need focusing further back than visible light and therefore still required resizing. Since IR is associated with heat, ordinary studio lights that emit quite a lot of heat require heavy filtration. The backing could be black drapes coated with a special dye that absorbs visible light and reflects IR, or an RP screen could be illuminated with suitable filtered white light. With this process there is no restriction on colours used in the foreground. As with UV, a specially coated reflector passed visible light and reflected IR and UV, with the latter having to be filtered out. Special IR film is used to record the matte. Results were excellent.

The most famous of these processes was developed by Rank in the UK with a specially designed camera, and Disney in the USA using modified Technicolor cameras. It uses the special feature of sodium vapour lamps (found in the yellow-coloured street lighting) that they produce a very narrow bandwidth (585.5–589 Nm). By using a special coating on the beamsplitter, only the sodium wavelength is reflected and all else is transmitted. Additional filtering ensures that only the pure monochromatic light reaches the matte and none of it reaches the colour negative. No special focus arrangements are required because sodium light is in the centre of the visible spectrum but, where matte edges are imperfect, the bright yellow of the background can be very intrusive. The system was very popular in the 1960s and was used for all the compositing with animation in *Mary Poppins* (1964).

Owing to the expensive and inconvenient special cameras, special lighting requirements and large amounts of light to compensate for all the filtering, these systems were eventually dropped when blue screen and then digital matting were perfected.

Video historic

Video colour separation followed a very similar development to film. In 1952 the BBC outlined a system which would use appropriately filtered blue- and yellow-sensitive tubes in a special television camera. By illuminating a subject with amber light and in front of a blue screen they could make a composite by feeding the output of the blue tube to an inlay switch as key and the yellow sensitive tube as foreground. The system was monochrome only and was delayed because of worries about registration and in the hope that a suitable camera would be developed in the USA for their colour service. In 1959 a test rig was finally assembled by Duncan Campbell for Graham Muir's *That's Magic*. This used two cameras through a beamsplitter, one with a yellow filter and the other with blue. The artiste was lit with orange light against a blue screen. The system dubbed 'colour separation overlay' (CSO) was reasonably successful, although plagued by alignment problems caused by the inconsistent geometry of early cameras.

The first frequently used system was CBS's 'videoscene', which employed a modified camera from their experimental colour service (1954–1965). Only two tubes were used for this black and white system. Most of the light was passed to the luminance tube whilst the remainder was relayed to one which was blue-sensitive. The two signals were fed to a 'montage' amplifier where a background was added. This transitional system was based on colour technology, but worked only in black and white.

In parallel with the development of colour was that of NBC's matting process called 'chroma-key'. This had the subject against a saturated colour screen (usually blue) and fed the image to an NTSC decoder to extract the required colour signal. If this were done along the B-Y axis, then a key could be generated from a blue backing. Rotating around the sub-carrier phase permitted choices of any colour within the NTSC gamut. The chroma-key process was used from the inauguration of NBC's colour service in 1954 on programmes such as *Tennessee Ernie Ford Show*. The term 'chroma-key' has been used as a generic term for all types of video colour matting processes but is actually a registered trade mark, only refers to the patented system as described above and, therefore, only relates to coded NTSC video. Owing to the fact that colour phase is alternated between each line in PAL systems the original chroma-key process is not applicable and, so, when the BBC started transmitting colour in 1968, a colour version of their CSO system was used.

The principle of all video and digital colour screen processes is to create a silhouette mask corresponding to the key colour in the foreground image, which can be used to key a video switch (see figure below).

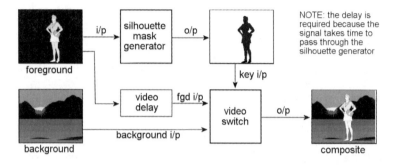

At first thought this seems very easy and simply depends on detecting the blue in the picture. However, this simple approach would produce a wholly inadequate key.

The synthetic luminance component of television (Y) is made up from a weighted combination of red, blue and green. Thus if the detector merely reacted to blue it would pick up on white (R + B + G), magenta (R + B), cyan (B + G) and any other intermediate colours containing an element of blue, as well as the intended 'pure blue' of the screen. This would not be a practical system, since what is needed is a process which can discriminate pure saturated blue from any other colours, including those with a blue constituent. The PAL system employs low-resolution colour components of B-Y and R-Y encoded within the synthetic luminance Y signal. If the B-Y signal, for which coders were already a part of the PAL and NTSC systems, was used, then it would provide a much more accurate representation of the unmixed blue component of a picture.

The Y signal is composed of approximately 60 per cent G, 30 per cent R and only 10 per cent B. So if we had a white subject against a pure blue backing, the B-Y formula would give us $100(B) - 10(B) = 90$ for the blue screen and $10(B) - 10(B) - 30(R) - 60(G) = -80$ for the white. In other words, the discrimination would be huge. The next most blue colour is magenta and B-Y would result in $B(50) - Y(5 + 15) = 30$, still vastly separate from blue at 90. In a B-only circuit magenta would be 50, 60 per cent worse than B-Y. Calculation would show that in R-Y red is only 16 per cent ahead of magenta (less than half the figure for B-Y) and the G-Y leads cyan (its nearest neighbour) by 25 per cent. Thus it is evident that on B-Y, at any rate, blue gave the biggest discrimination of all the possible colours and therefore was the obvious colour choice for chroma-key on purely technical grounds. The complement to blue (i.e., yellow) has identical characteristics and therefore, so long as there was no yellow in the foreground, was theoretically as good a key.

Early keying was not very good and a number of refinements were developed to improve matters. First the (Y) signal was replaced with (M) which gave equal weighting to all colour signals (i.e., M = 1/3R + 1/3B + 1/3G). With the B-M signal normalized to 1 V this would give a B-M = 1B − 0.5R − 0.5G, which results in far better discrimination against colours other than that selected. The final enhancement of these early keying systems was the so-called 'exclusive' key which was roughly equivalent to film's colour difference system. Here, the blue signal has red or green subtracted, whichever is greater. Applying this technique, only those parts of the signal which contain blue and nothing else are keyed. As soon as the blue has another colour added to it, it will drop to zero or negative and the negative parts of the signal may be gated out by a suitable circuit. With an exclusive key it is possible to have extremely bluish subjects against a blue backing and still discriminate against them in the key signal.

Another refinement was to replace the 'switch' with a so-called 'soft-switch' and, later, a linear keyer. In these systems the transition between foreground and background elements is a mix rather than a hard matte. In a linear keyer the background not only replaces areas that are blue, but does so at a density directly dictated by that of the backing. In other words if the blue screen were darker in a particular area then so would be the material inserted in its place (see figure below).

foreground with artiste's shadow but also with unintended shading

linear key with all shades of blue area carried over

background

composite showing artiste's shadow but carrying over the unwanted shading

This density control gave the system the capability of reproducing shadows, smoke and transparency within the blue set. In the analogue world this approach reached its apex with the 'Ultimatte', which applied film methods to video. In it, the foreground scene had all of the blue removed – taking the backing down to almost black and a complementary hole cut in the background. These two separately controllable signals were then combined. The advantage was that the transition could be much more finely tuned and very soft.

Basic colour matting facilities were built into all vision mixers (switchers) for live and post-production environments. Early systems were mostly blue, although yellow and green both had periods of popularity. Most systems offer at least three controls. Hue swings the colour wheel to the precise colour to be matted, threshold or clip level (signal amplitude) adjusts the density at which the transition is made, and softness controls the speed of transition (i.e., the extent of mix along the matte edge). Specific systems may introduce additional controls such as shadow density, transparency or foreground/background density and even hue.

The final improvement in the quality of colour separation matting was the development of key colour suppression (fringe elimination), in which any keying colour which had infiltrated the foreground subject was removed. Thus, for example, in a blue screen situation any blue contamination of the artiste would be eliminated. This enhancement was originally achieved using electronic filtering techniques, but was eventually perfected when digital methods came to the fore. A careful balance is required when using this technique if the subject's colour is not to be unduly distorted, as, for example, where removal of blue from skin tones usually goes unnoticed but yellow would be unacceptable. Just as blue cannot be used as the key on its own, so it cannot merely be subtracted from the foreground picture to remove blue bias. If blue (and particularly green, which is present in most skin tones) were simply subtracted, then it would both lower the luminance of the image and take blue from the subject's own natural colour. Key colour suppression systems use a formula to subtract the negative component of red or green (whichever is greater) from the blue signal (or red and blue in a green screen system). This does not alter the overall brightness or contrast of the subject, but destroys any blue cast.

Owing to the low colour bandwidth of the PAL and NTSC systems good results cannot be obtained from material encoded in them. This applies to both 'live' images coming down the line and off tape shots previously recorded. This means that blue screen shots had to be done live in the studio using R G B signals direct from the camera. This blocked a lot of creative possibilities and was very restricting. For a while the problem was circumvented by creating a separate key in the form of a black and white matte recorded on an additional video recorder. This added incredible complexity to the process since the matte and master would have to be synchronized to work properly. The off tape matte was full bandwidth, being luminance only, and therefore was almost as good as one directly created from the camera R G B. Analogue Ultimatte systems offered such a key output and it could be inverted if required. Being so cumbersome this process was only used to a limited degree and became unnecessary with the advent of component colour recording systems, such as Betacam SP, which recorded the three separate components of Y, B-Y and R-Y (although weighted slightly differently from PAL).

Blue and green screen were revolutionized by the advent of digital image processing. The noiseless and always first-generation quality of digital component tape formats such as D1 and Digital Betacam meant that colour separation matte processes could be accomplished off tape and in post-production with excellent and consistent results. However, it was in the actual compositing process that digital image processing improved results by an order of magnitude, whilst at the same time simplifying the entire procedure.

In a digital system each pixel has its colour and luminance defined by a set of numbers. In R G B (as used in most graphics, film and photographic software) this would be 0–255 for each colour in an 8-bit system. In colour video components (as used by most broadcast systems) the luminance (Y), blue (B-Y) and red (R-Y) components would each be defined by a number between 0 and 255 (in 8-bit). In such a system it is a relatively straightforward matter to analyse the particular colour of any point and modify it accordingly. A very narrow range of blue, for instance, can be pinpointed and all pixels with that value can be replaced with those from a different picture. Similarly, complex algorithms can be written to modify all of certain hues which may, for instance, correspond to areas where impurities have affected foreground colours. Special 'look-up tables' (LUTs) are often written to modify colours in particular ways depending on how user-adjustable parameters are set. Using digital techniques the subtlety, precision and possibilities of the process are limited only by the imagination of the system designers. However, in almost a century of phenomenal development the shooting methods for standing an actor in front of a coloured screen remain pretty well unchanged.

Choice of formats

The history of colour separation systems has been closely tied to that of recording formats. But now, in the digital age, any format can be used for acquisition since, whatever is chosen, it will end up being digitized or copied on to digital media (most commonly hard disks). In Chapter 1 (page 24) the difference between component and composite systems was discussed and it was made clear why, for colour screen compositing, it is essential to use a component recording system. As well as the video formats such as BetacamSP (analogue) and D1 (digital), 'component' in this context also includes film (which contains separate R, G and B layers), high-definition video and digital recording by streaming directly to hard disks (usually R, G and B). Choice of format can have a huge impact on the quality of the final composite.

When using film for compositing of any type, it is important to have the stability of 35 mm neg perfs. Standard 16 mm and super 16 are inherently unstable and therefore not ideal for matte work; however, with digital stabilizing they might be used in a tight (budget) corner and certainly are fine for background plates. By scanning into the digital realm directly off the negative, 16 mm can produce excellent results although, for effects purposes, if the final image is going to be 4 × 3 ratio, then standard 16 mm is more stable, having sprockets down both sides of the film. In VFX it is always best to scan or TK from the negative rather than a print since the KS perforations, generation and reduction in colour accuracy and resolution, could make such processes as blue screen very difficult. However, if a print is required for some reason (perhaps creative) then it should be made on stock with neg (B&H) perfs, which is available on special order. In general it is best to use the less grainy slower to medium stocks and to check whether there are any specialized stocks available for colour separation work. Where colour screens are being used it is best not to push, pull or otherwise manipulate the film in an unconventional way, which could effect colorimetry and therefore extraction of a particular hue.

The largest area of negative possible should always be used. For example, if shooting on 35 mm then open gate (full/silent aperture) should be adopted, even if a narrower aspect ratio will finally be used. This means that there is room for reframing if required, and there is the option to enlarge the image by a greater magnification with smaller, tighter grain and therefore higher resolution. Anamorphic lenses use the maximum real estate available, but also provide the widest ratio normally required, thus allowing various adjustments to be made in post. If super35 mm is being used for the main shoot then 'Scope shooting of effects should compensate for any losses generated in the various VFX processes. Using 65 mm, vistaVision or other large-format systems will obviously result in the very best definition, although it should be remembered that special stocks will only be available in the horizontal 8-perf, 35 mm systems and there will be far fewer facilities and processes available for the less common formats.

Having chosen a shooting format, a suitable post-production route and format must also be decided upon. Film for TV use needs to be digitized by means of a telecine and, for film distribution, on a film scanner. Speeds and line standards should be according to the local requirements but images should never have to be converted between line standards or frame rates when being used as blue/green screen elements. When standards conversions take place image quality, particularly with respect to motion, is severely distorted and this will make keying very difficult, if not impossible.

For colour-based VFX always use the best scanning system and data pipeline available. Blue and green screen keying depend directly on the quality of the images being worked on. Keying on a person's face will be much better at 2K (pages 20 and 219) than it is from 525 video resolution, because fine detail such as hair will be more clearly defined and therefore the individual pixels will represent specific keyable elements rather than an average (see figure below).

"A" at double the resolution of "B" will key much better as shown in the enlargements.

Thus if 'difficult' keying needs to be accomplished it may be better to scan it in at a higher resolution than the final job – do the compositing at that higher resolution and then downsize the image to the appropriate finishing format. With film for TV this is obviously very simple to do, since the film (even 16 mm) contains much more information than the video image. With the increasing use of high-definition systems it may be that an HD TK and compositing might be an economical route to achieving this, if the facility involved has invested in this technology. However, bear in mind colour space and sampling issues (see below). Most film finish work is done at 2K these days. This is not equal to the quality of the film, which is closer to 6K, but most producers judge 2K to be the best compromise between cost and acceptable quality. The argument goes that with the printing process and quality losses incurred at exhibition, the projected image is well under 2K. Whether this is true or not, it may well be best to scan and composite certain blue/green shots at 4K for the same reasons explained in respect of video.

7 Self-matting processes

A more tricky consideration is that of sampling rate, compression and colour space. Normal digital video (CCIR 601) as recorded by D1 and digital Betacam draws on historical colour component systems and records Y, B-Y and R-Y type components (see page 25). The system does record these three signals entirely separately, but the B-Y and R-Y colour components are sampled at half the rate of the luminance (hence called 4:2:2). At the time 601 was agreed it was deemed that this was sufficient for chroma-keying and, indeed, in most cases it is. DV formats are, however, 4:1:1 and in most cases this is not sufficiently good quality for even simple blue/green screens. It should be noted that HD-cam is 3:1:1 and therefore only suitable for some blue screen work – for complex or high-quality results, direct feeds from the camera to a disk array should be used.

However, not only is the low colour sampling rate a problem for colour separation work, but so is the colour space of Y, B-Y, R-Y. It is much more restricted in the range of colours reproducible than the R G B system favoured by most computer-imaging systems. The differences in colour range of the two systems is sufficiently large that conversions from one to the other result in distortions to the colour gamut (reproduced scale/scope) and the introduction of artefacts. Going back and forth a number of times between the two systems can produce quite extreme effects. Thus, it is essential to stay in one or the other of these two colour spaces and, for blue or green screen in particular, interchange is not really an option. For example, if a shot is being manipulated using computer-centric software such as designed by Discreet Logic or Adobe then it will be in R G B colour space. This should not be archived, as the work progresses, using a digital video tape system such as digital Betacam because each journey to and from tape would result in increasingly severe colour artefacts. So, in this case, archiving or transportation between facilities should be on data tapes or disks, rather than video tapes. Furthermore, it would be best to transport the signal from the TK via a 4:4:4 R G B feed, to stay out of the video component world entirely. This problem does not exist when working with film digitized on a 2K or 4K scanner, since these all work in R G B colour space.

Video tends to be recorded in 8-bit colour (i.e., 256 levels for each component) although pro-tape formats can record in 10-bits. Again, more bits means more accuracy and therefore a better key. With film for transfer back to film then 10-bit is the minimum and 12-, or even 14-bit are preferable. Some systems based on Kodak technologies use 10-bit log (as opposed to linear, see Chapter 8), which is more akin to the colour response of film and ultimately the human vision system which it mimics. Conversions between log and linear are reasonably non-destructive, but conversion to a lower bit rate and then back up again are unacceptable. The fact is that anything which affects the colour will also impact on a colour-dependent VFX process.

Last, but not least, is compression. Like those variables already mentioned this can distort or alter the colours depicted in an image and therefore will affect the ability of a process which needs to accurately analyse colours. If compression mushes up an image, then so too will it mush up a key! For blue or green screen work it is really important to work with lossless compression. Digital Betacam (2:1) is acceptable for most TV work but moving on to DV, which uses

5:1, is getting near the limit. Systems such as MPEG will not allow good results to be achieved.

Thus, open gate 35 mm film scanned to 2K or 4K in R G B colour space with 10-bit log colour would achieve the very best results. However, on the other hand, for TV use, a TK directly linked to the computer graphics department using R G B feeds would also be fine. If broadcast video equipment is being used, such as the products of Quantel (i.e., Y, B-Y, R-Y) then the material can safely be recorded on to a format such as D1 and played in to the system at a later stage.

Most of the comments above about video format's usefulness for blue screen in post-production apply equally to their use for acquisition. Any video format can be used for collecting backgrounds for compositing with shots also made on video, but only those shot on progressive-scan cameras may be used to back material shot on film. This is because standard video uses two fields per frame (page 13) which would be incompatible with the single frame per exposure nature of film. Obviously on specific set-ups, such as static shots with no movement in them, they are fine to mix but, where fast movement of either subject or camera is involved, then field-based and frame-based material should as a general rule not be mixed. For blue/green screen work, component 4:2:2 is the minimum requirement. 10-bit is preferable and R G B directly out of the camera and recorded on some form of data recorder (e.g., hard disks) will get the very best results. Where live keying is being used, then component connections, preferably R G B, should be made to the mixer or keying system (e.g., Ultimatte).

Technically, foreground (particularly blue/green screen) elements should always be shot at least with the format being used for the main part of the job, but in most cases it is advantageous to utilize a format one better than that in use for the main action.

Choice of keying colour

The colour used for shots containing people has traditionally always been blue. There are many reasons for this, but ahead of all the others is the fact that the human form contains very little blue. Elderly Caucasian ladies can have blue in their hair and females of West Indian origin can have blue pigment in their skin but, in both cases, the levels are very low and easily remedied by make-up. Apart from blue eyes, which only show up on close-ups (and can be corrected by using orange contact lenses), there is no other blue in people.

Early two strip Technicolor was able to comfortably reproduce human skin tones without having any means of recording a blue record whatsoever. This means that if blue elements can be kept out of the costume, then blue will give a very wide separation from skin tones which tend towards orange, a colour almost the complementary of blue. With a very saturated blue it should be possible to successfully pull a matte from objects which are still quite bluish.

However, on the downside, blue is the grainiest layer on film and also the noisiest chip in video cameras. For this reason many post-production houses now encourage the use of green, which is the quietest colour on both film and video systems. The argument goes that this reduces noise in the key signal and therefore creates a cleaner matte edge. On the other hand, there is a lot of green in skin tones and hair colour so the separation between subject and screen is much less – indeed it is only since the advent of sophisticated digital compositing that it has become a practical colour to use. Enthusiasts for green will observe that these modern keying techniques need much less latitude between subject and screen, so therefore it is worth a slightly tighter key to gain quiet edges.

The argument of blue versus green is hotly debated in VFX circles but, in the end, both work extremely well using the latest software, and the main determinant becomes whether the artiste, props or setting contain the keying colour. If somebody were wearing blue jeans then green seems appropriate, just as blue would be preferable to photograph Robin Hood's green-clad merry men. Additionally, due consideration should be given to the background colour. If keying our subject into a forest scene, then green would again be appropriate, because any contamination from the backing would be entirely appropriate and any matte edges would be lost in the background.

Any colour can theoretically be used and, when humans are not involved, alternative choices are perfectly practical. Blue and green automobiles for instance might be shot against red or yellow. Finally, black and white should not be forgotten since these are neutral in terms of reflecting off the subject, and in the case of black does not need such complex lighting as a coloured backing. Modern keying systems and particularly digital rotoscoping are so sophisticated, accurate and quick, that the imperfections of shooting against black can easily be corrected where the technique offers other advantages.

Creating the backing

One of the most important decisions in planning a blue/green screen shot is how to create the coloured backing. This is a complex decision, given that almost every single process discussed up to this point can be used. The main aim is to create a backing that has the purest colour and maximum saturation possible. Achieving this end will result in apparently quite low luminance, particularly when shooting blue. Increasing luminance will start to contaminate the blue because, to make it 'appear' lighter to the eye, it requires at least some green and red.

The simplest and most common way of producing the colour screen is to paint it on a cyc (cyclorama or large curved backdrop), canvas or a flat. There are numerous specially made paints from such companies as Fargo, Rosco or Bollum/Redaluma, although it is possible to choose a highly saturated blue paint from any paint catalogue. The specialist paints are based on the major compromise between durability and sheen. Ideally the paint should have a matt finish so that it does not reflect the lights, which would show up as bright spots and in worst cases have very little blue content. Having a matt finish eliminates this problem completely, but unfortunately, the more matt the finish, the more physically delicate the paint becomes. In the rough environment of a shooting stage this can be a big problem. If the blue paint has to extend to the floor, then only a few rehearsals or takes will 'scuff' it to the extent where a repaint is needed.

Even where no floor needs to be seen, avoiding marks, scratches and areas where the blueness has been reduced is very difficult to manage. Also, the paint appears to vary each time it is purchased, as the manufacturers reformulate the mix to deal with the continuously changing feedback they get from customers. To increase the durability they add more adhesive (effectively glue which is hard and shiny) and to reduce the reflectivity they must lower the adhesive content. By far the best results come from the more matt paint and it should be used if possible. To deal with its lack of durability, paper or light boarding should be laid on a painted floor for the rehearsals and kept there right up to the start of takes, and only the essential area should be uncovered at this time. If a backing will be used for some time (or is a permanent fixture), then it is worth having curtains to pull across it when not in use.

There is some discussion as to the 'lightness' of the paint. The two main alternatives are chroma-key (or CSO) and Ultimatte, with the latter being somewhat lighter and therefore less saturated. When shadows and trans-parency first became possible it was found that the normal chroma blue paint was often too dark for the shadows to show up clearly – certainly the more sub-tle ones. For this reason Ultimatte brought out their own paint which was con-siderably lighter in colour than standard at the time. However, modern digital compositing is very sensitive to blue density and therefore it is best to go for the most saturation possible. Green is inherently much lighter than blue so does not suffer from this problem.

Since the paint can vary between batches (and with age) it is best to mix large quantities so that the entire area will be covered from one combination. The paint should be applied as evenly as possible and should go over a pre-pared surface so that it does not alter according to either the flatness or the colour of what lies beneath. Holes, joins and other blemishes should be taped over before painting.

In many circumstances the use of a coloured fabric may prove more practi-cal than a rigid painted surface. For close situations, such as miniature or table-top photography, flexible coloured plastic may prove useful or, for larger areas, photo background paper (which comes in rolls) is ideal, although it can crease and wrinkle very easily (particularly if stood upon). The most popular material is cloth and the best is felt. Again, check out your rental/media supplier, since spe-cial blue and green rolls of felt are stocked for this purpose. Cloth backings should be hung so as to avoid creases or unevenness such that areas become slightly shaded. The material should be stretched like a screen to maximize evenness and to ensure that it will not move because of any draughts or air cur-rents. Rosco and Composite Components both make special fabrics for blue and green. Fabrics (particularly felt) have the advantage of being very matt, capable of supporting a good saturated colour and are easily stored and trans-ported. Should a small blue screen be needed on a location, then a cloth screen can be carried with the unit and mounted on a trace frame as and when required. Kino-Flo make screens specifically with this application in mind and even provide the carrying bag! The material has eyelets to allow fast and efficient mounting on support tubing. This approach might be needed in a documentary where a number of individuals are to be interviewed at various locations dotted around the world.

Whether fabric, paper or a painted surface, it may be that under white light the colour is not sufficiently saturated. This is easy to see when looking at the foreground after key colour suppression. In theory the coloured backing should be near black, but will often be substantially lighter and will often have a cyan tone. This is, of course, due to impurities in the dye or paint and also because some of the non-blue light illuminating the screen will be reflected back from it. The solution to this problem is to illuminate with only light of the key colour so that there is hardly any other coloured light incident on the screen. This will ensure that no other colour is reflected from the screen and that it appears purely the required hue and also very saturated. The coloured light can be created by either filtering it or using special luminaires designed to emit only the correct hue. HMI lights and arcs are much bluer than standard tungsten units so are particularly suited to this work but, in either case, it is still worth using filters. Blue or green gel on the lights is an expensive option since, on top of the cost of the actual gel itself, more light is needed to generate a given value at the screen. This is because the coloured filters absorb light and therefore reduce exposure of the screen. Manufacturers' numbering of light control media varies from company to company, as do the actual filters they sell, so it will be necessary to check out the available blue filters at any given time. 'Medium blue' is, however, produced by them all and provides a good starting point when researching the best filter for your requirements.

An alternative to filtering white light is to use specially made lamps which emit light in a very narrow spectral band. Best known of these are the 'kino-flo' fluorescent tubes which are available in both blue and green. These appear to be quite dim because of the very specific wavelength they transmit but they will provide a stunningly saturated screen and are strongly recommended.

A third alternative is to use blue light on a white cyc. This does not produce an ideal key, and additionally sprays blue light all over the entire studio, but in certain circumstances is a very useful technique. Take a live music show, for instance, where the star sings various songs sitting centre stage. Behind him is an enormous white cyc surrounded by cyc lights which can project any mix of the primary colours the lighting designer deems appropriate. However, for one sequence, the director wants to put pre-shot images behind the star, but there is no time to fly in a blue flat. In these circumstances, being able to do a lighting change to pure blue will be a stylistic godsend and, with appropriate flagging and control, should give a perfectly adequate key.

In any situation involving either blue or white backings great care should be taken when pouring coloured light down on the stage. It is imperative that none of the blue filtered light should get anywhere near the artiste or other in-vision set pieces. This would cause contamination of skin tones, nasty blue highlights and, in a worst case, mis-keying. Furthermore it should be noted that coloured light cannot be used in situations where the floor is in shot. This is because, to get an evenly illuminated backing and floor, they must both be lit by the same type of lighting and reflect the same level of saturation. Obviously if the floor is in shot, it is to permit full-length framing of the subject who will be standing on it and therefore illuminated by the same lighting – this gets particularly tricky where shadows are to be carried over into the composite.

In situations where the subject's feet are not shown then there are a huge number of alternative methods available for creating the coloured backing. All projection systems can be used. Rear projection screens can have blue light projected on to them or be backed by many small bulbs (e.g., PAR lights) or by fluorescent tubes. The lights can be individually blue or filtered at the lamp or immediately behind the screen. Using multiple lamps rather than projection avoids hot-spot problems but increases the complexity of setting-up. Special blue-dyed screens are available such as the Stewart T-Screen. The great advantage of a rear illuminated screen is that it gives a perfect colour backing which is not affected by what is going on in front of it. This is a 'switch on and shoot' scenario and is therefore used in many news and other permanent sets around the world. On the other hand, the blue is very intense and should not be allowed to ingress onto the subject.

FAP can be a brilliant source of colour keying. A very low-powered blue-filtered lamp can be reflected from a mirror at the camera (see figure below) with the advantage that it is so low-powered that there is effectively no blue spill on to the back of the artiste standing in front of the 3M screen.

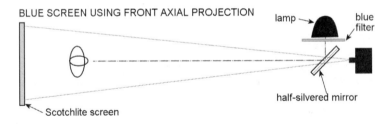
BLUE SCREEN USING FRONT AXIAL PROJECTION   lamp   blue filter

half-silvered mirror

Scotchlite screen

Chromatte is a recent system developed by the BBC and based on the FAP principle. Here, a retro-reflective material is used which, unlike Scotchlite, is designed to reflect a few degrees off-axis. This is combined with the proprietary 'lite-ring', which is a ring of blue or green LEDs around the camera lens. This does away with the need for the difficult-to-manage mirror and light rig, since the lights to the side of the lens bounce back into it thus simplifying the entire process. Where rear screens are somewhat limited in size, 3M or chromatte screens can be enormous but, of course, in neither case are they suitable for creating coloured floors or reproducing shadows.

Large-screen display technology, TV screens and electronic projectors can all reproduce an even field of a specific colour and so can be similarly used for colour screen work. For example, the large-screen displays in stadiums can be switched to blue so as to feed material into them directly rather than through their own electronics – this would, for instance, mean that sensitive material could be shown to the home audience without those present seeing it!

Finally where a large area of colour is required but only a small area is needed to back the subject (see top figure on page 105 substituting blue for black) the blue can be extended by vignettes, glass paintings or Scotchlite/chromatte material up close to the camera. In all cases the light level on the ancillary screen can be adjusted to match the main backing.

Lighting and setting up

Lighting blue/green shots involves three main tasks: matching subject lighting with the background shot, making the screen very evenly lit and ensuring that neither area interferes with the other. To make these three endeavours as painless as possible the subject should be kept as far from the backing as is practical. This will permit both to be independently lit and to avoid spill from either contaminating the other. A subject should never be closer to the screen than 10 ft, despite the fact that everybody seems to be hell-bent on placing them as close to it as possible!

The screen itself should be lit as evenly as possible – this can be done by any means the cinematographer prefers. Hard lights (arcs, fresnels, spots) with or without diffusers, bounce light from anything, soft lights (eggcrates, panels, multiple bulb, Chinese lanterns, spacelights) or fluorescent tubes. If the screen is not too big, then coloured fluorescents are the simplest to set up, and give superb results. If a large floor area and cyc are being used then spacelights probably win. But whatever system is chosen the screen should be very even (not varying by more than one-quarter of a stop) so that the keying can be kept tight and therefore offers maximum separation. Evenness can be checked from the camera with a spot meter, by using an incident meter physically against the screen and gridding it out (i.e., walking up and down its length – if it is very big then this might require a ladder) or by looking through a suitably coloured viewing glass which will instantly reveal any imbalance in saturation. However, a word of caution, meters are not necessarily accurate once you stray from white illumination. Many meters have a much lower response to pure blue light than to the rest of the spectrum and, conversely, most film stocks are more sensitive to blue. Therefore testing is recommended to find the offset required when metering blue-filtered or fluorescent lights. On the other hand, they are usually pretty good with green. An argument put forward by many for using green is that it has much more energy in it and, therefore, needs less light for the same exposure as an equivalent with blue. This is generally true and for the same material and lighting set-up green will usually come out about one stop in advance of blue.

A much disputed topic is the ideal exposure level for the screen relative to the subject. There was a time when an exposure on the screen equivalent to the keylight was considered necessary but now, with the excellent keying available in software compositing systems, it is well worth dropping the screen key level to one stop below the subject. This saves on lighting but, more importantly, drops the level of light reflecting back on to the subject and gives a more saturated result. Less than this starts to cut down too much on the colour density, whereas going to equal or above makes the screen much too bright.

Whereas setting up the screen is a largely technical exercise, lighting and adjusting the subject is somewhat more tasking. The subject must be placed as far from the screen as practical and all means taken to minimize any spill from the screen falling thereon. At the same time care should be taken to ensure that light from the subject does not contaminate the screen. This might not only be direct light hitting the screen or bouncing on to it, but also could be stray light escaping from, for example, gaps in a barndoor mechanism.

Having isolated the area surrounding the subject, it should be lit to match precisely the background image, which will be composited behind it. For example, if in the backplate the sun is shining from above camera left, then so should the key in the studio. If light is hard with deep shadows, then the studio foreground should be the same; if it is soft with no shadows then this should be emulated too. The entire look of the background should be matched in both camera framing and lighting of the foreground. As discussed at length in previous sections, lenses, DoF, camera position and angle should all be exactly reproduced.

The important thing here is communication. Whichever is shot first, and this will often be dictated by production logistics rather than VFX convenience, it is essential that the most detailed information possible is passed between units so that a good match can be made. Notes, drawings and photographs will all help in this and reference shots taken wherever possible. As well as written material, reflective and grey globes can be very helpful to see straight away what lighting is present. A white or light-grey globe held in the subject position will show the angle and density of light, whilst a highly reflective globe (mirrorball) will show the exact positions of bright light sources. Computer graphics may use a silver globe to aid the creation of reflection maps whilst a grey and silver globe may be used for automated lighting.

Matching the lighting exactly is an additional reason why spill light from the screen must be avoided. Modern compositing software can remove any colour bias from the subject. What the software does is remove, say, a blue tone from the spill light but it does not remove the spill light's effect on the overall luminance or brightness of the shot. If there would be no light falling on the subject from the rear in the background, then there should be none in the foreground element either. This is also the reason why the theory that straw backlights help hide any blue spill in a blue screen shot, or magenta backlight on a green screen, is not to be followed. Modern key colour suppression will fix any difficulties along these lines, but cannot remove actual light coming from the wrong direction. On the other hand, if the background shot indicates strong backlight then it must be replicated in the foreground on the stage.

Even with a good distance between screen and subject there will be some spill light, particularly if a very big screen and floor area are being used. In, for example, a very wide shot it may be that little of the blue actually backs the subject and the rest is merely 'filling in space'. In such circumstances (see figure on page 176) it is well worth the time and effort of covering over all of the redundant sections of blue and leaving just that which is directly adjacent to the action area. This is best achieved by using black drapes which can be hung on rails around the cyc and drawn across the screen as appropriate. The missing blue can then be either reinstated by garbage matting in post, or be reinserted into the picture by blue vignettes or glass mattes close to the camera.

artiste v large blue backing   unnecessary blue covered over   fgd vignette restores blue

Steps for a basic colour screen shot

The simple blue or green screen shot is so fundamental to modern visual effects that the following summary of basic procedures should be fully understood.

I   Consult with the post house, determine well in advance what components are needed and resolve the order in which elements should be most efficiently and creatively shot.

II   Coordinate the shooting of foregrounds and background to ensure that they will visually and photographically match.

III   Document details of camera, lighting and scenic set-up for use by crew shooting the foreground elements.

IV   Match foreground camera and lighting to background data very precisely, with particular attention to perspective and direction of light.

V   Choose keying colour, screen method and subject positioning carefully to maximize separation, evenness and thus quality of composite.

VI   Consider colour, texture and design of costumes and scenic elements in the foreground shoot to avoid technical problems.

VII   Provide full information to the post-production team detailing precisely what was done during the shoot.

VIII   Do not degrade the foreground image by filtering or abnormal processing.

Complex colour screen shots

Blue/green screen shots are the most common building block used in the complex composites of modern productions. Although two or three elements are typical, the tally can often run to several dozen components being combined into a single, apparently integral, image. For example, in an epic depicting the result of an earthquake, there might be a main background of the hills and sky behind the city, a number of miniatures all shot against blue with built-in collapsing features, two, three or more foreground elements of actors running away from the desolation (this is crowd multiplication, where the same group of extras are used in multiple takes to create a larger crowd) and then who knows how many individual elements providing sections of falling masonry, smoke, fire, dust and splashes where any of the materials hit water. Many of these elements may actually be shot statically and then moved during the compositing stage. For example, in space operas the ships of the Imperial Fleet will tend to be shot individually and then combined, resulting in sometimes 30 or more discrete elements.

But to make even a simple single-element blue screen shot work, there are many issues which need to be addressed if it is going to successfully suspend disbelief.

Careful matching between foreground and background is essential, but what really fixes the credibility of a shot is interactivity. If a person is shown in an environment and they cast a shadow on an object within it, then surely they must really be there! Similarly, if a shadow is thrown across a scene that includes a figure standing in it, then surely that figure is actually there. Shadows are very important to blue/green screen shots and they can be created in a variety of ways. Simplest to understand but often most difficult to execute is the creation of an actual shadow against the blue. For this, the blue screen must extend all the way across the floor on which the artiste is actually standing. This is, of course, the most difficult scenario to light evenly whilst avoiding variations in the blue, because of the paint's reflectivity. However, trying to create a shadow of the subject without spoiling the floor's overall evenness is pretty difficult, particularly when the shadow must extend in precisely the right direction, and with feathering and density exactly matching that depicted in the background. If the appearance of this foreground shadow does not match those in the background then the effect will fail.

A shadow can be 'carried over' to the composite by many modern keying systems such as Ultimatte and Primatte which are sensitive not just to the blueness of supplied material but also to the density of that blue. Where the blue is darker the background will be darker too. This technique requires extreme care in the lighting but the extra effort will usually be justified by the results. If the composite is being created in post-production then it is often the case that a lot of manual retouching will need to be applied in these circumstances, but this is a far better alternative to having to create the shadow completely from scratch.

Since a shadow is interactive (i.e., it moves as the entity creating it moves) and is dependent on the subject for its shape, it is not the easiest of things to cheat, yet often a naturally generated shadow just cannot be supplied. If the subject is static, for instance a package in a TV commercial, then the shadow can simply be painted on the floor, or added in post-production during the compositing process. Sometimes it may be convenient to do a separate pass to automatically generate this; one pass for the main blue screen, then a second with a powerful lamp used to create the shadow. For this pass the blue would be extremely uneven but the 'shadow' would be clearly delineated. In post these two foreground runs would be combined.

Depending on the shot content another trick is to use the foreground matte to create a synthetic shadow. Here the outline of the subject is used to create a black matte which is tilted, squashed, blurred and its density adjusted to roughly match the look and direction of real shadows. This can all be done either as a separate pass or as part of the workflow in a modern compositing multiprocess software suite. Getting the shadow thus created to stay connected with the subject in a realistic way and simultaneously look like it is on the floor is quite difficult, but the technique can quite often be combined with the final (and worst) alternative. If all else fails then there is nothing left but to animate, frame by frame, a shadow to provide the necessary element of reality. This process could either be hand-done or a crude (since it shall never be seen by the audience) 3D CGI model can be built of the subject and then animated to exactly move as the 'real' one does – this CGI figure can then be made to create a shadow which is added to the scene.

It will often be the case that the very lighting itself can contribute to the believability of a shot. So-called 'interactive' lighting is very important to the success of certain types of scene. Let's say, for instance, that the location shoot was done at a time when the 'star' was unavailable so it had become a blue screen. At the real location it was very dark and the lights on police cars had a major and eerie effect on the scene. To have these orange and blue lights continually scanning across the background but not our subject, supposedly standing there, would not make for a plausible scene. In this instance, the addition of mock-ups of the flashing lights would do the trick, but great care would have to be taken to avoid them having too large an effect on the blue screen itself. This would involve keeping the action well away from the screen and masking the lights from it. Needless to say if the lights were blue then a green screen would be necessitated. Precisely this same scenario applies to scenes using pyrotechnics, fire effects or other situations where bright or continually varying lighting will be expected by the audience.

Interactive lighting also works the other way. If the subject shot against blue is very bright or gives off some sort of unusual glow which would effect the surroundings, then this should be somehow applied to the background, preferably at the time of shooting. To use the example of a police car again – if the effect were done the other way around and the car was actually being shot in the blue studio with its lights flashing – then the same coloured lights should be applied to the background at the time it is shot. It goes without saying that in some scenes a method of synchronizing the beams should be found if the movement in the two halves of the shot should appear as one. This is particularly the case where, for example, a blue screen performer is shining a torch around the interior of an alien spacecraft constructed as a miniature.

Interaction between foreground and background can also be created in the very action of the shot itself. If an action and reaction appear to occur across the boundary then surely there is no boundary! An example might be where an item is handed from one character to his identical twin, or where a foreground player picks up an object apparently in the background. These aspects of interactivity are discussed in more detail in Staging colour screen shots, below.

The one remaining creative enhancement that can increase the reality of composite shots is that of motion. In modern media, images move constantly. Whether it be the smooth gliding shots of a computer-controlled camera, or the wobbly-cam of the pseudo news footage so loved of police procedurals, the sudden insertion of a static VFX shot will stand out a mile and alert the audience to the fact. Movement can be introduced to the action itself in a static frame, the camera can be seen to pan and tilt, or it can actually appear to move about.

Sometimes complex and fast action by the subject can suffice. This is most usually created by careful planning and staging and does not involve any especially advanced technology. However, the moment the camera moves everything changes and a number of extra techniques must be brought into play.

To believably create moving shots it must first be understood what is happening in a typical moving camera situation. An ordinary scene may show a single individual who is moving. In closer shots this may be suggested by either the foreground character moving against a static background or by the character being static and the background moving (see figure below).

camera pans with foreground actor   camera stays on bkgd while actor moves

These two scenarios are, of course, dependent on which part of the action the camera follows. If, for instance, the foreground character is walking past a static background (e.g., a building), then if the camera follows her, the character will appear to be static in frame and the building will move by her in the opposite direction. If the camera concentrates on the background, then the character will move through the frame. On the other hand, if the actor is stationary whilst a tram passes by, then the camera following the tram will produce static background and moving foreground.

In a blue/green screen shot these scenarios can be recreated easily by either having a static or moving background plate and a static or moving foreground camera. Any combination will produce a shot with movement in it. For example if we wanted to depict a camera following somebody as they walked along the side of a building then we could shoot a pan along the building as the plate and then shoot the foreground subject either walking along a blue cyc or walking on a treadmill in front of one. As long as we do not see the feet of the actor in the studio, absolute synchronism in the apparent movements of the two shots is not required. However, it is necessary to match focal lengths of the lenses of both taking cameras otherwise two apparently different depth of fields and angles of view will be evident.

Although it can produce good results and has served well in the past the above method does require pre-shooting of the move and, on wider lenses, may not always create a result up to current standards. There are two ways to accurately synchronize foreground and background camera movements. The first and more obvious is to use some form of repeating head for the camera. This would cause the camera to pan or tilt in exactly the same way whilst photographing both the foreground and the background. Although in the 1950s analogue systems were built for a few specific shots such as in *Samson & Delilah* (1949) this technique has only come into its own with the development of computerized systems such as motion control and field heads.

These systems are dealt with in the next chapter but essentially permit the camera's position to be determined by a computer-controlled program. Thus you could shoot a stand-in walking along a wall and looking at its features. Sensors on the camera head would precisely record the operator's movements. A second take would then be made without the stand-in but with the camera moving according to a replay of the original actor-led take. The first take would also be kept for reference. On returning to the studio the camera would be set up to repeat its move but now against a blue cyc. Obviously for this to work everything about the camera and its relative position would have to be identical. The actor would now act out the same rough movements as the stand-in had, whilst the camera performs the identical movement. This technique is often executed in the reverse order with the main actor being shot against blue first and the repeat move being done for the background. The choice as to which way round to do this will be a combination of scheduling and practical considerations – the technology can deal with either method.

The problem with such computer-controlled systems is that they require the presence of bulky equipment – not often practical on difficult locations. Worse still, they require the shot to be predetermined whilst shooting one of the elements and the other element to be subsequently locked to this. In the example of a character walking along a wall and looking at its features we can see that this method is not particularly helpful. If the actor is shot first without any reference he may not look in exactly the right places to fit the wall's features but, on the other hand, if the wall is shot first, it could be very difficult for the actor to synchronize with the movements made in the pre-shot plate. Neither approach is ideal.

An alternative is to use large plates or even 'tiles'. Here the theory is that a much larger plate which covers most of the blue screen is put in as the background (see figure on page 22). This plate should be on a larger format than the principal photography or be made up of multiple shots pieced together. For example, if the foreground is shot using standard def video then the plate might be HD or, if it were on 35 mm film, then the plate might be vistaVision. In either case, if the background shows a motionless subject (such as the wall of a building) then an even better and more economical solution is to use a still photograph.

Where the plate has to be really large and cover a much wider field of view then the use of tiles may be called for. For correct perspective the same focal length lens should be used for the plate as for the foreground and yet if the plate has to be three frames long to permit a pan then the shot will not work unless the camera shoots three passes representing the two sides and middle of the shot (see bottom figure on page 128).

However it is created, we now have a much larger plate than the foreground and must tie the two together in post-production. Special tracking software exists for this purpose (discussed in the next chapter) and is basically able to fix on to a point in the image and to move another image in precise synchronism. Since we are in an evenly lit blue screen studio no such feature exists naturally, so it is necessary to fix identifiable targets (tracking markers) on to the screen so that the software will have something to latch on to. Using this system the camera can freely pan and tilt with the actor as he walks about looking at the screen. In post, the plate of the wall can then be dropped in and the appropriate movements will be automatically added (see figure opposite).

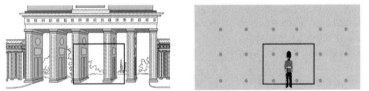

the camera can freely pan about on the blue screen as long as there is sufficient background material to cover the movements and some means of tracking the shot

A single marker in shot will permit locking on to pan and tilt movements (i.e., using a fixed camera head). Two markers visible at all times will also make rotation and size adjustments possible (i.e., will allow a hand-held camera) whilst four markers allow software to calculate perspective also (permitting combination with 3D computer graphics). Because of the pre-existence of the background any significant features' position can be marked on the blue screen or on appropriately positioned stands. This enables the actor to get the correct eye lines even though the final background is not visible, the foreground and background to move synchronously without restricting the studio cameras movements and minimum set-up in both locations. However, this method does impose quite a bit of work on post.

Finally, shots where the camera moves in three dimensions – such as tracking into the action – will require a motion control camera or more complex 3D software tracking. A motion control system (see page 205) will require extensive and complex equipment to be taken on location and then set up again on the stage. Using this technique is complex and time-consuming but can achieve excellent results. It is particularly well-suited to shots where the scale of the foreground and background are different. This could be where, for example, the foreground is live action actors and the background is a miniature. The software can be set to scale the move appropriately and so the apparently same move can be executed in the full scale studio and 16th-scale miniature.

Much more flexible, but extremely time-consuming in post-production is to use camera tracking for both parts of the shot. Here the shot is made in one of the locations – let's say the location shoot. Tracking markers are included such that they are visible throughout the shot. For 3D programs there may be specific requirements for how these are laid out, depending on the software chosen. In addition there is some really excellent software such as 'Boujou' which can derive tracking information from within the image content. In this scenario tracking information is also derived from the blue screen studio (using tracking markers) whilst a move 'approximately' the same as that done of the location is repeated. Part of the trick here is to make sure that the studio screen shot never loses the edges of the subject out of frame and therefore they can be placed wherever is necessary in the background shot. An additional trick is to shoot at least one of the two components on a wider frame area – e.g., shoot open gate whereas the main photography is all at 1.85:1. With time, care and money, it is possible to marry up the two shots. Like a lot of modern techniques this method is used since shooting time is very expensive and to be avoided if possible, whereas time in post-production is not such a big issue and can therefore be justified, since it saves stage time.

There are additionally a number of technical innovations which have aided the realism and believability of blue/green screen shots. These originate in the continued improvements of the 'switching mechanisms' and 'soft mixers' which developed alongside early colour television. Most importantly was the linear keyer, which assigns density to the background image in proportion to the density of the foreground keying colour (see page 164). Thus, as discussed, a shadow can be carried through from the foreground to the background but also, with careful alignment, transparency (basically a lightening of the area in the foreground) can also be reproduced. For example, a pane of glass shot against blue will desaturate the background colour and therefore will cause less of the background to be keyed through – this density change will 'look like' glass in the final composite. Another special instance is smoke, which desaturates the blue, however, if transparent enough, will still permit the background to show through but with attenuation proportionate to the density of the smoke. Getting the levels exactly right is very difficult with these processes. Originally only special devices such as the Ultimatte were able to execute such complex effects – and only when the many controls were in the hands of a very experienced technician. Now with the development of digital effects software it is relatively straightforward to make these enhancements work well.

Most important of the technical enhancements is the fringe eliminator, key or foreground colour suppressor (see page 165). One of the biggest problems with colour screen work is the way the keying colour can infect the foreground subject. This can occur as a fringe around the edge of, or as a wash across, the subject's surface (or indeed both). Key colour suppression allows this to be removed but without altering the tonal or colour levels in the shot. In early standalone devices this involved complicated electronics and was limited in its adjustability, but now, with special software designed specifically for blue and green screen working there is almost infinite flexibility possible to solve these problems. Nowadays these systems are so sophisticated that this age-old problem does not cause concern on the shoot to the same extent that it once did but, on the other hand, a heavy blue cast or corruption of the edges of the subject will result in mis-keying, which is a totally different problem.

The last improvement to keying options is that of softness. It is now possible to make a soft key work, but because of DoF issues it is still not a good idea to deliberately shoot soft elements. This is much better done during post-production where the process can be properly controlled, since sharp pictures with as much information as possible really are a better starting point to work from.

Staging colour screen shots
There are many techniques and tricks which can greatly simplify the efficiency of a blue screen shoot both during and after the actual photography. These can be divided into 'assistance towards successfully executing the shoot' and 'support to those working later in post'. However, before the actual shooting begins careful pre-planning can solve a lot of problems before they ever happen.

Where appropriate and particularly on big effects movies, 'pre-visualization' (pre-viz) may be used. This once took the form of 'animatics' – photographed and edited storyboards – but is now more likely to involve filmed rehearsals and simple effects shot using consumer DV-cams, animations and images taken from videos and DVDs of previous productions (sometimes called 'steal-o-matics'). The most flexible and accurate method is to use low-resolution 3D computer graphics to create virtual versions of the scene or sequence. Pre-viz is often used to map out complex sequences dramatically, to help the director argue their case and to aid in costing.

Smoothing the shoot

Working in a blue or green set is very tiring and depressing because it is void of any reference points either in regard to the shot or indeed from a psychological point of view. Having done major effects-laden productions many artistes refuse to ever do one again! One of the most important tasks is to offer crew and actors as much helpful visual stimulation as possible. To minimize the principal actor's time in this environment the main lining up should be done without them. This initial lining up will use information gleaned from the previous shooting team and/or the CGI department (depending on where the background originates from). It is usually best to work backwards from the main artiste position so that it can be established well away from the back wall of the cyc. Using a stand-in, this can then be lit according to information provided about the scene into which this subject is to be dropped.

With the actor's position established, some easily understood means should be adopted to identify a correlation between the location and the blue stage representing it. This might be in the form of a grid painted on the floor in a slightly different colour from the screen so as to be sufficiently different for people to see, but blue enough (if using blue screen) for the process to ignore. Blue camera tape is ideal for this and can be used to delineate the position of furniture, walls and so on. Once this is all mapped on the floor, blue posts or stands draped in blue should be positioned where appropriate to give good cues to the actors without them having to look down at the floor. These can be aligned with features with which the actors must interact, such as doors or windows. At the same time as accurately fixing these points the camera should be positioned too. As discussed previously, this will require accurate data describing the camera settings such as focal length as well as positional information including inclination, height above floor and distance from subject. If necessary, pre-measured posts or other marking devices can be positioned to help determine the exact camera framing.

Once the actor and camera positions are determined, all areas of blue/green should be covered over with something like black felt to minimize spill and visual strain. If there is a lot of rehearsal necessary and the floor is painted then it is best to protect it with strong paper, card or cloth. To help precisely frame the shot and to give everybody a much better chance at properly aligning and timing the action, a video replay system is invaluable. If the background has already been shot then it should have been loaded into this but, either way, a replay of the scene being filmed should be available.

7 Self-matting processes

The video replay will be of no use whatsoever if its image does not positionally align with the replayed material. The best way of absolutely ensuring that this is accurate is to set up a chart on which the viewfinder graticule can be marked and then filmed. There is no other way of guaranteeing in post-production where the actual framing should be within the frame if it is not thus filmed. If this were done during the shooting of the background then this chart should be included on the front of the clip to be used with the video tap system on the studio floor.

Some means of comparing the pre-shot background and current shot should be included in the video assist package when working with VFX. Most common is a tape replay of something such as miniDV, Betacam or digi-beta, or alternatively the images are pre-stored on hard disk. In either case it should be possible to mix and wipe between the pre-recorded and live images. On a system with good colour reproduction it should also be possible to do a rough key. Obviously on all video systems from miniDV right up to HD a full quality key will be possible straight away but on film equipment the 'video-tap' may not offer such a good image. By shooting a caption aligned to the viewfinder graticule (see figure on page 103) life is made very easy for post-production who simply have to align the grids shot on the blue screen and background shoots, respectively. However, aligning these may be slightly more difficult during the shoot. Even on a given camera the position of the video tap may vary between elements shot a long time apart and obviously the amount of the frame scanned in a telecine (or scanner) will also depend on decisions taken. Thus it will usually be necessary to have some mechanism capable of resizing at least one of the two elements so that the graticules (live and pre-filmed) can be equally sized for the shot. Once this is done then elements in the live studio can be lined up with reference material in the background with total confidence.

To line up a scene the best all round method is to have a 50/50 mix between foreground and background but, if fixed linear material is to be aligned, then a horizontal or vertical wipe slowly moved to and fro may help even more. This can be used to check the alignment of a straight line – say the frame of a door which is being replicated in blue to match a real one in the background. Another technique favoured by many is to draw important aspects of the background image on to the monitor with chinagraph pencil and then to align the foreground to this. The one problem with this approach is to allow for the thickness of the monitor glass, which means only one person in one precise position can accurately use the marks. With LCD screens this problem is less, but not removed. Once aligned, and judging the actual action by the actors, a full chroma-key will give the best representation of what the final image might look like. There is much argument about the best way to use video assist, with some arguing it should *not* be shown to artistes and others believing that it is a big help to them.

Once everything else is ready it is important to establish the artistes' eye lines and help them to fix on these. Posts, crosses on the cyc and various other physical markers can help, but there is nothing to beat another actor (preferably the one they are supposed to be eyeballing – if possible) who can stand in the appropriate position and even feed the dialogue. This will often be done by a stand-in or assistant, but on occasion is a responsibility the director or VFX supervisor like to take on themselves. Sometimes it may be convenient to place a video monitor on the eye line so that the actor can actually see what is happening in the other half of the scene. Where the background will be some enormous CGI monster, for example, then a head on a stick or some such representation which can be moved in similar fashion to the final entity will be a big help. This really is important and there are sadly all too many examples where the eye lines have not been properly established and the actors given nothing to 'act to' – with wooden, hammy results all too familiar in even big-budget effects movies.

Finally, having lined everything up it is necessary to consider the peculiarities of the actual shot itself. Most scenes are simply putting the actors into relevant backgrounds but some require interaction with that background. It may be, for instance, that they operate equipment in the background (but it will be part of a CGI image) or shake hands with their brother (but it is played by themselves in another pass) or they lift up an object from a table (which is in a miniature set). Very careful thinking is required in the design of these effects. For example, if the character is to pick up an object that is in the background, then, unless there is some really good reason, this should be physically in the blue set with him and positioned to be in the correct place in the background. This way the actor can pick it up and move it about without any complexity. However, if this is some artefact which is impossible to construct outside of a CGI model then a similarly sized representation will have to be used (see figure below).

| real object shown in the background but interacted with is best shot in the fgd | a substitute for a cgi character which is being added later in post production | final composite with cgi character added over top of working substitute |

It will be necessary for this to have distinctive markers on it which will provide three-dimensional data on its relative position as it is moved about. Quite often such representative models are painted blue or green to make it easy to key the artiste's fingers over the replacement object. What is not a good idea is to ask the actor to mime holding something with nothing provided at all. This is very difficult for the actor to do believably and provides no means for the post team to 'fix' the inserted object to the artiste's movements.

Where the interaction is with something apparently fixed in the background, such as a lever or switch, then a blue/green representation in the correct position on the stage is the best method. Once again the actor needs something to home in on and the post crew need him to be gripping something from which they can get a key around his fingers.

Reactions with other actors are the most difficult, the best known being where an actor apparently shakes hands with himself. As with all such things there are many ways of facilitating this, the most common being shaking hands with a stand-in dressed in blue apart from the hand, or totally in blue or wearing blue gloves and having the hands completely replaced. The difficulty with this is to precisely position the character in the two respective takes. This is down to very careful use of a video assist system and alignment stands in the studio.

One clever solution, if the shot is static and dark, is to have an entire arm shake hands in the blue set and then attach this to the person at the elbow (see figure below) but this, of course, necessitates the actor to stand unnaturally still. This effect has even been tackled in recent times by removing the lower arms of both shakers and replacing them with CGI models, which of course, can be positioned and adjusted with infinite variance.

| actor plays left role shakes hands with dummy hand | actor plays right role holds arm out of shot lines fed by stand-in | hold back matte for actor's chest | composite |

Smoothing the post

Although generally much cheaper than a studio, time in post is still expensive and if it can be saved through reasonable measures during the shoot, then it should be – the adoption of some simple procedures during the shoot can save colossal amounts of time and ensure a much better end result.

First and foremost is the provision of information for the team further down the line, which might be another shoot, CGI models to be added or the compositors who will stitch everything together. In all cases they need information about all aspects of the blue studio shoot. From camera data, through information about the action, including carefully measured geographic data, to accurate lighting plots (see VFX data sheet on page 59). Most useful is reference material to help automate the process of compositing. If the camera moves then there must be usefully positioned tracking markers. These can be tape crosses on the backing or small clearly defined spheres (such as ping pong balls). The requirement here is for these to be as small as possible whilst still being absolutely clearly defined. Since they will have to be removed they should be minimal but must still be clear to the software which uses them. As a general rule there should always be at least four visible, but the requirements of the software being used should be clearly understood for any given shoot. Lighting references using large white, grey and reflective spheres should be shot to show clearly how the light was working. Other important references should include a white out of black grid (if this had not already been made for the lens being used) to map any distortion in it and a pure grey card to show any colour or shading problems.

Within the action it is always good to have a stand-in adopt the position of any person who might be added later to show expected framing, where shadows will fall, and so on. Similarly with photographic effects, if there is some kind of filtration used throughout the shoot but which is inappropriate for a blue screen then a version of the shot should be made with this in position to define how it should look after the effect is simulated in post-production. Finally it is always a good idea to shoot an empty pass (i.e., with all actors and props removed) since this can be used during compositing to improve the key. This 'clean pass' shows what was shading on the background and what was shadows belonging to the foreground and also provides information for potential difference matting. If there are rigs this also makes it easier to eliminate them.

There are also a number of procedures which can simplify the post processes. It is possible to shoot in an empty blue studio and provide all masking and other similar effects as part of the composite but many of these are easy to do during the shoot and should therefore be done at this time if possible.

It has already been stressed that unused parts of the blue/green should be covered over to eliminate spill but additionally some of the areas outside of the action area may contain ancillary equipment or parts of rigs. So-called garbage mattes are particularly useful here. These may be small cards close to the camera or large flats or cloths further away, but if the same colour as the screen, they can help to automatically fill the frame with blue so that a key can be done without further masking in post. With masks close to the camera this can also reduce spill and glare into the lens from lights which may have been positioned within the frame but outside the active action area.

The actual action itself can also be modified on the stage so as to simplify things in post. For instance if we have two characters talking, but only one is being shot live then it is beneficial to have someone standing in for the second character so as to provide reflections, shadows and shading which would be expected if someone was really there! Finally, if the subject will be walking through a door or behind a pillar, or some other similar interaction with the architecture, then it is much more convenient for everyone if this is done live on the stage by having a suitably positioned and coloured flat (see figure below). On the other hand, this should only be done if the shot is known to be accurately aligned because if it is not, then the studio door may prove impossible to line up with the one in the background.

blue flat representing door frame

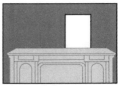
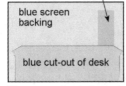

pre-shot background   blue screen live action set   actor masked as though coming through the doorway

Special uses of blue/green screen processes
The process of detecting and replacing a coloured material can and is used in other ways than photographing action against a large screen. These techniques

basically reverse the blue screen process by having a small blue screen within live action, rather than having a live subject in front of the blue screen. A very simple example would be where an image is to be inserted into a television set. Here the TV screen would be covered with, or painted, blue (if the shot was to move, with tracking markers on it) so that the on-screen image could be added later but foreground action within the scene could pass in front of it. Similar procedures deal with the view outside a window or door in an otherwise completely built set. More exotic examples would include where a stand-in is being used to provide interactivity for a CGI fully animated character. It could be argued that as the entirety is to be replaced it does not really need to be blue but, the blue has the advantage of letting the main character's limbs be laid on top of the CGI character when they cross the stand-in. If he was not blue, then this would have to be painstakingly rotoscoped (see figure on page 185 – where the ball is now blue to allow overlap). Complex rigs may also be dealt with in this way. Say a character is to float through the air, the armature which carries him can be painted blue and then replaced with an empty pass, shot without rig or artiste – inevitably some retouching may have to be done, but the majority of the work will be thus automated.

There are an almost infinite number of variations on this technique including where particular objects are required to change colour during a scene. A flower, for instance, might alter magically from white to red – the subtle and multi-coloured nature of flowers often means that using a real flower's colour would be impractical – or even because of the heat the flower itself might wither – so a saturated coloured flower can be used and then whatever colours are required keyed into it. Invisibility, too, can be created by an actor wearing a blue mask which is replaced by a clean pass on the background. Care has to be taken not to see down the collar – although a false shirt can be built in front of the actor's head which would be hidden in blue.

Compositing colour screen shots
The combining of blue/green screen elements may be done in many different ways and at various points in the production process. In video, electronic or digital systems it can be done live as the foreground is actually being shot or in post-production. In film systems the combination will always be done in post-production, but could be made electronically, digitally or even optically.

Video and digital systems
In an electronic system the output from the camera may be fed directly to a keying device and combined, on the fly, with a background either generated live from another source (e.g., camera or computer system) or with a pre-recorded scene. In a live combination of this nature the key signal must be near perfect or a compromise on quality accepted, since no sweetening or cleanup of any consequence will be possible. On the other hand, this is the staple diet of current affairs and news programmes the world over and fills their needs admirably.

Live keying may be done with a stand-alone device such as Ultimatte or via a vision mixer (video switcher). The former offers some very sophisticated controls including inputs allowing live garbage mattes to be applied and also permitting very fine control of the keying signal and, where the staging is appropriate, will even reproduce shadows and transparency. The video 'switcher' will usually permit control over the adjustment of keying, but also offers a lot of control over garbage mattes, permits wipes to be manually applied to control transitions and vignettes aligned with elements in the setting. It will also allow mattes and vignettes to be cut invisibly in and out of a scene.

Thus, for example, in a scene with a door (see figure below) a wipe is aligned across it so that our character can appear to pass through.

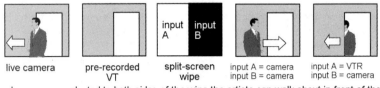

| live camera | pre-recorded VT | split-screen wipe | input A = camera input B = camera | input A = VTR input B = camera |

when camera selected to both sides of the wipe the artiste can walk about in front of the door, but when the VT is selected to the right hand side he will appear to go behind door

The character could walk across the setting as he enters from off-stage and then, whilst on far side of frame, the wipe to a freeze frame or pre-recording of the empty set would be cut in. On his return to the door, he would appear to walk through it. This is typical of the sort of effect done live where a large but empty cyc is used in combination with vision mixer effects which can easily be preset.

The great advantage of live working is that you can see the composite in real time and make adjustments to it with immediate visual feedback of their outcome. The downside is that, particularly where all of the image components are made live, an error in any single element will bring down the entire shot. High quality work will never be done this way, but excellent results have been obtained and for pre-visualization and previewing this technology is very useful indeed.

For post working, composite recordings are not acceptable (for reasons stated earlier), although it is possible to record a monochrome full-bandwidth key on a second recorder. This technique was used in the early Ultimatte days before composite recorders were available, since it had a separate key output which could be used later on as a key signal for post combining. It was a very expensive and tricky process to use, since at the time recorders were expensive machines and synchronizing the two decks was not trivial. The results produced were remarkably good.

Component recordings of course record the colour signals separately and are therefore entirely practicable for post-production keying. However, it should be remembered that the standard broadcast recorders sample the chroma signal at a lower rate than they do the luminance and therefore the key will not be of as good resolution as the main black and white component of the image. To minimize this effect the least compressed systems should be used with D1 and D5 being superior to digital Betacam and HDcam and all of these being superior to the various DV formats. For the very best quality, direct feeds from the camera chips should be fed to hard disk systems so as to capture the full bandwidth of all the colour channels. Where possible R G B should be used rather than Y, C^R, C^B since the colour space of the former is far superior.

Once the video image is on tape it can be processed using any technique available. The tapes may be played into a stand-alone video solution such as Ultimatte or into a video switcher and treated as if live, but with the advantage of being able to repeat the process until the desired result is achieved. Alternatively, the material can be combined in an online edit suite where automated mixing and wiping facilities are available and a certain amount of frame by frame work is possible (see below). The material can also be digitized into a non-linear editing system such as Avid and the combinations made there. Finally, the material can be fed into a fully fledged VFX computer system such as the hardware solutions made by Quantel or a software system such as Inferno or Shake (see next chapter).

The main technical peculiarity of video-originated material is that it is interlaced and therefore measures must be taken to ensure that images being combined with it are produced in the same way or stuttering motion will result, which will draw attention to the effects. Most HD cameras are now available with progressive scan modes usually indicated by the letter 'p' written following the speed, e.g., 24p, and these should always be used if possible since the image quality is better, but also for a matte shot there will be half as many positions to rotoscope. Apart from consideration of this temporal issue there is no difference in how post-production will deal with video frames rather than film.

Film systems

Film can be manipulated in post-production using either traditional mechano/chemical processes or electronic systems. The film route is analogue and suffers very badly from generational losses, which are manifested as increased grain, contrast and colour saturation. The gamma is altered and the image will lose detail. With the ever-decreasing cost of digital compositing methods and the gradual erosion of the skill set necessary to do film opticals, this method is really disappearing and will not be considered in detail here.

To manipulate film electronically it must first be converted into either analogue video or digital form. In the latter case this might be digital video or high-resolution data. Film is converted to video by running it through a telecine which works in real time and permits colour grading on the fly. The colour adjustment is necessary to choose which part of the film image information is thrown away, since video has a more restricted colour and luminance range. It is very important that, at this stage, the colour is kept as neutral as possible where VFX are concerned, particularly if processes which depend on colour are to be used. Obviously in blue and green screen shots the colour information must be preserved as best as possible. It is not a good idea to try to grade in more blue or green at this stage if the screen is imperfect, since this can severely distort the entire colour range of the shot. If adjustments are to be made they should be made by the compositor doing the shot.

Many telecine machines have a control variously called AK, VAC, detail or aperture correction, which is used to sharpen the image artificially. For VFX, particularly blue/green screens, this should be turned off because it can create 'ringing' (thin lines along a subject's edges) which make it very difficult to get a key without a matte line. If all the other material is being artificially enhanced then this process can be applied after the compositing has been done – indeed this will help the illusion because it means the effect will be applied over the demarcation edges and thus help to sell the idea that this is one shot.

Most telecine machines output an 8-bit/linear Y, C^R, C^B 4:2:2 signal and if the work is to be done in a CCIR601 or analogue hardware environment then this is fine. However, if the job is to be done using VFX or graphics software on a workstation then this is not a good format since it will have to be converted to R G B colour space where most computer systems operate. The differences between the two colour spaces result in artefacts and losses in image quality on each conversion made. Thus shots on computer systems should not be archived to video tape formats as errors will be introduced. For CGI systems then, it is better to output from the telecine at 10-bit/log, R G B 4:4:4 which will pretty well preserve most of the information that is in the photographic image. It is film's ability to be output at a variety of formats and quality levels which makes it so much more appropriate and convenient to use for VFX purposes.

Some TK machines randomly output in either field dominance. This is not acceptable for VFX and the machine must be set up to produce first-field-dominant output. If this is not arranged then the two fields of a film frame (originating in one instant of time) will be distributed across two video frames with field one of the film on field two of video frame one and field two of film being field one of video frame two (see figure on page 15 and figure below). This creates jittery frames which are not easily correctible in an online environment, although the problem can be fixed in a non-real time computer system.

when a telecine is in the wrong field dominance film frames will be split and so jitter

If the material will be processed with the intention of going back to film again or for HD or other future systems then it is usual to scan the material on a high-quality film scanner. These are preferred because of their kinder film handling, their superior stability (they use registration pins) and full range 10-bit/log R G B files in usually 2K (2048 × 1556) or 4K output image size. Like TKs these machines offer edge enhancement and this should be OFF, as discussed, for VFX work. Scanners do not have built-in colour grading systems since the idea is to capture the entire dynamic range of the image and therefore decisions about how to change this can be deferred to later in the pipeline. For VFX purposes this is the only choice, since to get the best keys in a blue screen you need to have all the original image information as accurately as possible. If some colour grading is necessary – say matching to a match grade clip – then for blue/green screen work this must be non-destructive, that is, it must not create alterations which cannot be restored to their original state.

For example, if a shot is made darker, then some dark tones may be reduced to black – this means they will be 'clipped' (see figure below).

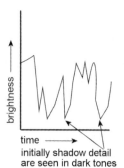

time ──────▶
initially shadow detail
are seen in dark tones

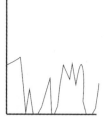

making the entire shot
darker by "sitting" signal
clips the dark tones

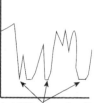

but lifting it again will
not be able to regenerate
what was clipped before

If at a later stage the information that was in those shadows is required it will not be recoverable. In a blue screen where shadows were being reproduced this would be very destructive. Far better to match grade the background shot, match the foreground to it as part of the compositing process so that the two elements gel and then afterwards match the completed image to the surrounding shots.

If the film is telecined to video SD (standard definition) or HD then all of the real time processes such as can be performed via a vision switcher or online edit suite may be applied to it. Thus, it can be played into a live show, used as an element in a 'live' chroma key or composited in real time during an online using digital Betacam or some such format. Basically if transferred to video then film 'becomes' video and will behave as described in the previous section.

Once film is transferred to a computer the possibilities explode and almost anything becomes possible. This will be discussed in detail in the next chapter; however, suffice it to say that depending on size and power of the computer in use, resolutions from less than SD all the way up to 6K can be manipulated at speeds ranging from real time to many minutes per frame. In a digital system, colours are divided up into 256 levels (8-bit) or even 1024 (10-bit) for each colour. Software can be written that can do anything imaginable to these values and for instance pick a particular range of blue levels and determine that anything within that range will be replaced by another image (i.e., a blue composite). Since these systems do not need to be real time the software can be as complex and sophisticated as the programmers can dream up. Thus all of the special techniques such as key colour suppression, edge blurring, shadows and transparency can be accommodated.

The greatest advantage of doing the work in a computer environment is that the entire shot exists as individual frames. If there are holes in the key or shooting off the backing or places where the foreground action breaks the active screen area, then on a frame by frame basis the image can be hand-painted to correct for these deficiencies. There are many tools and techniques to help with these shots, for example, if the key has holes in it then a black on white version representing the matte of the shot can be created and then black simply painted into the thin areas (see figure below).

| live action shot against blue | very imperfect composite from the bad key | the matte from the live action is not good | the matte after being manually retouched | resultant key is now perfect |

Similarly it is very easy indeed to create vignettes corresponding to opaque elements in the shot. A doorway can very easily and quickly be painted, for instance, and cut in and out at appropriate times to allow the action apparently to pass in front of or behind it. Most software has 'timelines' which enable events to take place at certain moments through time so that, for example, mattes can be predetermined to cut in and out at the required instants or keying levels adjusted at appropriate times through the shot.

With the subtlety possible in such software and the fact that there are no generational losses in the digital world it is possible to build up extremely complex effects shots from what might be quite simple but numerous elements. The secret to successfully producing such multilevelled composites is in the planning. To combine six or ten or twenty discrete elements into a single image requires very careful planning and attention to detail. To shoot all of the required elements requires considerable forethought and scheduling, so that all of the elements may be collected together and are shot in a fashion which permits them to be seamlessly joined in a reasonably efficient manner.

Let's imagine, for example, a scene in which a speech is being made in a large town square and which is about to be hit by an earthquake. For the 'hero' shot, in which the whole place starts to collapse on an extreme wide angle, we may these days see 20 or more separate elements being used. The lower part of the setting might be built in full scale and photographed with extras looking towards it and then running away when the quake hits. The mayor and his party could be shot on a small balcony to be matted into the upper part of the building which would be a miniature rigged to collapse. Tops for the surrounding buildings in the square and the dome of the main building might all be 3D CGI elements (two each right and left sides and one for the dome, making five in total). These would all be designed to collapse at the appropriate time. Additional crowd elements would also be needed to come close to camera (say three passes against blue screen for right, left and middle). Finally, there would be lots of passes of rubble, dust and masonry shot against blue screen to matte over the collapsing buildings both back and foreground; further passes could have dust and smoke shot against black and additional smoke and atmosphere could be created in CGI. This adds up to over 20 elements which could be matted together digitally to make an apparently single live action scene in which characters would miraculously appear to be enveloped in falling masonry and debris.

One of the great advantages of working in the digital domain is that images can be resized and reframed or cropped very easily. This process can actually be dynamic too, so that a CGI or animatronic bird, for example, might be delivered in a fixed position centre screen against blue. The intention here is to 'fly' the bird by means of reducing it to the required size and then positioning and flying it across the frame (see figure below). The kind of multilayering and subtlety possible in post is demonstrated where this shot might show the bird flying near a white wall – in which case the bird's matte could be shrunk and blurred and then laid as a soft shadow of a density to match other shadows in the backplate. With this put in place the bird could then be laid on top and look much more believable (see figure below).

original cgi bird flying in a fixed position   resized the bird can be flown across the frame as it flaps its wings in the animation   with blur the matte can be used as a shadow

Despite all of the fantastic tools available for compositing colour screen work there are times when a key simply may not be good enough. This may be where, for example, an actor has very fine blonde hair against a green screen. This will transmit and reflect a lot of the coloured light and so will simply key through as if it were not there. In such cases a solution may be to scan and composite at a higher resolution so if, for instance, we were working at SD we may rescan at 2K or if already working at 2K then could move on to 4K. At higher resolutions the software will run much more slowly but will often do the job with much less of a problem.

There are no special rules for shooting blue/green screens for digital/computer-hosted compositing compared with any other method, indeed the requirements can be slightly relaxed given that almost anything can be 'made' to work. However, having said this, the better the key, separation, evenness of screen, lighting of subject, sharpness of image and matching with background then the easier it will be to do the composite and thence possibly the better the result (there is always a limit to how long can be spent on a shot before the producer declares it acceptable). There are, however, a number of things which will make life a lot easier for a digital post crew. If the shot moves, always include tracking markers such that at least three and preferably four are always visible. Always do a pass without the foreground action so that the shading of the background can automatically be determined. If filters are being used, do a pass with them, but *do not* have them in place for the actual action takes. Shoot a grey scale, a grid, a reflective and white globe to provide grading and lighting information. Shoot a line-up chart which delineates the precise positions of the viewfinder graticule so that element positions can be instantly aligned. Slate shots and document them such that it can easily be seen which elements belong together and how they are supposed to combine.

Difference matting

This is the only conceptually new compositing technique to have developed from digital technology. It is very similar to blue/green compositing and indeed can be used as an alternative method of combining colour screen elements or to aid in their keying. Difference matting relies on the fact that a digital image is made up of individual elements (pixels) each of which is described by three numbers relating to their R G B values. Within a computer anything involving numbers can be mathematically interpreted.

If we have a locked-off camera and record an empty set for a few seconds and then do a second pass with an actor walking across it – on any given frame we can subtract the equivalent empty frame from the one including the actor and in the specific position where the actor is, in that frame, the pixels representing the actor will be different from those where she is not shown (see figure below).

A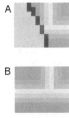

B

live action pass (A)   clean pass (B)

resultant matte

A and B are enlargements of a small section
C shows the mathematical difference between
these two - any pixels other than black will be
converted to full level white

C

With special software that detects whether there is a difference and its size, it is possible to specify that any pixels which do not have a difference greater than a pre-determined value will be replaced by another image – just as one would for values representing blue in a blue screen. This is a fantastic tool and effectively allows one to do a blue screen *without the screen*!

The main problem with difference matting and the reason it has a bad name in some circles is that the computer does not 'know' what it is doing and, therefore, if by chance the colour of an actor's face in a particular place just happens to exactly replicate the colour and brightness of the setting behind him, then no difference will be established and the background will be punched through. If the camera moves then it will be necessary for that movement to be identically repeated for the difference pass and this will involve the use of some form of computerized camera mounting. Worse still, if the background is moving, such as trees and/or grass blowing in the wind, then the background itself will differ between one pass and the next. Thus, difference mattes often need substantial sweetening in post to make them work – but, it has to be said, so do many blue and green screens even when adequately photographed.

On the other hand, there are many reasons to use difference matting and in controlled conditions it can work extremely well. From a creative point of view it provides a really simple way of shooting scenes such as where an actor wanders around a set which then slowly dissolves through to a different time and place. It is the definitive method for depicting an actor playing multiple roles within a scene, since it allows her to be solidly laid into the scene, pass behind and in front of furniture as required and yet neither require the building of a duplicate set nor to black out the existing one. Let's say that we want just two characters in our scene, but both will be played by the one actor. Firstly she plays the entire scene as one character then, after costume changes whilst ensuring that *nothing* in the set or its lighting is altered, she plays her second scene. Finally, a third pass is made without the actor present, to provide the differencing information. If one were to be pedantic, then a difference pass would be made immediately after each acceptable action pass. This is usually best done by leaving the camera running and having the actor rapidly get out of the shot.

Ironically difference matting can provide superlative composites when shot in the same controlled circumstances as a chroma screen. One of the main complaints about, say, a green screen is that in most real world circumstances you would never have a completely flat and even light source/backing and the effect of this will rarely match the background that will go behind the action. For example, in a scene with a couple on a park bench, you will often have a very bright top third (the sky), grey or brown mid sections (distant buildings or trees) and a relatively dark bottom third (grass or paving). Replacing this with an even green will not result in the best tonal/colour effect along the edges of the subject. Now, using difference matting you could replace the green screen with a cyc painted with colours which would roughly match the plate – it could even be painted, roughly to match a photograph of the location (see figure below).

location background

live action pass of studio painted bkgd

clean pass of studio backing

composite using difference matte

The advantage here is that the lighting could approximate that which would have been in the original background scene, say brightly lit at the top and darker across the middle. This provides the cinematographer with an extremely flexible additional tool to help in making the image more believable. Finally, if there were a slight matte line, say as a result of displacement of the key to either side, then the shoot-off would not be a highly saturated and unlikely green but of a colour and tone roughly the same as the background. This might help hide the matte line and thus make the post much easier. Less importantly it also provides a much pleasanter environment for those working on the stage.

Difference matting also offers a fantastic convenience factor and can save money. Lighting of green and, even more so, blue screens, can cost a lot both in resources and time. It is a tricky and time-consuming activity to light a blue screen evenly and requires special lights and/or coloured gels and a specially prepared backdrop. A difference matte does not require special lighting, it does not have to be even and it can be much darker than a typical blue screen. It requires no filtration nor does it require a specially prepared backdrop unless it is using a painted backing, in which case it can use ordinary paint and not the special high-priced material used for blue and green.

In rushed circumstances a difference matte is infinitely simpler to set up than a coloured screen. In a documentary, for instance, it is possible to create an impromptu matte where none has been intended. This may not be perfect and in post might need sweetening, but at least it gives some help in fixing the shot – the alternative would be to rotoscope the entire scene. Where a blue screen is particularly uneven and there is not the time to sort it out, a quick pass without the talent can allow it to be used as a difference matte or more likely a combination of both techniques.

Although by no means a perfect technique, difference matting can be used in association with many other techniques to produce far superior results or to enable imperfect material to be fixed.

7 Self-matting processes

8   Computer-based systems and techniques

From the producer's contract to the final profit and loss spreadsheet, and from the film camera to the automated ticket machine, computers have conquered the entire motion picture industry. Nowhere is this more true than in VFX, where digital methods have rapidly replaced most other techniques.

The terms 'digital' and 'computer' are gaily bandied about, but it is important to understand the meanings of these terms. A modern computer is a programmable machine which can perform logical and mathematical functions. This means it can be set up to execute specific tasks according to how it has been programmed. In other words, it may be configured to act as a 'virtual machine'; a device which to the user, appears to be job-specific, even though 'behind the wall', there is a customized standard machine. Contemporary computers work digitally but could be analogue, like mechanical calculators.

Digital and analogue are alternative working methods. In analogue, a value is represented by a continuously variable signal, whereas in digital it is assigned one of a set of specific known values (see figure below).

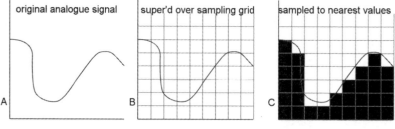

A: an original continuously variable analogue signal

B: with a grid superimposed on it showing the permitted sampling values

C: in a digital system only specific values can exist so the original signal has to be "sampled" or mapped to exactly coincide with the nearest relevant value

D: the resultant digital signal is much coarser than the original analogue - obviously a higher sampling rate - closer lines - would give an improved rendition

This could be a decimal value (0–9) or a duo-decimal value (1–12) but in all modern digital devices the binary scale (0–1) is used, because it is easy to represent electronically by 'on' or 'off', logically by 'true' or 'false' and mathematically by 0 or −1. The simplest piece of information (YES or NO) can be symbolized by a single 'bit' of information.

Each additional binary 'place' doubles the information stored, with a two-bit (2-bit) system having four states, and subsequent increases as follows:

1-bit	=	2 states	5-bit	=	32 states
2-bit	=	4 states	6-bit	=	64 states
3-bit	=	8 states	7-bit	=	128 states
4-bit	=	16 states	8-bit	=	256 states
5-bit	=	512 states	10-bit	=	1024 states

There are 8 bits in a byte so	1 byte	=	256 states
A kilobyte is 1024 bytes	1 KB	=	1024 bytes
A megabyte is 1024 KB	1 MB	=	1 048 576 bytes
A gigabyte is 1024 MB	1 GB	=	1 073 741 824 bytes
A terabyte is 1024 GB	1 TB	=	1 099 511 627 776 bytes
A petabyte is 1024 TB	1 PB	=	1 125 899 906 842 624 bytes

The process of converting a value into digital form is called sampling. Using too few samples to represent a signal would result in coarse reproduction, whilst the higher the sampling rate the closer it gets to recreating the original (see figure below). This is why some believe that analogue vinyl disks sound superior to CDs, on which the sampling rate is perhaps too low.

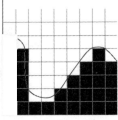
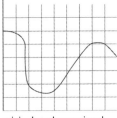
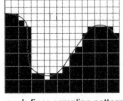

coarse sampling pattern   original analogue signal   much finer sampling pattern

Anything can be represented in digital form once a suitable system has been designed and implemented. Without a predetermined format it would be impossible to read back the information contained in the digital file. A simple example is 'ASCII' text which uses one 'byte' to represent the characters on a keyboard. Since there are only 26 letters in the alphabet (52 including capitals) and ten numbers, many other symbols and keyboard actions (such as 'return') are also classified since the 7 bits used can represent 128 entities. The process of converting an analogue object into its digital representation or code is called 'encoding' and the process of converting back again is called 'decoding'. A device for performing this task is called a 'codec'. Nowadays this is often a single microchip included on the computer circuit board.

In VFX many devices are based on digital technology. Images are stored on digital video tapes, disk drives and data tape drives, all of which store digitally coded images but which are not computers. Even film records digital information In the form of keycode, timecode and Dolby digital soundtracks. However, it should be noted that all of the above use analogue recording techniques. Watches, exposure meters, film cameras all have miniature computers buried in their innards – whether these devices are computers is a philosophical question not to be considered here!

Computers fulfil two functions which are useful to VFX. They can store and act on supplied information or create it and they can talk to off-board devices. This means that information can be loaded into their memory enabling it to be manipulated and changed, or, be used to control external equipment.

Computers – external processes (for control)

Computers have many methods of talking to the outside world such as firewire, USB and other connections. We are all familiar with the mouse and keyboard, but all manner of other devices can be hooked up to a computer and it can control pretty well anything. A computer can send on/off signals, digital code or, using a suitable codec, signals of varying voltage. All of these external communications may then be interpreted and used to drive analogue and/or digital devices in the outside world. Many devices can be controlled in this way, but some specific tools have been developed as spin-offs from computerization.

Most important of these to VFX is the stepper drive which is a motor whose rotation is divided up into a number of precise steps. According to the control signal fed to it, the rotor will rotate by the appropriate number of steps (see figure below). This provides two very useful functions: it allows the rotor to be very precisely controlled but, much more importantly, it enables the computer to know 'where' exactly the rotor is positioned at any moment in time – an essential ingredient where very accurate repeatability or precise line-up is required.

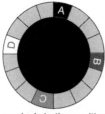

nominal starting position

rotate +2 steps (22.5')

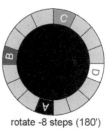

rotate -8 steps (180')

There is no limit to the number of devices which may be connected to a computer nor to the complexity of control functions applied to them. One of the principle advantages of computer control is that individualized programs may be written which enable very complicated controls to be applied from a relatively simple-to-understand interface. This ability to customize the control interface and to build into it complex but hidden intelligence about the system it is overseeing is the reason that computer control has become pre-eminent. Finally, the ability to very precisely, reliably and repeatedly manage systems in a simple but sophisticated way allows many complex processes, which were previously out of the question, to become practicable. The very first applications of computers in VFX were of this kind, using rigs which moved cameras in special ways.

Recording/post systems

Being able to precisely access particular frames and view or record them, jump on to other frames and vary the speed and direction in which they are viewed has been made possible by the use of digital techniques. These simple-sounding processes have made the whole of modern post-production possible. Analogue tape systems can have a timecode number attached to each frame either on a soundtrack (LTC – linear timecode) or encoded in unused lines of the picture (VITC – vertical interval timecode). Film has keycode numbers along its length (effectively barcodes) and can also have timecode in one of a number of different flavours. Digital systems have timecode or frame numbers embedded in their data.

With a timecode reader built in to the video or film viewing machine and control of its transport mechanics, it is possible to take charge of the system from a remote computer. This allows for the design of editing systems where one machine is nominally a recorder and the other a player: simply jumping from play to record on the record machine makes an electronic cut (see top figure on page 115). This can be grown to the number of machines required, such as three machines to make a mix (two into one) or four machines to make a rotoscoped composite (one each for foreground, background, matte and recorder). Much more complex schemes can be achieved using even more machines. This was the basis of the very earliest editing suites in the 1960s and, when allied to a vision mixer (video switcher), was capable of very sophisticated effects.

These very same facilities also make it possible to execute animation and stop frame effects using video or digital equipment, with the advantage over the original film method of being able to review the shot up to and including the frame being worked on. Because of its instantaneous frame locating and better mechanical stability it is preferable to use hard disk systems for these latter, since on a tape system it would be necessary to rewind before each replay with subsequent delays and mechanical strain.

Finally by having full control over devices such as video recorders and film scanners or telecines, it is extremely easy to manage input/output to/from the digital domain. Specific frame start and end points can be pre-determined and then the material required can be automatically loaded without further human intervention.

Camera systems

Computer control of camera systems takes two forms – control of the camera mechanism itself or control of its position and movement. Digital controllers for stop frame, timelapse and animation can be purchased off-the-shelf or special software written to control the camera. Most special control software is built-in to modern systems such as those made by Arri and Panavision.

The use of sophisticated software enables simultaneous adjustments of functions not otherwise easily coordinated. For example, if speed changes (ramps) are required, then an adjustment of the aperture or preferably shutter angle will be required to compensate for the resultant exposure variation.

With computer control this can be set up as an automated process which will track precisely, whereas manual movements would be very hit-and-miss. In activities such as timelapse, software can take into consideration various factors other than purely arithmetic inputs. For example, the software could be programmed to adjust exposure for a consistent image until lights are turned on, at which point it would remain at a pre-determined exposure until they are turned off again. It might also check the image before recording, to see if it has changed and only record if it has.

Although effectively re-discovering what Muybridge had done in the nineteenth century, 'timeslice' photography (see page 46 has only become possible since the arrival of computer control. In timeslice many single cameras can be set up and fired off simultaneously to permit an apparent track around a frozen subject. At 24 fps this requires 120 cameras to record just five seconds of footage. With the special software used in these systems it is now possible to select any combination of coincident or successive exposures, thus enabling seamless combinations of frozen and moving images.

Although a visual effect in itself, timeslice may also be set up in 'consecutive frame' mode (where each camera is fired after a delay) so as to mimic the effect of a motion control system (see below) but without any of the inaccuracies created by physically moving a camera around in space.

Computer technology was first adapted to VFX from flight simulators and other military developments. It was initially used to create multiple pass elements for TV commercials such as those made in the 1970s by Robert Abel & Associates. For pack shots (as discussed) it is often necessary to shoot many passes, say a beauty pass, an internal lighting pass and a matte pass. The problem with this technique is that it does not allow for movement; however, using a computer-controlled camera which can precisely repeat an identical movement every time, multiple exposures of an inanimate object with a moving camera suddenly become possible.

Computer-controlled camera movement

Field cameras

The simplest motion systems generally control the pan and tilt of the camera. These are usually known as field, repeating, memory or mimic heads, or as 4-axis systems. The latter refers to the four parameters such as pan, tilt, focus and zoom that the system will generally control. Some special heads have been manufactured specifically for this purpose but many more have been built from a geared head such as a Moy or Arri which has been motorized using stepper drives.

Early systems were controlled by arcane interfaces which involved typing in numbers relating to X (horizontal) and Y (vertical) coordinates and time counts for moving between them, usually measured in frames. The latest systems permit an operator to pan and tilt the camera as normal. The system records the movements and then allows them to be repeatedly played back with or without modifications. Most of these heads permit movements to be around the nodal point or the centre of gravity as desired.

The hardware involved in these systems generally has sensors and motors connected to the pan and tilt axes of movement. The sensor will often be a shaft-encoder which measures rotation of the relevant axle. The shaft-encoders are most usually optical and read the light reflected off alternating reflective and non-reflective stripes. The results are measured against time and therefore express speed as well as motion. The sensors keep the computer informed of where the head is and how far it has moved. Motors are used to move the head on replay. The best and most common are stepper drives. As described, these can be very accurately adjusted and, in systems which do not allow the head to be moved manually, steppers can be used without additional sensors.

Software generally uses a timeline along which 'keyframes', 'way points' or 'nodes' represent the positions of the variables at given times (see figure below).

Current Positions			0.00	0.00	0.00	0.00	0.00	0.00	0.00
Frm	Posn	Target	Track	Lift	Rotate	Pan	Tilt	Zoom	Focus
0	1	154.0	112.05	10.00	-22.40	-3.05	-12.45	3.00	
25	2	156.9	78.45	23.00	-21.65	3.49	-12.25	3.00	
179	3	170.0	54.67	45.40	0.00	3.99	-12.75	3.00	
250	4	166.5	5.50	30.45	-36.60	5.78	-12.86	3.00	
325	5	166.3	-34.63	30.34	-29.48	6.34	-12.75	3.00	

reproduced courtesy of Mark Roberts Motion Control

When run, the system will attempt to synchronize the various components with these way points. Usually the operator will be given the choice of linear or smoothed (curved) moves between these points. In a smoothed system a spline or logarithmic algorithm will be applied so that movements appear to naturally speed up and slow down as they start and finish or to avoid sharp changes of direction or speed when passing through a way point. Most systems permit the camera to be positioned (either manually or via computer control) and an 'enter keyframe' option used to enter the positional details. As many points may be entered as required and the camera may then move between them in the specified time in either a straight or curved line depending on the option chosen.

The software will usually allow for limits to be placed on any movements, since unrestricted travel with an automated head could result in damage such as snapped cables or tilting beyond the capabilities of the head. Another feature often available is that of scaling. This allows the move to be scaled differently

8 Computer-based systems and techniques

between passes. Thus for instance an actor could be shot in a live action studio against blue with a pan following as he walks and talks. The background is shot later on a miniature of 16th-scale and, to accommodate a matching move, the field software is set to 16th-scale. This will match all the elements apart from camera speed, which will of course remain constant between takes. Like many such systems field heads can display eccentricities and these should be understood and noted before use. Most common will be slippage where on resetting, the start point may drift. Necessary precautions should be taken before each take such as checking a physical mark on the head or a suitable target aligned with the viewfinder crosshairs.

Field heads are often used where inhospitable locations need to be shot as background plates, or where locations are too restrictive to permit the use of larger gear but the production have requested that the plates have movement in them. It is always better to shoot the foreground action first and then have the move applied at the location, since this will not involve actors trying to match something they cannot see. However, it is still worth having a stand-in of similar height to aid in lining up the start and end positions, so as to get a properly matching angle. If the plate must be shot first, then a stand-in really should be used in at least one pass to give the studio crew a guide.

The easiest way to align the shot is to set the camera to its start position and mark up the actor's position, then set the camera to its end position and mark that too. It will be much simpler for the actor to time his performance between these two known physical positions, rather than trying to fit with a move he cannot see. If there are any elements in the scene requiring interaction such as to be looked at or passed behind, then it is worth putting some markers or poles in those positions. With a hard disk video replay system it should be possible to synchronize the replay of the background image with the position of the head on set. This means that stopping the movement at a given time on the timeline will present the appropriate camera position and using a super or wipe it will be easy to accurately position the actor's aid (see figure below).

background

live action with
post to help actor

split screen to
check alignment

composite

All of the recommendations made for matching and setting up composite shots are even more important here, since it will be much more difficult to fix any errors where the camera is moving in post since the various elements must precisely fit in time as well as position. It is essential that a memory head rig should be absolutely rigid and capable of no movement apart from that dictated by the computer. Any additional moves during a given pass would result in its having a different movement over time and therefore not fitting with the other elements;

the composite would therefore fail. As mentioned, precise positioning of the start point is also imperative if the moves are to fit.

Field heads can be used in situations where multiple passes must be made *in situ* such as making space models drift across frame. They can also be used to collect data taken from their sensors where computer-generated backgrounds are to be added later. This latter usage is typified by the 'virtual set' in which a 3D computer model is rendered live to provide a scenic background which is moved about according to data fed from the camera heads. The data can also be used for pre-visualization purposes such as checking that digital matte paintings or CGI models provide sufficient coverage.

Field heads are relatively light, transportable and easy to use – they are, on the other hand, not very sophisticated and limited in the shots they can handle. For more advanced uses a full motion control system is required.

Motion control cameras (MoCo)

There are many motion control systems dotted around the world and even though a number of companies manufacture off-the-shelf systems, few if any of them are the same! However, the basic principle is very simple, with a camera mounted on some form of computer controlled mover.

This can be as simple as a portable flat base with rubber wheels which travels on conventional track (see figure below). A tripod or other mounting may be attached to the base, perhaps with a field head. The computer simply controls forward, possibly reverse movement and the field head if there is one. In such a system the exact start position would need to be marked since it would be highly unlikely that the dolly would accurately return to it after a move.

A MoCo can also be an extremely sophisticated installation with its own customized stage, suspended from a ceiling-mounted track, with a long telescopic arm and special underslung head permitting 360° rotation in any direction.

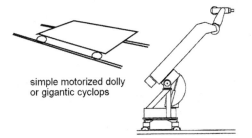

simple motorized dolly
or gigantic cyclops

Every conceivable variation between these two extremes exists. Many rigs have been built for specific productions or even single shots and quite a few of the independent owner/operators have, over the years, built up flexible modular systems which can be configured to match almost any eventuality. The principle components are outlined below but many exclusive elements have also been fabricated.

Computer   The requirements for a MoCo system are quite elementary in terms of processing speed and memory requirements. Proprietary systems will usually come in a black box with plugs and sockets specific to the system, however inside the box will be a pretty standard PC. Since their reduction in size and cost and increase in power, laptops are now frequently employed for portable systems.

The important requirement is a good and fast method of communicating with the hardware which will usually be in the form of special drive cards to talk to the stepper motors. It was the propensity of these cards to burn out that gave many early systems their reputation for unreliability.

Software   The brain of the system and its public face, the software enables an operator to communicate his requirements to the system, calculates the necessary operations and communicates the requisite commands to the various motors sensors. Early systems involved typing-in the required positional information at a command prompt (e.g., pl25 for pan left 25°) but all modern designs employ a graphical user interface (GUI) in which the various specific functions are represented as sliders or other standard Windows controls. A typical system might provide 16 or 24 axes of movement which might include:

- *control of the camera*: start/stop, advance (by specified number of frames), retard (by specified number of frames), speed (adjust to specified rate), shutter alignment (set shutter to required synch point), shutter angle (adjust to specified opening in degrees), exposure (time shutter remains open), focus (to specified distance) and zoom (to specified focal length);
- *control of the head*: pan (yaw), tilt (pitch), and rotate (roll);
- *control of arm*: elevate/de-elevate (crane up/down), swing (jib) left/right, crab (slide) left/right, extend/contract (track in/out);
- *control of dolly base*: track forward/backward (by specified distance);
- *control of ancillary devices*: one or more control axes may be reserved to control additional devices such as a model mover (see below), lighting control, fan or firing mechanism.

Hardware   Motion control rigs come in many shapes and sizes but the basic principle is the same. A field head is connected to a moveable base by some system which may additionally allow vertical and/or horizontal movements. The head will always allow pan and tilt and usually be nodally centred. It may also permit rotation and in some systems all three movements can be through a full 360°. The base will usually be attached to some form of track. This may be flat and the dolly move by friction on simple rubber wheels. More intricate systems may have cogs which fit into serrated track or be pulled by special flat cables with teeth along their surface. Some smaller rigs are motivated via a very long worm screw. The track may be floor- or ceiling-mounted. Ceiling-mounted rigs are particularly adept at flying over miniatures and other large horizontal settings. The centre section connecting the head and dolly is optional but may be either in the form of a crane arm or an elevator (see figure below) with the former being able to swing up, down, left and right whilst the latter consists of a horizontal armature extending to either side of a central column.

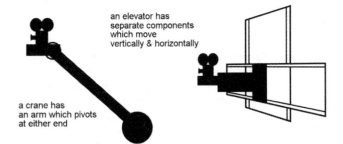

an elevator has separate components which move vertically & horizontally

a crane has an arm which pivots at either end

The head can move along the armature which in turn can move up and down the elevator. Although some large rigs are built in to vast stages specially created for the purpose, the majority are portable and often modular to allow them to be set up in a variety of locales from the studio to the deck of a ship. These will often run on track which can be slotted together so that moves can be over considerable distances. Some of these portable rigs are capable of moving quite quickly and can achieve speeds suitable for real time live action.

Throughout this section it is assumed that a film camera is attached to the rig. It is of course possible to fit a video or digital camera but many of the features of the system such as long exposure times and the use of special lenses are not ideally suited to video, or the relevant accessories are simply not available. With a fast real time system video would make sense particularly with its superbly steady image. With the advent of the latest digital cameras and hard disk recorders it certainly has become much more practical, but R&D has tended to be directed towards software tracking systems to create movement rather than MoCo.

Operation Each axis of movement has its own timeline along which are positioned 'way points' (keyframes or nodes) representing the state of that function at that point in time. Thus for instance, focus could be set to 20 ft at the start of an event and after 100 frames might have a second node set to 20 ft, after a further 100 frames (i.e., at 200 frames along the timeline) it might have a third node set to 30 ft. The above would result in the focus continuously changing from 20 ft to 30 ft over the period of 100 frames. If the move were linear then it would be focused at 25 ft when at 150 frames along the timeline and so on (see figure below).

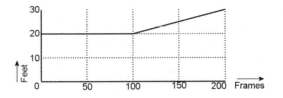

Each function controlled by the program will have a separate timeline and all of these will be synchronized together – however, whether this will be visually represented as a linear timeline depends on the design of the particular software. Whatever method is adopted it will be possible to state the start point of any given action and the time over which it will be executed.

A choice between 'linear' or 'smoothed' (chamfered) will be offered, often with various smoothing options such as spline or log. This will specify whether changes in the timeline are made instantly or by accelerating/decelerating in a more natural way. It is important to realize that if the smoothing option is engaged, then repeating just part of a move may not result in that take matching the same part of a move made on a full run.

For example (see figure below), imagine a shot in which a motion controlled dolly moves 100 ft past a tree, a post, a telephone kiosk and another tree. We have the same actor playing different roles in each of these sections and use the various objects to hide the split screens which are used to matte them together.

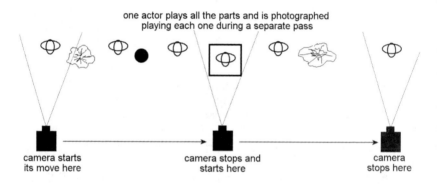

one actor plays all the parts and is photographed
playing each one during a separate pass

camera starts
its move here

camera stops and
starts here

camera
stops here

The shot starts static on the first section and then accelerates passing the first tree and post and then coming to rest on the kiosk to see the player do some business. It then moves off past the other tree finally coming to rest at the end of the track. All of the movements are smoothed out. Six passes are required, one each for the six characters portrayed. On many systems the entire move would have to be made for each pass (certainly up to, and from, the point where the dolly stops) because the smoothing function would be unable to calculate the precise speed at any given point if it were not actually executing that part of the move. Some more sophisticated systems can calculate this, but it is a good example of the flaws which need to be understood in these highly individual systems.

Some software is capable of extremely complex calculations and can offer facilities such as precise vertical elevation even if the system has a pivoting arm (see figure opposite). This is achieved by the body of the MoCo moving to compensate for any change of distance created by the arc of the arm's movement. Very precise movements such as pivoting around an object can also be easily programmed in, or moving very accurately between extremely close objects, as in some miniatures or commercials pack shots.

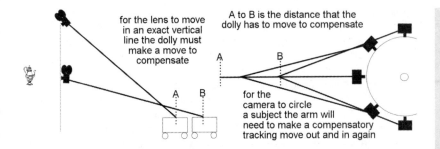

for the lens to move in an exact vertical line the dolly must make a move to compensate

A   B

A to B is the distance that the dolly has to move to compensate

A   B

for the camera to circle a subject the arm will need to make a compensatory tracking move out and in again

An essential function is a 'reset' option. This puts the entire program back to the nominal start state, meaning that it will return to its zero or default position. Prior to activating this function or indeed any other motion control activity which sets it moving, all personnel in the studio should be made aware. Although there will be an emergency stop facility these are usually very heavy devices with considerable inertia. Motion control systems have wrecked many sets and valuable objects over the years, including a fair share of humans! A horn or loud announcement is essential when a MoCo rig is set 'on the move'. From simple to extremely complex systems it is important to have a physical check of some kind to ensure that the datum is accurately attained – slippage will often mean that the nominal start is not found. On some systems this can be automated by having various sensors seek an optical or other marker.

If a real time move is being made it is essential that the shutter is controlled by the computer. If it is not, and the camera is merely started by a run-up-to-speed switch, then the shutter is unlikely to be in the same rotational position on each pass and thus the apparent camera position will be different for any given frame in each pass. Let's imagine we have an 180° shutter (see figure below) and the camera is doing a long and fast horizontal movement in real time at 24 fps.

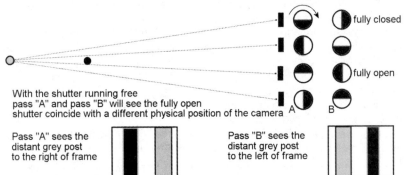

fully closed

fully open

With the shutter running free pass "A" and pass "B" will see the fully open shutter coincide with a different physical position of the camera

A   B

Pass "A" sees the distant grey post to the right of frame

Pass "B" sees the distant grey post to the left of frame

This means that if the shutter starts a half-phase differently on our two passes then it will actually be 1/48th second further down the track on one pass than the other or at a speed of 4 ft/s it would be displaced by 1″ easily enough to make it impossible to ever marry together these two passes without hours of work in post – if indeed it would ever properly composite at all. To understand the significance of this difference simply close one eye and move your head by an inch and notice the difference it makes between close and distant objects.

Lining up the shot can be achieved on most systems by slowly jockeying the rig to each position using manual controls to frame the shot visually via a video tap (or the actual picture if using a video/digital camera). Some systems boast joysticks or other interactive analogue controls to make the process easier. By far the most useful option is a portable control box which is either connected to the terminal by a long flying lead or, most luxuriously, by wireless link. On long and complex moves, particularly where the camera is in close proximity to the subject matter (e.g., in a large miniature), a flying control box is essential since it will be the only way to safely move the rig between the various elements of the scene. Clear vision of the set will usually be blocked by the body of the rig so the only alternative to a portable controller is to shout or radio instructions to an assistant operating the console – a frustrating and far from foolproof method, and to be avoided.

Whatever method is used to find the various keyframe positions they can usually be entered by pressing a single button. This procedure is sometimes called 'targeting' and each position can be aligned to a chosen point on the timeline. Timings can also be entered separately and all elements can be edited retrospectively. An alternative 'learn' mode is sometimes available in which the rig is flown through the desired move manually and then the timing adjusted to the actual speed required. Unfortunately most motion control systems are not capable of real time speeds because of their mass and inertia and moves are therefore made at a fraction of the speed required to be seen on screen. This situation is exacerbated by the fact that on many typical motion control shots very small apertures are needed to get sufficient depth of field and therefore long exposures are required to make exposure. For these reasons MoCo shots are often effectively stop frame in nature with very long exposure times of ¼ s, ½ s or even longer required. When operating in this mode two alternative scenarios present themselves – either the camera comes to a halt before each exposure or is deliberately moved during it (sometimes called go-motion). With a stopped camera the resultant moving image stutters just as with traditional stop frame animation and therefore it is preferable if possible to create motion blur by moving whilst the exposure is being made. Normally this is done by positioning the camera and halting it, then starting the move and exposing prior to moving on to the next position – it is not usual to open and close the shutter during a continuous move through the entire length of the shot.

Data relating to a move can be exchanged with other systems, allowing for example, computer graphics to be synchronized with the motion control move. In some instances this will be the sole purpose of using a motion control system and only one pass will be required. Some special, real time rigs have been built specifically for this purpose. In turn, data from a 3D CGI system can also be generated to drive a MoCo rig. For some complex miniature work a 3D CGI model is built and a virtual camera rig is animated to fly through it as required. The data generated from this is subsequently used to operate a physical

MoCo rig flying through a 'real' miniature. With very expensive studio time and crews this can be a very cost-effective way of creating extremely complex shots.

Accessories Spare axes can be used to control all manner of devices which may be required to operate at specific instances along the timeline. For example, lights may be required to fade up, down or flash as the camera passes particular points and similarly pyrotechnics may be required to fire at appropriate moments on each pass. Most important of these offboard devices is the so-called 'model mover' which is effectively one or more additional motors used to control moving elements in the subject of a shot. For instance, a model helicopter might be shot against blue, with a matte pass, a beauty pass and an internal lighting pass. For total realism the rotors should be seen to be turning but, with a MoCo move to depict the 'copter swooping in to shot, they would have to recreate exactly the same motion on every pass. By having the rotors connected to one of the axes of movement they can be made to behave identically on every pass – even slowing down and stopping if that is required. Similarly if a model plane is fixed to a pivot then by simply rotating the plane as the camera moves in on it, the impression of the plane flying past us will be given (see figure below) and, if available, another axis could rotate the propeller.

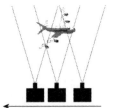

as the camera moves along its track the resultant image is no different looking than if the subject had passed by

direction of camera move

Other accessories in motion control are the periscope, snorkel, pitching, probe lens or endoscope. Although slightly different in their specifics (see page 53) all these lenses consist of a long thin tube with a viewing aperture at the end. This permits the viewpoint to be placed in small spaces into which the full camera body could never fit (see figure below).

a snorkel lens is often used for shooting close in on tabletop set-ups

The downside of these optics is that they often have a very small aperture of f/11 or lower and so therefore will usually require long exposure times. On the other hand, there is nothing more impressive than a shot whizzing along a model, table top or even grass verge less than an inch above the surface.

Uses Motion control can be used for shots requiring very precise movement and framing, to collect data for computer processes or to make exactly matching multiple passes. The latter can be used to depict the camera moving with respect to the subject or to create the impression of a static camera with moving subject.

Usually only requiring a single pass, MoCo systems are ideal for creating very precise tracking shots through and close to small objects. This is typified by commercials table top scenarios such as a mouth-watering display of fruit and vegetables through which the camera tracks at close quarters to discover the branded pack which supposedly contains them. These shots will usually be made with a snorkel lens of some kind and involve extremely careful line-up. If the shot is to end on a specific object it will frequently be shot in reverse since many rigs using long arms may exhibit a certain amount of instability when stopping. A slow acceleration from rest will be much easier to handle and is certainly the direction in which the shot should be initially built up. Organic materials do not fare well under hot lights and yet a large depth of field will be required in this kind of venture, so these shots are rarely made in real time. Despite not being inherently multipass shots the repeatability is used to align the move precisely and also permits alternative versions, say with a different pot of jam at the end of each. The only special considerations in designing shots made this way are to plan a suitable trajectory for the lens when building up the setting and also to take into consideration the proximity of the lens which can make for very difficult avoidance of shadows and reflections of the lens tube.

Precision tabletop shots will often overcome the depth of focus problem by using oversized props. An example might be the shot described above but this time flying over a garage workbench and eventually finding, say, a tin of adhesive. Where plastic, wood or metal man-made objects are the subject, double-, triple- or even larger-sized special props are often built and on camera appear indistinguishable from the real thing.

One final use often made of the repeatability of such shots is where a series of mixes or wipes are made between different subjects. In the produce shot described above it might be that a pass would be done over root crops, then a pass over citrus fruits, then greens and finally exotic fruits. In post-production a transition might then be made from each group to the next. With a portable rig these various passes might even be made in the actual fields and gardens where these things are grown. If the shot is simple this might be done by careful timing of a manually tracked camera, but if the move is made slightly more complicated, then a MoCo system is essential.

On complex effects films involving a large number of CGI models being added to live action it will enormously improve efficiency if data accurately detailing camera movement can be passed to the animators. This can be done by using a MoCo rig or field head (depending on complexity) or by fixing suitable sensors to the various moving elements of the camera mounting or by using a single 3D sensor attached to the camera and analysing data received from three or more transmitters placed in known and measured positions. Obviously, tracking markers could be placed throughout the scene and the camera movement back-calculated by analysing their movement; however, if a large number of shots are being made, then a huge improvement in efficiency can be generated by collecting live data on the set. Where these procedures are being used it is important to provide additional data about the actual set in which the camera is moving. If parts of the set are being replaced or altered then actual drawings and measurements of it will be essential to the post crew so that, if necessary, a CG model of the set can be built to precisely track the live action. It will also be necessary to provide accurate lens data including a grid and grey card and reflective and white sphere with associated lighting plot so that the lighting can also be matched. If the subject or implied light source move, the globes should be moved along the appropriate path.

The classic use for motion control is multiple pass photography involving a moving camera. Many of the situations where this might once have been used can now be achieved using tracking software or with a timeslice rig set to consecutive frame mode. The reason for this is that even so-called portable rigs involve substantial pieces of equipment, their inevitably long set-up times and then quite lengthy shot line-ups.

There are also problems on many rigs with absolute repeatability. By any normal standards even the worst rigs can achieve a remarkable degree of replication but, unfortunately, the degree of accuracy required to exactly lay two or more image passes on top of one another is in a different order of magnitude. Rigs are built mainly out of metal although some use carbon fibre – in either case they are subject to changes due to temperature and other external variables. With such complex devices involving lots of mechanical elements as well as electronics various combinations of otherwise harmless factors can result in differences between passes. The number of testimonials the author has had to write indicating that shots are un-combinable for insurance claims is proof enough of these difficulties. Just one example will suffice – a rig which had to do one pass at sunrise each morning and therefore had to be left rigged on a desert island beach. All precautions were taken, including laying a concrete bed for the entire system to sit on. Unfortunately the entirety slowly but surely sank into the ground below it – an imperceptible change until trying to marry the elements.

These observations aside, MoCo systems have been used to great effect on numerous film, and particularly commercials, projects. All of the usual requirements for both compositing multi-element shots such as front-light/back-light and shooting stop frame apply to motion control.

MoCo can be used to give apparent motion of either the subject itself or the camera. Imagine, for example, a spacecraft miniature being shot against a rear

8 Computer-based systems and techniques

projection screen depicting a rotating planet. This scene will require four passes to be made:

1   the screen fully exposed to show its background;
2   beauty pass of the spacecraft lit with bright point source + screen off;
3   matte pass with all lights off except rear illuminated wash over screen;
4   miniature lighting pass to expose model's internal lighting (very dim).

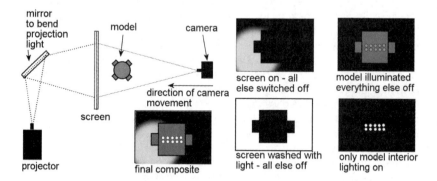

Two alternative scenarios are possible with this arrangement.

In the first the spacecraft will appear to move – not the camera. Element two would be shot first and the move would be set up to suggest that the model is approaching the camera rather than the other way around. Next, the matte pass and miniature lighting passes would be executed using precisely the same data. Finally, camera element one would remain stationary but would use the focus adjustment from the move used for the other passes. When combined, the spacecraft would appear to drift towards camera with the planet below going slightly soft.

In the alternative scenario all of the elements would have the same move applied to them and the camera would now appear to approach the spacecraft.

This very simple example embodies all of the principles of the technique and can be used as the basic building block for incredibly complex shots. The above example alone could be turned into a marathon exercise if used to create the imperial fleet. With 20 different camera moves and a massive 80 passes, 20 spacecraft could be shown to dart in all directions. As with all complex shots the trick is in the planning – figuring out which ships go in which directions and which are to the fore and the rear is the complex problem, not the actual shooting which is a purely routine task.

Motion control rigs can also be used to shoot conventional blue/green screens just with the added element of movement and portable rigs can be taken to all manner of locations to provide the backgrounds. It should just be borne in mind the intricacies of setting up these shots and replicating that set-up in another place and at another time. One of the most important applications is that of placing actors into miniatures. The basic rules such as matching lenses still apply even when the foreground and background are scaled with respect to one another. When scaling, all measurements will have to be divided by the scale factor but the focal length will remain the same – this is easily imagined if you think of a plan of the full scale and miniature scale sets – both of which must be identical apart from the linear measurements. Thus if you were to draw two lines on the live action plot from the lens position to the frame edges in the set and measure the angle of view it would be identical to that determined by the same procedure on the miniature plan.

MoCo can also be used very effectively to make numerous passes in a conventional set where perhaps an actor is to play multiple roles. It should be remembered that, on average, setting up a MoCo shot will take three to four times as long as a conventional similar shot. To have a player make multiple characters is once again down to careful planning and figuring out the choreography as to who goes in front of, or behind, whom. Once this is done the move can be set up with a stand-in for every character to be included in the shot. Once the move is predetermined it is just a matter of repeating the move for each character. It is imperative in these situations to make sure that nothing is moved from one pass to the next and also to always shoot an empty pass to enable clean ups of unwanted shadows or to be used as a difference matte to help in the compositing of the various elements. All techniques in the VFX toolbox may be used in conjunction with this technique so blue screens could be brought in, rear or front axial projection systems can be used to fill windows and/or doors or even fully back the performers, and travelling mattes (say, following an architectural feature) or rotoscopes of the actors themselves may all be used to combine the various passes.

One final example of how this can be used to great effect is the standard 'Dracula' shot in which Count Dracula looks in a mirror where there is no reflection. In many versions this is badly muffed, but using MoCo we can actually track in past Dracula to reveal that there is no reflection. This is simply done by making three passes – one with the actor in position and the camera tracking in past him on to his reflection in a real mirror. A second pass is made as before but this time with a blue insert in the mirror – this is the take which will be used so should be replayed until the actor's performance is satisfactory. Now the insert is removed and a third pass is made without the actor present and therefore with an empty mirror. The first pass is for reference only and may be omitted but is always useful in the decision-making process.

Finally, motion control will allow 'magic' or appearing/vanishing elements to be created, for example where special stunt or support rigging needs to be eliminated. Say a magic floating wand is required. This can be flown on wires with the camera following it and then, once a good take declared, a second pass without either wand or rigging can be made to provide a 'clean pass' for post-production to use for wire removal.

Computers – internal processes (for digital imaging)

Formats

As well as holding information about how an image is formed the actual image itself can be digitized. There are many formats and variants on this, but essentially the picture can be divided up into a mosaic of individual picture elements (pixels) and then each of these can be allocated a group of numbers to describe its attributes (see figure below).

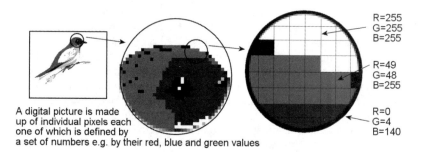

A digital picture is made up of individual pixels each one of which is defined by a set of numbers e.g. by their red, blue and green values

R=255
G=255
B=255

R=49
G=48
B=255

R=0
G=4
B=140

Film, photo, computer and art applications tend to allocate values for red, blue and green to describe each pixel's colour and luminance, whereas broadcast and video systems use B-Y, R-Y and luminance (Y) values. There are other systems too, such as hue, saturation and luminance and yellow, cyan, magenta and black (K) used in print; however, anything that can be expressed as a number can be turned into digital form and subsequently be stored and manipulated by a computer.

Quality is not just determined by the number of pixels however, it also depends on the number of samples into which an analogue original is divided. This is generally known as 'bit-depth'. In an 8-bit system (which allocates exactly one byte per value) the analogue signal will be divided into 256 levels. In a 10-bit system it will be divided into 1024 levels. Video and digital systems normally represent this division in 'linear' space where the samples are equidistant (see figure opposite) whereas film systems tend towards using 'log' which spaces the levels out with increased value and more adequately represents the film sensitometric curve.

The human eye can see approximately the equivalent to 8-bit colour (i.e., 256 levels each for R, G and B), however film can register in the region of 14-bit log. The compromise currently adopted for film work is to capture it at a value greater than 10-bit (depending on the process) and then down-sample to 10-bit/log. Part of the reason for this is that the duplication process used for distributing feature films downgrades the quality and VFX require the maximum information practical to make systems such as blue screen work effectively. Video, on the other hand, is generally worked at 8-bit with 10-bit for the higher

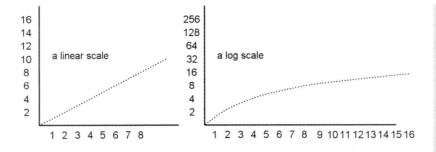

quality systems. Current TV sets are not even capable of reproducing the full quality of 8-bit.

Just to complicate matters further, digital video does not sample the colour and luminance information at the same rate. D1, D5 and Digital Betacam all sample according to the 4:2:2 scheme wherein the two colour difference signals are sampled at half the rate of the luminance and thus squeeze the three channels into the bandwidth which would otherwise be used by just two channels. HD-cam is effectively 3:1:1 and the various DV formats are 4:1:1. Obviously if 4:2:2 is only adequate (see page 168) then HD-cam and DV can be problematic for processes such as blue screen.

Aspect ratio also needs to be considered in the choice of a digital file. HD is 16 × 9 (1.77:1), SDTV is 4 × 3 (1.33:1), most feature films are 1.85:1 with some using the anamorphic ratio of 2.35:1 (see table on page 219). Most systems have symmetrical or square pixels but, for compatibility reasons, digital video in the PAL and NTSC regions have rectangular pixels: tall and thin in the USA, wide and oblong in Europe. This latter is a major problem for VFX and when video-originated material is being used the software should be set up accordingly. Unfortunately some VFX software does not recognize this and therefore the image becomes distorted. It is very important that computer-generated material is created with the appropriately shaped pixels if it is to be combined with 625 or 525 line video.

Quality is also reliant on compression. File sizes for moving images are enormous and to make their recording and distribution practical it is necessary to reduce the quantity of data. A great deal of research has gone into the creation of compression systems which appear to have minimal impact on quality and yet reduce the data stream enormously. These systems are extremely sophisticated and complex – the following examples are much simplified compared with the real thing. In a still image there are often areas of uniform colour; a compression scheme might state that the current pixel colour should be repeated for the next 40 pixels where there is a block of colour. This scheme can result in incredible space savings in material such as cartoons. In moving images lots of areas of the picture do not change from one frame to the next so some compression methods only record the changes, thus reducing the data stream considerably. Even cleverer are systems which look at movement in the frame and predict what the next frame will be like, the predicted frame and real one are then compared and only the difference between them is sent.

There are two types of compression: lossy and lossless. With the latter the displayed image will be exactly as the original, but lossy algorithms will lose some picture content or quality – that is, the displayed image will not be exactly as the original. Lossy compression is not acceptable for VFX work since it can destroy some of the information essential to compositing. One of the problems with compression is that although it appears to cause no problems at one point in the pipeline, it may prove problematic later on when it has some wholly different method of compression applied. Like drinks, compression systems do not mix!

Frame rate is not a problem in computer-based systems since each frame is stored independently and is not related to the final display speed – replay through the computer can be set to whatever speed is required. However, the issue of video fields does have to be dealt with (see page 13) and even in the digital domain, video interlace causes precisely the same problems as in the world of analogue and cannot be mixed with non-interlaced material for VFX.

Combining all of the above, the most common VFX formats used are those shown in the table on page 219.

The video formats are indeed formats and can be recorded straight to tape or captured by a computer system where they can be worked on immediately in their native format. The film specifications described above are, however, just that and have to be encoded into some form of standardized file to allow exchange and a variety of software to be able to read them. In the VFX world the two most popular are DPX and Cineon, both of which allow quite a few variations in their content. Other popular file formats are SGI, TIFF and TARGA. These are raw data formats which simply store the data relating to an image as viewed. Many programs such as Photoshop and After Effects have their own proprietary formats which store the image in multiple layers and information relating to them – for example, a foreground, background and matte (called alpha channel in such software) would all be stored separately so that the composite could be altered sometime in the future. The final output (or 'render') would be to one of the standard formats. For a given job, one format should be standardized on and maintained across all departments or ludicrous amounts of time will end up being squandered on conversions from one to the other. Finally, backing-up of data offline can be done on any one of a score of formats. In-house it is possible to fix on some really obscure format but, if exchange with other outside facilities will be required, then what 'they' can handle should also be considered. At the time of writing the most popular formats are DTF, firewire/USB portable hard drives and DVD-R discs. For temps (quickly made place holders used until final VFX are completed) at lower resolutions CD-R is practical but not much use for exchanging 2K Full Ap. since one CD will only hold 2 s.

From the table opposite it should be noticed that digital film file sizes are enormous. The most common size is full aperture 2K and even that at almost 13 MB/frame will eat up disk space voraciously. A 5 second shot at 2K would use up 1.542 GB. Just a simple VFX shot would involve a blue screen foreground, a background for it to be laid over and then somewhere to put the result, this would already amount to 4.626 GB, not to mention any additional elements which might be required. It is not surprising therefore that the larger VFX houses now measure their storage in

Format (All 35 mm is 2K unless stated)	Pixels (Video not sq.)	A-R	Bit depth (Most common)	Size (MB/frame)	Notes
Digital Video – NTSC region	720 × 486	1.33:1	8-bit	0.691	4:2:2: B-Y R-Y Y
Digital Video – PAL region	720 × 576	1.33:1	8-bit	0.829	4:2:2: B-Y R-Y Y
HD 16 × 9	1920 × 1080	1.77:1	8-bit	6.2	Various formats
4K 35 mm Full Aperture	4096 × 3112	1.32:1	10-bit/log	51.09	R G B
35 mm Full Aperture	2048 × 1556	1.32:1	10-bit/log	12.85	R G B
35 mm Academy	1828 × 1332	1.37:1	10-bit/log	9.84	R G B
35 mm widescreen	1828 × 988	1.85:1	10-bit/log	7.3	R G B
35 mm 'Scope – anamorphic	1828 × 1556	2.35:1	10-bit/log	11.48	R G B
35 mm 8-perf. – vistaVision	3112 × 2048	1.52:1	10-bit/log	25.27	R G B

8 Computer-based systems and techniques

terabytes and, if a film is to be digitally mastered, then one is talking about, say, 100 min or 1.807 TB. Thus a major consideration in setting up a large VFX project is the pipeline along which the data will pass from scanning-in, through the actual effects processes and then recording back out again to film or tape. The scheduling of all this is a major headache and not to be underestimated. Large VFX facilities actually have entire departments whose job is specifically to wrangle data in terms of moving it to and from various workstations and backing it up. These data ops will frequently be found doing longer hours than the compositors and CG animators! As a cautionary tale it should be noted that in the past some smaller effects facilities have lost jobs because of missing deadlines – this a result of data handling problems and not inability to execute the effects.

Input to digital world

As mentioned, digital video formats such as HD, for example *Star Wars Ep. II – Attack of the Clones* (2002), can be fed straight into a computer and are therefore pretty well ready for use instantly. Indeed if they were recorded on hard disk to begin with, that disk can literally be plugged into a post-production system and work started immediately.

For VFX purposes 35 mm film is still the preferred choice. But being an analogue system it must be digitized before any work can take place. For television a real time telecine machine is used but, with just a single megabyte per frame, the data throughput is not too horrific. There are some HD telecines around which are real time but unfortunately these are not really suitable for VFX purposes since their film registration is not stable enough. Thus for effects work film needs to be digitized using a 'scanner', a register pin machine which typically runs at between 2 and 10 s per frame depending on the format of choice.

Scanners can be of two types, CRT or CCD. In a CRT system, as typified by the machines made by Cintel, a dot of light scans across a cathode ray screen (same principle as a TV monitor) and is focused via a lens on the film. A light sensor on the other side of the film reads the transmission level which is then sampled to give a digital value (see figure below).

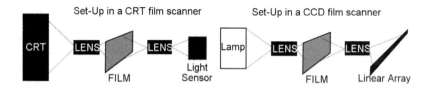

In a charge coupled device (CCD) system a linear array (i.e., a row of receptors equivalent to one line of the picture) is positioned on the opposite side of the film to a lamp. The film is drawn across this and a series of readings taken according to how many lines are required. This is why one set of values are always the same (e.g., 2048 on a 2K scan). Obviously if a frame area less than the full width of the film is used then this reading will be smaller, which is why Academy (which allows for sound track area) comes in at 1828.

For VFX it is absolutely essential that at the scanning-in stage all of the information is captured from the film. There must be no destructive colour grading done to the image which might impede processes such as blue screen. For example, imagine that we have a blue screen foreground shot on a stage. The shadows are very dense and might be difficult to key. If the image at the scanning stage is shifted slightly downwards towards the black ('sat-down' in video parlance) then these areas might become 'black-clipped' (see figure on page 192). In this case the small amount of blue that was there and could have been useful to a compositor would be lost and he would probably end up having to rotoscope that area. This is why anything 'destructive' of information is not acceptable at this stage. Obviously, once keying information has been extracted the image can have anything the artist feels appropriate done to it so as to match with other shots or even the background plate.

When the idea of digitizing movie film was first considered, 35 mm resolved around 4K (4096) and so this seemed the natural choice; however, current stocks far exceed this resolution. When Kodak first set their digital intermediate standard this was indeed the chosen resolution with a full frame being 4096 × 3112. However, the practicality of dealing with frames of 51 MB in the late 1980s, let alone today, was totally impractical and thus it was that 2K (or half rez) became the compromise. Even now, with the vast advances in digital technology and particularly memory and disk storage, 4K is still largely impractical to deal with and out of the question for 3D computer animation where render times would go through the roof. However, VFX may on occasion need to use 4K scans, particularly in the case of blue/green screen shots where there is very fine detail. This will often be resolved at 4K but just a blur at 2K. Of course, once the composite has been made the resolution can be dropped back down again to match the rest of the film. The native resolution of most scanners is 4K and they then downsize to 2K by either reading every other pixel or using software (slower but better quality). An effects supervisor will have to be cognizant of this and make a carefully considered decision (given the time and cost implications) of whether certain shots will need to be worked on at a higher resolution. The very latest machines are capable of 6K but, looking at the resolutions chart, the advantages of that very old VFX format, vistaVision, can be seen to continue into the digital age as a front runner.

If CGI is being used in combination with 'difficult' live action material then it is always possible to do the latter at 4K and then 'upsize' the CGI from 2K for the compositing side of things. However, when doing this sort of thing it is important to establish that all of the elements are in compatible formats and that sizes involving incompatible numbers are not being mixed.

As with all things involved with compositing the inward-coming material should be on compatible formats which can be combined without undue conversion work since this will inevitably result in quality and/or compositional loss.

Output to analogue

The formats to which the end product are converted do not technically have much impact on VFX although it is always well to be cognizant of what they might be. Once compositing and other processes have been executed anything done to the image will not alter the quality of the combination. However, if the final display format is to be much larger than was apparent during production then matte lines for instance, which were not readily visible on a 20″ monitor, suddenly take on epic proportions! It is therefore very useful to know from the outset what will be the delivery format – if it is only to be SDTV then 4K scans for difficult keying really would be a waste of resources and energy.

Re-digitizing material that has already been around-the-houses is to be avoided. However, sometimes this cannot be avoided. Work done on a sequence by one facility may have to be revisited for some obscure reason. Again, although production may not consider this to be a problem, no stone should be left unturned in the quest for first generation material. If you are handed film negative make sure that the original data really is not still available or how it can be passed on to you if it is.

The VFX department may be responsible for recording out their own shots. Again, if it is video then this is a straightforward matter of recording on to a suitable format. For film it will require a film recorder. There are two main technologies here, laser and CRT. The CRT has a high-resolution monochrome picture tube which is effectively photographed through R, G and B filters by a camera. Although it sounds crude, systems built by the likes of Celco produce excellent results. Laser recorders use three coloured lasers to burn the image on to the film. CRT systems tend to shoot on to camera negative film (e.g., 5245) whilst laser systems usually employ colour intermediate film (e.g., 5242). Laser recorders are normally set up to produce an internegative but can be adjusted to record an interpositive instead. This may be useful where the entire piece is being shot out (e.g. for a Digital Intermediate or Master) and not just some effects shots. In general, however, interneg is necessary so that the effects can be cut in with original camera neg (for non-effects shots). Thus when an interpos is struck from this spliced master it will be clean of joins and can happily be used to make multiple negatives for release printing. Finally, because the technology may only be available there, the VFX department might be asked to do a digital squeeze on their material. This occurs where so-called super35 is being used. This is a shooting-only format which puts a 'flat' 2.35:1 image across the area of the full aperture. For final release an interpositive is usually optically squeezed at the lab to produce a standard 'Scope Negative. If the material is all going through a digital process (such as digital intermediate) then it may make sense to do the squeeze digitally and avoid an optical process. This basically involves a translation from 2048 × 872 to 1828 × 1556.

Digital image manipulation

Once an image is converted into digits and stored inside a computer absolutely anything imaginable can be done to it. Add a couple of digits to every single pixel value and the image gets lighter, subtract and it gets darker. Tell the system to replace every pixel of a certain shade of blue with the equivalent pixel from another image and you have composited a blue screen.

Very sophisticated software and user interfaces have been written to achieve all manner of image manipulation, but also to use the computer as an image creation tool in its own right. Digital VFX can now be divided up into two distinct categories: 2D or image manipulation and 3D or computer-generated imaging (CGI), also sometimes called computer animation. 2D works on flat two-dimensional images and could be likened to work done in a graphics workshop or photographic lab. 3D creates three-dimensional models in virtual space around which a virtual camera can observe them, akin to architecture, where plans are drawn and 3D constructions derived therefrom. Nowadays many effects are created by building 3D models and then compositing them via 2D software into live action plates.

2D digital image manipulation

The explosion in digital effects grew out of what is now called 2D. It began with the development of framestores for TV broadcasters. These were the first devices that could hold a single frame of video. Initially they were used to solve technical problems such as delaying pictures so that isolated (ISO) feeds on the end of long cable runs or microwave links could be synchronized with studio pictures without the complexities of 'genlock' and other arcane methods. Quantel (from quantized television), seeing that these machines mostly went into newsrooms where a camera was always set aside to shoot a monitor to fit the blue panel behind the newsreader (see figure below), hit on the idea of providing a quarter-sized version of the input picture and key which was moveable to anywhere in frame.

Inserted shot from remote feed or off tape is reduced in size and positioned by a digital device

Live action studio shot of newsreader.

This was very easy to do (simply taking every other pixel and every other line) and was added almost as a gimmick – however the requests for embellishments poured in and soon they produced the DPE5001 which, as the name 'digital production effects' implied, was a tool specifically designed for effects. This was before the powerful personal computers of today and involved very complex, customized and exceedingly expensive hardware but it opened the floodgates and was almost singly responsible for the first fad of TV digital effects best described as 'flying logos'.

Around the same time Vital Industries produced their 'squeezeZoom' which did much the same things. It was however a glorified video switcher with a whole raft of preset effects. What set the Quantel device aside was that it was programmable and the user could define their own effects. These devices basically provided all of the facilities that an optical printer could do in film, but in real time video. Included were an infinite zoom from infinity up to full size, slide vertically (V) and horizontally (H) to anywhere on or off frame, squeeze both H and V, mirror and flip. What was most impressive at the time was that there were a set of pre-set buttons which meant that a box could be set to ¼ frame top left in one pre-set, then full frame in another and a transition time set between these. Thus with a suitable time set, the image would reduce down to ¼ frame at the press of a button and back up again with another. The frame size and position was matched by a matte from a separate output. Initially these devices were used mainly for graphics and title sequences with little boxes and lettering flying about the screen in increasingly random and senseless ways. However, a few dramas attempted to use them more intelligently for multiscreen sequences, or by the BBC's *Dr Who* for actual VFX.

Shortly after the Quantel device Ampex brought out their 'digital optics' ADO which added the missing function of perspective so that, where previously a spin had been approximated by a squeeze shut and open, now it would actually turn correctly as a piece of card would do if spun (see figure below). This second generation device sealed the broadcaster's fixation with spinning logos about and meant that this style of title became pretty standard and is still popular on sports and current affairs programmes to this day.

simply squeezing the image gives a   a true 3D rotation gives the correct
crude impression of it being rotated   perspective of a rotating plane

The really important gift that these devices gave to effects was access to the individual frozen frame, which meant that rotoscope effects could be applied to video pictures for the first time. By means of a video camera focused on a light box and a monitor showing a mix of the freeze frame and the output of the rostrum camera, mattes could be drawn on cells much as they had been on film. This was a painstaking process and subject to many potential areas of failure, particularly at the recording end of things, but inspired producers to see what was coming.

From the same two companies came the next advance which was the electronic paint (or video art) system. Quantel's 'Paintbox' and Ampex's 'AVA' for the first time gave the necessary tools to create an electronic art piece completely from scratch. With an eye to newsrooms again the idea here had been to do the same thing for weathercasters' maps as had been done by the caption generators used to produce end rollers and name captions. Just like you could pick a font, size and colour for a title, the idea of the paintbox was to pick a colour, brush size and draw a map or graphical element. This device, however, provided the means producers had been searching for to draw mattes and achieve many of the things possible in film opticals with a much faster and more efficient turnaround. The commercials industry almost immediately saw the incredible possibilities of the paintbox and adopted it wholesale. Suddenly the names on pack shots could be changed at will, and extremely complex composites could be made. The only problem was the inefficiency of the recording process, which still required a VTR to run at full speed to record even a single frame.

The appearance of the unsung hero Sony 2500 1″ C-format recorder was the turning point for the burgeoning video effects industry. This machine for the first time allowed single frame recordings to be made one after the other without the machine having to go into standby with the heads down. This meant that the problem of so-called invisible edits (which displayed a small but obvious sideways hop) were a thing of the past and that the paintbox and, in parallel, early 3D CGI systems could for the first time be realistically used for animation. The additions of digital disk recorders such as Quantel's 'Harry' and Abekas' 'A64' and finally the D1 digital video recorder to permit sensible back-up procedures all helped to accelerate the already rolling train.

All of the machines mentioned so far were hardware systems with discrete boxes built to do specific tasks. Such systems are, however, hard to update quickly such as to fix bugs or add new features requested by clients for specific jobs. The next great stride forward was the advent of software solutions running on generic platforms (i.e., standard off-the-shelf computer systems). Initially this was limited to workstations such as those made by Sun and SGI (Silicon Graphics) since only these very expensive systems were capable of the speed necessary to process video in real time. Best known of the early systems was Discreet's 'Flame' which was a direct competitor to Quantel's 'Henry' – an integrated compositing/storage solution. One major difference was that 'Flame' used the hardware built in to the SGI host and was therefore a full R G B system, unlike all previous systems which were Y, B-Y, R-Y. Additionally, since these systems were entirely defined by the software and not the hardware they could be resolution independent.

Although a few experiments had been done with digital effects for film, such as the robot's vision in *Westworld* (1973), the requirement of Cray supercomputers made them few and far between. When Kodak designed their 'Cineon' system for scanning and recording to make possible digital intermediate they also discovered that their system could run on the large SGI boxes. However, when it was realized that only 2K was practical to do film effects, 'Flame' was quickly adopted as a film tool and the age of film digital effects was ushered in. Nowadays all systems run on generic computers, with PCs under Linux or Windows NT being most popular.

There are basically two models for VFX software. One system allows the operator to build a 'virtual machine' from a set of 'nodes' or tools by means of a graphical flow chart, and only once the method is set up and tested using single frames are the final full sets of images processed and rendered as a final viewable composite. In this model many individual processes can be lined up for simultaneous execution and hence an entire finished composite created in one go. These schematics can of course be saved and reused for later shots or kept in a library to solve similar problems in the future. These saved processes can themselves be used as elements in further virtual machines so that any given operator can build up a collection of favoured procedures.

This method tends to be used for film and other long form work and to be operated without a client present. First made popular by Cineon, the interface has since been adopted by many others and is usually available in two versions – 'GUI' (graphical user interface) licenses which are used to design and test the effects and 'render' licenses which are typically run from a command prompt. Common practice is to have the software loaded on all workstations and the licenses run from a server. As any given operator runs the software the license server is interrogated and gives permission or not depending on the number of operators accessing the software and the number of licenses available. These systems are designed specifically for doing VFX compositing and are generally only practical to deal with one shot at a time – they are neither designed nor suitable for editing sequences. This type of software is relatively inexpensive and runs on PCs; it will often be found on floors jammed with workstations and with sometimes hundreds of licenses running.

The other common style could be described as 'performance' software and derives from the original 'Harry' interface which is extremely simple to visually understand and is based entirely on working with the actual images being processed. The screen is divided with the top part confined to images usually presented as though in film strips and the lower part a series of menus. The pictures are moved around by a graphic cursor controlled by a pen and tablet rather than a mouse and apparently laid on top of one another for multilayered effects. The systems are extremely interactive and provide almost instant results as long as not too many processes are run simultaneously – which they tend not to be. Typified by the products of Discreet and Quantel, they are designed as complete post-production environments and are fully capable of editing sequences together and synchronizing sound. This interface has been most popular with short form productions, is used mainly for commercials and music videos and is commonly run with a client present. They may be used in film production where extreme interactivity is required such as colour grading a sequence of shots which are difficult to match. Running on very expensive high-end workstations, facilities will tend to have only a few of these systems where they might have hundreds of the schematic variety for a similar cost.

Since all these systems now run on generic workstations it is possible for third-party suppliers to create specialized nodes or 'plug-ins' which add extra abilities or productivity to the system. This is a fantastic bonus since it means that a high level of customization is possible and also that small, often one-man companies can make a living out of writing very specialized applications.

Ironically there are not that many things which modern software can do that it was not possible to do previously. The main processes such as blue screen, rotoscoping and travelling matte were all previously possible by other methods; however, what digital brings to the party is generation-free working. What this means is that an image can be copied and adjusted, copied and adjusted over and over again an infinite number of times and will never suffer any loss in quality. After all, it is simply copying numbers. Thus processes can be perfected to levels never previously dreamt possible by adding layer after layer and revisiting an imperfect result over and over. Additionally, sections of an image may be worked on seamlessly without any perceptible joins being visible and this permits effects to be attempted which might previously have been considered impossible.

The most common digital tools are as follows.

Colour grading and image quality

Digital colour grading is incredibly flexible. The whole image, or just individual tones or colours, can be varied and made to change over a stated time period. Since every imaginable colour is represented by a specific number it is possible to set the software literally to change any given colour to another one. Matching two shots, an essential in VFX, can easily be achieved by having them side by side on the same screen. Most software permits all functions to be used together so it is possible to apply colour grading to, say, a foreground while it is actually being combined with its background, making the eternal problem of balancing the elements of a composite much simpler. If a particular area is to be colour graded differently from the rest of the picture it can be rotoscoped and the grade applied to only the inside of the matte.

A vast array of adjustment methods are available in all of the common colour models such as HSV, RGB, CYMK and even Pantone swatches. Adjustments can be made through the use of colour wheels, histograms, faders, knobs and even simple numerical entry. Some systems allow the addition of hardware control panels to give the same operability as telecine grading systems.

Fully matching images to surrounding sequences or photographic references is fundamental to making VFX work and there are many additional tools to aid in this. All of the variables which you would expect to adjust alongside colour grading such as luminance, gamma, contrast and sharpness are available, but there are also some unique processes such as degraining and regraining. These permit the grain to be removed from the shot and, if required, grain with the desired characteristics (e.g., that of a particular film stock) to be added. This can be used to match 3D CGI shots which will inherently have no grain or video to live action film elements which display a preferred grain structure.

Colour matching also must take into consideration the various systems being used. Particular scanners and recorders, monitors and film stocks will all have differing colour characteristics and these must be factored into the VFX pipeline. If the VFX artists cannot see the correct image on their monitors then it will be impossible for the shots to fit into the sequence being worked on. This is a continuous point of annoyance and development work and in most systems is addressed through the use of special look-up tables (LUTs). These are basically conversion tables which modify colours according to the particular characteristics of the equipment being used. Thus many facilities will have a particular LUT for their picture monitors that attempts to match the monitor to the output medium which might be, for example, projected film. This is a can-of-worms, however, since although it might reproduce the colour and brightness of images in that particular company's screening room it may match no other theatre in the world. It is this imponderable which has resulted in the well-known dilemma of 'which monitor do I look at' when in a control room they all look completely different. Almost impossible to match in the analogue world there is no doubt that one day digital techniques will solve this problem through the use of flat screen panels and digital projectors which should be much more consistent – at the time of writing however this still poses a major dilemma.

Geometrical tools

These replace the optical printer and the DVE or picture mover of video post. In addition to conventional sliding of the picture around the screen, flip and mirror, resize and squeeze, apply perspective and output mattes, they also provide tools to bend and twist the image in all manner of shapes and fragmentations such as cylinders, spheres and shattering glass. In all cases transitions are possible from any one effect in any condition to any other effect in a particular state. Thus, for example, it would be possible to have a raster-shaped image fitted to a set element change into a spherical form, representing a picture on the wall transforming into a floating spherical robot. The timing of all these effects can be via a timeline and are infinitely changeable up to the point when they are output.

Digital geometrical manipulation scores against other methods in the control interface available. Really simple to understand and operate but very complex controls permit extremely quick and accurate setting-up of effects. Of particular importance is so-called corner-pinning which enables a rectangular image to be drawn by the corners to precisely fit a shape in the live action over which it is being matted. For example, if an image is to be put into a screen in the set, the four corners of the insert can be literally drawn to the corners of the set-piece.

As with everything else in these digital software packages the resize and other geometrical functions can be combined with other tools. Thus, for instance, in a blue screen composite where the elements do not quite fit, adjustments can be made whilst viewing the actual composite. Where an element has been deliberately shot at a different size, for instance because a character is to appear very small and the camera cannot be pulled back far enough, then given measurements provided by the studio crew a scaling can be worked out and the numbers simply typed into the resize tool so that trial and error can be avoided. Another important technique is 'morphing', made popular by *Willow* (1988). Here geometrical distortion is used to pull one image into the shape of another, say a man's face into that of a wolf. The reverse process of distorting the wolf's face into the man's is also applied. With both of these effects animated over the same period of time, going in the same direction (man to wolf) and slowly mixing between them, we see the man's face apparently physically change or 'morph' into that of the wolf. The same visual effect can be achieved using 3D computer animation by building photo-realistic CGI models of man and wolf and then animating between them. This is usually termed a 'transformation'.

Paint and draw

There are two systems by which a computer can store an image – raster and vector. Paint systems use 'raster' graphics and work the same way as video and other digitized image systems. The entire image is divided up into pixels and each is allocated numbers which quantify their state. A live action image which is digitized can therefore be read straight in to such a system.

Raster graphics are very inefficient in terms of storage. If one had, say, a frame which was entirely red with just a single black line across it (see figure opposite) it would still take up the same amount of storage as a photograph of a forest.

image defined as a raster graphic

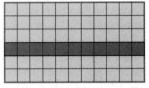

66 pixels of which 55 are red and one
row of 11 are black - however a set
of values will be required for every pixel

image defined as a vectorgraphic

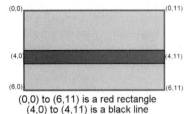

(0,0) to (6,11) is a red rectangle
(4,0) to (4,11) is a black line

Every pixel would have to have a set of numbers allotted to it – even though they would mostly be exactly the same (i.e., red). In a raster graphic system every frame takes up exactly the same amount of computer storage.

In a paint system everything you do is destructive to the image you are amending. In other words, if you were to extend the black line on the red ground the actual image itself would not hold the means to backtrack, that is, the black would replace the red and, if you wanted to go back again, you would have to repaint the red. For this reason software has an 'undo' feature which allows you to step back by one or more stages of your work, but this is a resource-hungry facility and on many machines setting a large number of undo levels will slow the machine down by a not inconsiderable amount.

'Draw' programs use 'vector' graphics which work on an entirely different principle. In a vector system the file representing an image describes to the computer how to construct the frame – but does not digitize it. In other words our example of a black line on a red ground would generate a file which would simply create a full frame of red and then draw a black line of stated thickness joining two points specified by their X and Y coordinates (see figure above). This would be a tiny file indeed and, of course, when viewed by means of a vector graphic draw program would be infinitely changeable, since all specified points, 'nodes', 'control points' or 'vertices' can be moved as often as desired. Vector graphics are constructed more like a computer aided drawing (CAD) program and offer tools appropriate to the draughtsman's office. Unlike a raster program, which is in output-ready form all along, a vector program needs to be rendered (converted to a viewable image) to whatever final form is required, but has the great advantage of being able to be output at any resolution, since the file only describes the various forms and their positions, not how many pixels they consist of. In terms of software sophistication the vector system offers greater opportunities since, by definition, the computer understands what the image consists of, whereas in a raster system this is not the case. Knowledge of component parts will obviously allow programmers to automate a number of processes such as to soften all objects of a particular specification – this sort of thing would be impossible in a raster program. Special conversion programs exist to interchange between these two methods which are respectively called 'rasterizers' and 'vectorizers'. Obviously, the special qualities of either system will be lost as soon as such a conversion is made.

Originally software was restricted to one type but nowadays programs such as 'Shake' offer elements of both methods.

Paint tools will generally emulate all of the tools contained in a graphic's, artist's and photographer's studio combined. Brushes, pencils, chalk, airbrushes and any other tool used for making a mark on paper are all represented, with an almost infinite number of options to set width, softness, edges, density, colour and solidity. Colours can be mixed according to any of the popular spatial systems (e.g., R G B, HSL, CYMK) but, much more importantly, can be picked up from anywhere in the image being worked on. Thus, for instance, if there were a particular colour in an image, the blue of the sky, say, which was to be used for the lettering of a title then this can literally be picked up from the picture with no need to mix it. This is a very powerful tool and offers the kind of productivity which makes these systems so invaluable. Using paint systems with any combination of imported images and material originated on the system it is possible to create stunning 'digital matte paintings' with the ability to make perfect matches to the live action elements.

All systems provide the means of drawing mattes (and therefore effectively doing rotoscope) which is often presented as a 'stencil' option. In a raster system this will tend to allow a single continuous line to be drawn around the required area and then, once perfected including any changes by rubbing out sections and repainting them, the area can be automatically 'filled'. Usually this matte or stencil drawing mode will be done using a transparent and obvious lurid colour such as saturated red or magenta (user definable). In raster systems it is very important to check the continuity of the perimeter line and complete closure of the 'join', since if there is a hole – and it only needs to be one pixel – then at the fill stage the colour will pour out of the hole like water from a puncture. In a vector system, which many matte artists prefer for this purpose, a line can be drawn 'point-to-point'. In this mode each tap of the pen will result in a line being extended from the previous point until a double click will join the last to the first, thus closing the figure. The great advantage of this system is that it can be very quickly used initially to roughly surround the subject and then painstakingly adjusted thereafter until a perfect fit has been attained. The reason compositors so value this tool is that the same matte may then be copied across to the next frame where it can easily be adjusted to match any movement in the subject. Nodes may be added or deleted at any stage. Mattes can be attached to the image they represent and only rendered once the sequence is finished and tested 'on the run'. To further aid in the creation of mattes all manner of standard shapes are available to be used either as solid or skeleton objects which can then be modified to fit the desired shape as required.

All image editing programs provide a huge raft of productivity tools including the ability of zooming in or out to do detailed work, moving around large images and cropping, resizing and altering all manner of image parameters such as softness and texture.

A few of these special tools have made it possible to do extremely complex work easily where it may otherwise have simply been too time-consuming even to consider. The 'clone' tool allows direct real time copying from one part of an image to another part of the same or a different image, with the size and shape of the area being copied user definable. This tool is almost like magic because it makes so simple the age-old problem of, for example, painting out unwanted modern accoutrements which spoil an otherwise perfect medieval setting.

A simple example (see figure below) would be a TV aerial. By cloning from the sky on either side of it and from above at the extremities it can be made to vanish. The great advantage of doing this rather than simply painting out the guilty party is that it not only guarantees the correct colour and density but also the grain and texture of the original, which would be lost in straight painting.

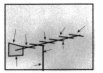

the aerial can be painted out by cloning from immediately surrounding areas such as indicated

half of the aerial removed using cloning from the neighbouring areas

the aerial removed

When using this technique in a sequence, each individual frame cannot be separately cloned, as this would result in 'boiling' since the painting could not be guaranteed to match well enough from one frame to the next. In this sort of situation it is usual to prepare a patch of clean sky to fit over the aerial and then to position and stick it down on each consecutive frame.

The other paint tool which is unusual is the 'edge definer', sometimes called magic wand/brush, which attempts to automatically create a matte edge around an object according to its colour or brightness. Success with this tool is very much down to the image content but it can be used to find the edge of an object which is very different in tone or colour from whatever surrounds it.

Finally, all painting systems also include sophisticated tools for 'cutting and pasting'. These will normally allow the normal paint tools to be used to define a 'selection' area – like a matte or stencil – which can then be removed, replaced, multiplied and pasted down in one or more positions with or without modifications done to it during the operation. Although used extensively on individual frames this method is not used very often on motion picture projects, wherein more sophisticated tools designed to deal with multiple frames are available elsewhere.

Compositing software

Central to VFX post-production are the various types of compositing software. No matter how complex it may get, the basic principle involved here is always the same. The software will combine two images (e.g., foreground and background, master and insert) as specified by a third image (e.g., matte, stencil, alpha-channel, key). It may be that the matte is drawn around an element of the foreground (a rotoscope) or automatically derived from blue in the foreground (a blue screen) or from a pre-made animated shape (a wipe or travelling matte), but the basic mechanism is the same and the main variables will also be the same – threshold, tolerance or key level to control the range within which the picture will be replaced, transparency or opacity of the overlaid image and softness/hardness of the matte edge.

In any given program a vast array of different keying options will be on offer with the basic difference being in the range of additional tools offered to help make the best composite possible. Titling work, for example, may have features added to help define edges and ease the placement, colouring and width of drop shadow or black edges. Blue screen might have facilities to shift the insert within the matte hole, to adjust the overall coloration of the foreground with respect to the background, to blend the edges of the two images together, to compensate for blue spill, to precisely select the keying colour and to add various enhancements such as transparency or shadows. Blue/green screen software is so important that there are specialist plug-ins such as Ultimatte and Primatte available which offer increased quality and options to those offered by the host software.

It is important to realize that it is not the options or even quality of digital matting that makes the end result so much better than older systems. The reason why such superior results can be achieved is that all digital post resources are available to help make a composite good and also that because of the generation-free nature of digital it is possible to break a matte up into many parts. Additionally, the ability to rotoscope so accurately and so easily means that any places where the key really does fail badly will still be relatively easy to fix. Given that an entire scene can be rotoscoped anyway, anything that the blue screen can do to help ease the situation is a bonus!

Imagine a blue screen where the backing is extremely uneven with both shading and reflections on the painted cyc, not to mention a bad shoot off. In normal live video or even post keying the level would have to be set for a compromise between the too-light and too-dark parts of the cyc and the threshold would have to be widened to accommodate the worst case, even though parts of the image would have been keyable at a much better level. Finally, to garbage matte out the shoot-off would be quite difficult since the levels would not precisely match. When keying this shot with blue screen software, however, the screen could be broken up into a number of areas each of which could be keyed slightly differently and optimized for just that blue density. Any area where the key is really too weak can be enhanced by hand-drawing a matte. One useful way of analysing a key in these circumstances is to use the foreground to generate a black and white matte and then, by hand, fill in all of the areas which are incorrect – shown by having holes or shading in them (see figure on page 193). Of course, if the advice given earlier in regard to shooting for digital post was taken, and a clean pass had been made without the action elements, then a difference key could have been derived in addition to the blue screen information and so help to eliminate the variance in the blue backing. Finally, all of the tools such as colour grading and resizing are there to instantly fix any problems identified and with these tools difficulties such as colour spill can be completely eliminated.

Conventional mattes such as split screens and travelling mattes can very easily be created using electronic paint systems. For static shots only a single frame is required and this can then be either repeated or held depending on the operating method of the software being used.

The great thing about vector-based mattes is that they can be repeated frame by frame until they appear to slip too far and then adjusted so that it is not necessary to do a complete follow through matte (see figure below).

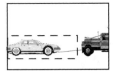 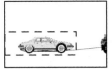 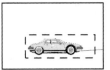

frame 1: the matte is lined up to give max movement in 1 position

frame 6: the car nears the matte so it must be adjusted next frame

frame 7: the matte is moved on to accommodate the next few frames

With softening tools it is possible to blend edges where there is no obvious architectural feature to follow; however, with all the digital tools available, problems can easily be hidden by painting or compositing extra objects on top.

New life into old methods

A number of very old techniques, little used for decades, have new life breathed into them through the use of digital methods. Rotoscoping has been mentioned a number of times. This was used quite a lot in the black and white classic cinema with effects such as buildings collapsing on to running crowds. The expense and difficulty of doing this to a decent quality level cut back its use latterly but now a single operator at a workstation can create mattes in a very reasonable time, but more to the point, can do so to an extremely high standard. Techniques such as softening the edges to match out of focus or moving elements in the image and adding in extra atmosphere such as dust, mist or smoke, can all contribute to the believability of the final combination. Because of their easy creation and accuracy, digital hand-drawn mattes have been used extensively on commercials and music videos and some directors and VFX supervisors have insisted on abandoning coloured screens altogether and relying totally on this most ancient of arts. The problem with this is that although it can be very good indeed it is still a relatively time-consuming activity and pretty labour-intensive. However, for something like a commercials pack shot, where multiple backgrounds are to be slipped in, it would be foolish to use any other technique.

Of even greater significance is the technique of rig or wire removal. This has utterly changed the way certain types of scene are shot. Using a mixture of techniques including rotoscope, cloning, painting, airbrushing and matting, this technique basically removes rigs or wires from the live action shot. The preferred and easiest way of achieving this is to shoot the action with whatever element is supported on a rig (see figure on next page) and then, following a good take, a second (clean) pass without the subject and rig.

RIG REMOVAL USING A CLEAN PASS

| full scale model pulled by a series of cables | a clean pass is shot to allow for rig removal | the rigs removed in post production |

Obviously, if the shot is moving, then some form of repeating head should be used. The outcome of this is that a version of the shot with, and without, the rig should be available to the compositor.

Assuming that nothing has changed in between, this means that all that is necessary is to copy over, reveal or restore through the clean background in any places where the rig is visible. The one problem occurs where a rig goes in front of the subject and this is to be avoided at all costs. Painting a clean version of the image over the action-take is easy and relatively quick to do, but painstaking. However, painting out a wire going across the hero's face is an extremely difficult and time-consuming (read 'expensive') activity. Sometimes through an error or problem this cannot be avoided, but should never, ever be planned as a solution. Another difficulty which is sometimes unavoidable is where the subject and/or rig cause a shadow so that the background is a slightly different level of brightness. This can usually be ironed out but involves extra work.

On occasion it is impossible to create a clean pass such as where a hand-held camera is being used. In this case it is useful to do an approximate walk through of the shot without the subject and rig. Although this will not be exactly right it may provide some sections of material that can be cut and pasted. This will tend to be needed if a large and bulky rig is being used, however if it is only thin wires that are to be removed, then cloning from immediately to either side of the wire or, if there is sufficient movement in the frame, from the frame before or the frame after (see figure below) should provide sufficient data. As with all of these digital techniques, if all else fails then the missing data can be laboriously painted in but this could take a very long time if it is to be done invisibly and without the boiling which is inevitable from hand-painting a fixed area through a sequence of frames.

| area in front of rig in this frame can be used to matte out the rig in the next | rig can be matted out by using the previous frame | in turn the previous frame can be used to provide the necessary elements for this |

Rig and wire removal have made a much wider set of stunts and realistic-looking effects possible. It has made practical again the oldest method of all for doing daring tricks – that of shooting it for real, as in so many silent films such as those of Buster Keaton. Many years ago insurance companies put a stop to this most realistic of methods but now safety equipment removed in post has put it back in vogue. Take, for example, a shot of a major star climbing up a mountain face with a vast panoramic view behind. Safety and insurance considerations would dictate in the past that this would be done on the mountain with a double working in long shot, and then on stage, with close shots of the star taken on a section of prop mountain built at ground level and with scenic projection or a blue screen behind. Generally this would have a fake air about it and would certainly limit the director's options in what shots he could frame. Now with wire removals the star could actually do the shot himself on the real mountain surrounded by as many safety wire and cables as the riggers would require. Camera movement would be possible and, if desired, the shot could pull back from a big close up to show the entire mountain with the star clinging to its side, courtesy of a helicopter shot. By shooting real actors in real environments it is suddenly possible to let the camera roam at will and create much more believable scenes with a lot more flexibility than if confined to a blue screen stage. This is one of the techniques which has made the *Tomb Raiders, Spidermen* and *Matrices* of recent years display their hair-raising scenes of dare-devil stunts, all very obviously featuring the lead players in the closer shots whilst once out wide we will unknowingly be looking at entirely CGI representations invisibly substituted before our very eyes.

In summary, keep the wires as thin as permitted, avoid them crossing the subject, avoid them causing shadows on background or even worse the subject, try to get a clean pass, avoid anything changing between the action and clean takes and ensure that focus is exactly the same on both passes. Brilliant recent examples of wire work are *Mission Impossible II* (2000) and *Crouching Tiger Hidden Dragon* (2000).

Perfecting the illusion

A number of digital techniques aid in modifying motion within the image, be it wanted or unwanted. Motion blur occurs naturally in all photography and is caused by the motion of subject matter whilst the camera shutter is open. As discussed earlier, lack of motion blur on animated material added to a live action shot can be a big give away. Although motorized miniatures under the control of a computer and cameras, too, can be programmed to move during exposure, there are many forms of animation such as claymation where this is quite impossible. Computer animation, too, will not inherently have motion blur and if the facility is available will be difficult to match to the live action it is to be combined with. For these reasons special software has been written to emulate motion blur. There are usually at least two parameters which it needs to be fed – 'direction' of movement and 'extent' or duration of blur. The effect can be applied to the whole frame or, using an appropriate matte, to just one element of the scene (the moving object). By comparison between the elements with which it is being combined and exhibiting the 'real' blur and the synthetic element which is having blur added, it should be possible to obtain a pretty good match. If the effect is not being matched to a particular shot, for example a CGI model which is being digitally moved across screen, then it is usually best to find some reference material since it is very difficult to estimate the look of motion blur for a given object at a given speed.

Originally developed for military targeting, extremely sophisticated software exists for tracking and stabilizing, the former applying 'within' the frame and the latter to its entirety. For all forms of compositing it is essential that the various elements are stable and certainly not moving in contrary ways. If there is weave or camera instability on a backplate, say, then a stable foreground laid over it will appear to be floating (since it is the smaller element and not the one containing the ground) – the audience will always assume that the ground is fixed. A far greater sin, if it was known to be a VFX element, would be where a camera had not been locked off and was drifting during the shot. Fortunately, stabilizing software can now fix on to chosen pictorial elements and track their movement within the frame.

If we were, for instance, combining two elements, one of which was unstable and the other OK, there would be two alternative solutions. Initially the unstable shot would be tracked by choosing a suitable component in the image (see figure below) and running the program. The result would be tracking data defining the movement of the frame.

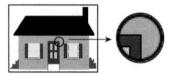

precise and easily recognizable geometrical features are well suited to targeting by tracking software systems

This data could then be used in one of two ways. In the more obvious, the unstable frame can be stabilized and then the two perfectly registered shots combined with no movement between the foreground and background. In a more obscure alternative, the tracking data can be applied in reverse to the stable image so as to make it weave precisely like the unstable master. This may sound odd but is often done where old material is having new elements added to it, since the audience expects these scenes to be imperfect. An example is the famous series of commercials in which a modern comedian was inserted into scenes from classic black and white movies.

The downside to this technique is that depending on the amount of movement between the most extreme displacements the entire frame is having to be moved and could therefore reveal a black bar along one edge of the picture (see figure below), depending on the extent of the travel. The only way to compensate for this is to enlarge the frame slightly so as to avoid the shoot off.

stabilizing this frame has required it to be moved down and to the left which leaves a black border

the only solution is to enlarge the image which may not be a good option

However, it should be remembered that if the frames have originally been matched then the shot which does not need to be stabilized will have to be enlarged by the same amount too. When using the special stabilizing software built into most VFX programs this resizing will be automatically taken care of, based on the discrepancy between the most distant tracking deviations – it can however be manually overridden to be increased or reduced as required.

Tracking software uses the same technology. This enables one frame to be locked on to another and is most commonly used to 'glue' an inserted element to a point (moving or not) in the target image. It is to enable this software to do its job that tracking markers (see page 180) are required on moving blue screen and other shots. As with stabilizing software the operational requirement is to select suitable points in the image for the program to track (see figure opposite) one point for panning/tilting, two points for rotation and four points to allow perspective to be matched. Tracking can be either of an entire frame to lock something on to it, such as to put an image into a television screen in a hand-held shot, or it can be of an object which is moving within the frame, such as a moving car on which the number plate needs to be changed.

The software itself is built into most VFX programs such as 'Inferno', 'After Effects' or 'Commotion'. Generally the user can define a number of points which are to be tracked and then the software works through the frames of the shot. Once done the track can be refined with reference to the timeline, and in sophisticated programs the points tracked can even be changed during the shot to allow for such problems as the points going out of, or coming in to, the image. The software identifies a specific set of pixels and searches for that pattern from one frame to the next and charts their movement. The data thus produced defines the movement of the shot and can be applied to another element to make it move identically.

If a scene is to have something added to it and is moving, then it will have to be tracked. An example might be where a digital or traditional matte painting is to be added in digital post while the shot is moving. It is best to have some form of markers in the part of frame where the element is to be added and preferably at the same sort of distance. If the markers do not coincide with the place where the inserted material would have been, had it been real, then there might be some sort of drift as a result of parallax or other variables within the frame as the camera moves. For example, imagine that we are shooting a scene in a room with a window. Beyond the window is a blue screen to pop in the background which should be there. If the scene were real and the trees beyond the window were really there, then, as the camera within the room moves about, the window frame and trees would slip against each other owing to parallax. Thus to get the background to behave correctly, it will be necessary to have tracking markers on the blue backing and not on the window frame since this would lock the background plate to it and it would therefore appear to be stuck on – as if just a picture stuck to the window itself. For this very reason a number of markers would be necessary since, as the camera moves, the part of the blue screen which is seen will change and therefore any given marker will move in and out of visibility. When shooting locations it will be necessary to ensure that the markers are visible. If the camera is moving a lot, then round objects are best so that they remain the same size as viewed from different angles and they should be easily apparent – tennis balls, ping pong balls and footballs in yellow are popular since they are so easy to obtain. If the scene is at night then patches of Scotchlite or small illuminated bulbs will be required.

It should be remembered that the tracking markers will have to be removed in post-production if they are in parts of the frame where they will not be covered up by the material to be inserted. Thus very careful consideration should be given to the placing of tracking markers since there have been many cases where the removal of the markers has taken longer and used more resources than the addition of the pictorial element they were there to help insert. Although obvious, it has to be stated that things like smoke drifting across tracking markers is an absolute no because this makes it very difficult to get rid of them.

If at all possible the use of obvious tracking markers should be avoided and preferably elements usable for this purpose should be integrated into the setting. For example, window frames or other architectural ornamentation can be used and often can be added to look like it is part of the original design (see figure below) with the excellent result that it does not need to be removed once used. Objects which are to have images inserted into them are good examples so, for instance, a book or mirror which is to have a magical image inserted can simply have a pattern or ornament of some kind around the frame.

 tracking this shot will be difficult using the door frame since the actor will go past it and cover it up   by adding a mirror with an ornamental frame tracking will be much easier

As in this latter example, tracking software is also used where subject matter moving within the frame is to have an element attached to it. A magic book being carried by a character and with moving images on its cover or a TV set in a moving shot both illustrate where this technique might be used. As mentioned the use of design elements to track is preferable to specific markers since if, for example, a magic mirror into which non-reflected images appear were being created, it might be that it sometimes goes back to being a real mirror; so crosses on a blue patch for example would not be practical. Similarly, TV sets will often have any low density reflection on their glass surface laid back over the composite, again to give a realistic effect. The old method of putting a blue card on the surface of the screen is no longer favoured since the result looks very 'stuck on' and modern digital techniques make it easy to track and insert with a mix back of any reflections off the screen – so the best technique is to simply turn the TV off!

The best-known use of tracking markers is their addition to blue/green screens. This can be used to attach static backgrounds to moving studio foregrounds or to fix the blue screen element to a moving background (which will also require some means of tracking so that the foreground may be attached to it). Tracking markers on a blue screen can be flat and are often simply camera-tape crosses stuck to the backing. Tape the same colour as the backing is often used, chosen for example, to be blue enough to key but sufficiently different to track.

As long as the blue screen element has blue surrounding it then it can easily be put into much wider shots without any special precautions apart from ensuring that the perspective is correct at all times. If the camera were going around the subject, for instance, then it would have to rotate or have the camera move around it in a complementary way. However, if the camera on the foreground is moving substantially, then the plate going behind it will have to be effectively much larger than the foreground shot (see top figure on page 128) because, if the shot were real, the camera would be panning over a much larger area which must be depicted in the background. This can be achieved as described earlier (page 180) using either a larger format or a number of tiles stitched together. Most modern VFX software will make this extremely easy to do since images of different sizes can be combined. It is also possible to build in slippage between the two images so that parallax can be realistically imitated.

Some particularly clever tracking software such as 'Boujou' and 'Synth Eyes' is now available which can calculate the movement of the shot in 3D space from the elements within it. The data provided is accurate enough to be used to animate 3D CGI elements to fit the shot even where both the camera and the subject matter are moving.

3D computer-generated imaging (CGI)

Also known as 'computer graphics' and 'computer animation', CGI is the basis of an entire industry and is already the subject of many books. It is used extensively in the design of everything from toasters to cars and in the simulation of everything from landing an aeroplane to the gyrations of the planets. A separate branch of the motion picture industry uses CGI to create animated television series and major feature films such as *Shrek* (2001) and *Toy Story* (1995). Computer graphics were, however, first used for VFX and play an ever more important role in their execution. This section will therefore be confined to the use of CGI for effects and what a producer, supervisor or cameraman needs to know to make use of them.

3D computer graphics are an extension of the principles used in vector or 'drawing' systems. A file of information is created which describes a three-dimensional object. Special software has been written to enable the building of such 'models' in an interactive and intuitive way. This usually involves plan and elevation views which may be sized according to requirements. Most of this software will also permit the results to be viewed on screen as seen from the point of view of a user-defined virtual camera. Once a model has been built it can be animated by moving it one frame at a time, just like traditional stop frame animation; however, computer animation software offers no end of tools to simplify this process by allowing key frames to be defined and then automatically in-betweening them. Once all of the frames have been defined along a timeline it is possible to go in and interactively adjust any frame which is incorrect. Next comes lighting the scene to set a suitable mood or match live action with which the CGI is to be associated. Lighting systems will also create the appropriate shadows and shading. Many enhancements of the basic process are available,

The side text reads "8 Computer-based systems and techniques" (vertical).

8 Computer-based systems and techniques

such as permitting imported textures to be applied to the surfaces of models (texture mapping), or for imported images to be reflected off shiny surfaces (reflection mapping). The final process of computer graphics is 'rendering' which is the system by which the image is output to a chosen viewable format. A given animation sequence could equally be rendered as 50 field 8-bit/linear video, 24 frame 2048 × 1556 10-bit/log R G B for transfer to film or any other image file format.

To summarize, the process of computer animation generally consists of four stages: building the model, applying technical processes (e.g., textures and lighting), animating and rendering. CG artists often restrict themselves to modelling or animating while 'technical directors' (TDs) handle other facets of the work such as shading and rendering. On very large productions every single process is handled by a team of specialists dealing with just one aspect of the work such as 'textures', 'lighting' or backgrounds.

Large features can take three or more years to make whilst employing a staff of hundreds. VFX, on the other hand, may employ a single 3D animator generating mattes or calculating match moves. 3D use in VFX covers a wide range of tasks. CGI models can replace miniatures, natural phenomena such as smoke, clouds, fire and water can be created in the computer, crude models can be used to mimic the movements of blue screen actors and thus create realistic shadows, spectacular backgrounds can be created without visiting the original locations, huge armies can be amassed and annihilated, whilst CGI characters can replace actors in dangerously impossible action sequences.

Computer graphics were first used in commercials to satisfy a series of visual fashions. Robert Abel & Associates were using crude wire-frame graphics to pre-program motion control moves. In the late 1970s when a creative from an ad agency saw this he demanded to use the green on black wire frame instead of the miniature shoot and so doing kicked off the craze for computer graphics in commercials. As each new enhancement of the process was invented it became a fashion in titles and TV spots, thus giving birth to flying, chrome, glass and liquid logos.

The first use of CGI in a mainstream film was *Westworld* (1973) but this was for a purely image processing function. Fully shaded models were used for some scenes such as the light cycles in *Tron* (1982) but most of that film's effects were pseudo computer graphics created by laboriously rephotographing the live action through coloured filters by means of a rostrum camera. The 'real' CGI was done on multimillion dollar Cray computers and most of the companies involved eventually went bust. Many of the personnel reassembled to work on *The Last Starfighter* (1984) in which all the model shots were done by computer graphics, but unfortunately, like *Tron*, the film was a box office disaster and the studios' brief romance with computer animation ended. George Lucas' ILM had a considerable R&D department working on 3D and they contributed the 'Genesis project' scene to *Star Trek – The Wrath of Khan* (1982) but because of the gigantic costs of this group Lucas sold it off to ex-Apple boss Steve Jobbs and it became known as 'Pixar' which, under the creative direction of John Lassiter, went on to produce feature-length CGI features such as *Toy Story* (1995). Eventually 3D computer graphics re-emerged at ILM in the VFX department using smaller, cheaper machines and first appeared in the stained glass warrior sequence of *The Young Sherlock Holmes* (1985). 3D computer graphics finally grabbed the audience's imagination with two James Cameron-directed movies: *The Abyss* (1989) water creature and, in *Terminator 2* (1991), the liquid metal morphing robot. Computer graphics then became the star of the movie with *Jurassic Park* (1993) and since then there has been no turning back.

These early films all depicted things which were outside of human experience: nobody knows how a machine inside a video game would look, nor a liquid creature or robot, nor indeed a dinosaur. The progression has moved on with people too small to make out clearly in crowd shots for films such as *Titanic* (1997) right up to Gollum in *The Lord of the Rings: The Two Towers* (2002), an almost human character. At the time of writing, the ultimate goal of a truly believable 'synthespian' or totally convincing human character has not been attained.

Nowadays all VFX companies have a 3D department and hardly a job goes by without some element of computer animation being used. The most obvious instance is the use of CG models in place of traditional miniatures. Particularly for objects which are freely floating about, such as a spherical robotic which flies around a room rotating as it does so, CGI really does have the edge. Depth of field and rigging for full rotational movement are no longer problems and precise timing of the model's interaction with the scene can be created whilst looking at the two images together. CGI models have everything going for them and are gradually taking over from the traditional miniature.

Rendering times and costs were a major disadvantage at one time but now a moderately priced workstation can be used to generate extremely sophisticated animated models. Modern software such as 3D Studio MAX, Maya, SoftImage and Lightwave contain suites of tools for all the processes of CGI at very acceptable prices. The only area in which models may fall down is their ability to appear totally real, but this is often directly related to cost, with a simple rule being that if the audience are unlikely to be familiar with the subject of the model then CGI will be fine, whereas if the model represents something well known, then perhaps a miniature or full scale model will be preferable.

As with everything else in VFX the trick is to 'match' the CGI element with the live action it is being combined with. This applies to both the possible scenarios: where the CGI is added to live action or where the live action is added to the CGI. The former might be a computer model of the exterior of a space station shown through the window of the live action control room. The converse is where live action of the control room is inserted into a window of a computer model of the entire station floating in space (see figure below).

computer graphic inserted into live action

live action inserted into computer graphic

The lens on the CGI virtual camera will need to be the same angle of view as that in the live action, with the same settings such as focus, physical position and camera angle. Remember that what the camera sees is not just determined by focal length, but by its combination with image size. Thus setting focal length alone may not generate the correct image parameters and it may be necessary to drill down the menus to find a setting for image format too.

Lighting and general 'look' also need to be matched if the illusion is to be real. If a computer model is going to react with its surroundings it is often a good idea to build a rough version of the location inside the computer so that the action can be exactly aligned – this is even more essential if the camera is moving. As previously stressed, provision of data from the live action set will make all of this much easier, since the information can simply be keyed in to the relevant settings. Reference material such as reflective grey and white lighting globes will also help enormously.

Camera lenses are by no means perfect and it is therefore most important for the CGI crew to be provided with lens information. A white grid on black for each lens used and a grey card will be very useful for analysing any optical distortion. This distortion may be mapped using special software which compares it to the computer camera's theoretically perfect virtual lens. The difference between the real lens and the virtual lens would mean that images created in the two media and expected to fit might not match correctly owing to, for instance, geometrical distortion in the camera lens which would be absent from the virtual camera (see figure below).

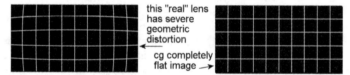

this "real" lens
has severe
geometric
distortion

cg completely
flat image →

photography with a real lens will always be imperfect compared to a virtual lens

Using the data generated from the grid two possible solutions become available. Either the camera original can have the distortion removed or the computer-generated image can have the distortion added. Both methods will make the shots match and the decision as to which is more appropriate depends on the shot content and context. If there is no specific reason to choose either way, then the most natural looking is usually to distort the 'perfect' CGI material to match the live action.

If the CGI is being shot first then it is necessary to be aware of the limitations of live action filming. Choosing focal lengths that are not available to the crew or placing cameras beyond the physical limitations of the set (e.g., beyond the studio walls) must not be done. Additionally a common measuring system should be defined before anybody shoots anything – having to convert from metric to imperial in the middle of a busy set is not to be recommended.

Finally, the lessons learnt from stop frame animation can be applied to computer animation. Problems such as animating fur and suspending heavy armatures disappear with CGI whilst it is always possible to revisit a piece of animation which is not quite perfect without having to re-animate the entire sequence. In particular, problems with motion can be easily dealt with in computer animation where, for instance, motion blur can be either automatically created by the software or eye-matched to the live action footage. Computer models can have textures and 3D paint systems can match them precisely to the look of real world 'dirty' objects.

3D computer models are now used for the full range of VFX requirements. They can be used to create individual objects which are freeform and can move, such as spaceships or flying creatures; they can be used to create subjects attached to the ground such as trains, cars or even people; and they can be used to create whole environments such as cities or forests. Once such models exist they can be animated to act naturally or to do what would be impossible with a real or physically built miniature.

CGI can also model natural phenomena or the more ethereal sorts of subject such as snow, rain or fire. This is fantastically useful for effects where precisely the size, shape and form of an element can be defined and made to order. Thus, for example, small fire elements could be created to fill in gaps in a physical fire which had been created on set. But far more importantly, unscaleable natural phenomena such as fire and water can be much more realistically created using computers. Water has always been the most difficult effect to create in miniatures and yet one of the most in demand. Now, in features such as *Titanic* (1997) and *Perfect Storm* (2000) it has become possible to tame this most uncontrollable of the elements. Water can be created as a totally separate element into which a miniature, full scale or computer-generated boat may be placed or it can be created alongside a CGI boat. If the sea is being created for the insertion of an externally sourced vessel then it may be necessary to created a crude CGI representation of this so as to create the necessary interaction with the computer-generated water (e.g., displacement and wake).

Animation of the model is done by means of a timeline. A model can be simply altered frame by frame as with conventional stop frame or it can be animated using keyframes and the computer's automated inbetweening. It is also possible to build the model to have a set of specific controls or nodes which allow it to be animated in a predetermined way. This facility will often be used to force the animator into a style of movement which only permits realistic options and refuses to allow what would be physically impossible in the real world. On large productions technical directors and/or model builders will often use this technique to allow non-technical artists to animate complex models and to maintain a consistency of approach, even where 20 or more animators may be working on scenes depicting a single character. Many animation directors favour different software packages for animation and modelling.

Digitizing (getting information into the computer)

It is not always necessary to fully model or animate CGI subjects since the necessary constructional or motion information may already exist. Wire frame or even fully formed models may be available in some other context, from an earlier project or simply from a model vendor. In this case all that is necessary is to import the data into the CG software and make any necessary alterations to adapt the model to the purpose at hand. Examples might be for a car commercial where the car had originally been designed using a CAD system and therefore computer models already exist. Many objects and even creatures are built by third-party specialist companies who then sell or license their designs and indeed will often create your subject for a very low price in exchange for being allowed to add it to their catalogue.

If a model is not available there are still some options to pursue before having to do the entire job from scratch. If the subject is quite small then a 3D digitizer can be used. This is a device which basically photographs the entire object from all sides and in 3D. Using associated software this will produce a model of the item as a single solid object. This will not immediately make it possible to animate this object and considerable work will subsequently be required to break the model up into independently moveable elements (if this is a requirement). However, the point is that a very precise representation of the subject's physical appearance can be automatically generated and this is a big step in the process. For larger objects such as people or cars a 3D scanner can be used and it basically achieves the same purpose as a digitizer but on a much grander scale. Environmental mapping equipment can now be used to do this for large-scale subjects such as entire buildings, natural features or movie sets. In the past this could only be done by traditional surveying or photogrammetry, both of which are expensive and very time-consuming, but recently developed laser-based 'Lidar' scanning may now be used to very quickly scan and map large areas to a high degree of accuracy.

CG animation can also be aided by external data. Where the talents of expert traditional stop frame animators are required it is possible to attach motion sensors to the physical armatures they animate so that, as they have made each move to their model, instead of firing a camera exposure the 'take' button records the data detailing the model's positional status. When the sequence is complete this data can then be imported into a computer animation program and used to animate a CGI model. This method allows experts such as veteran dinosaur stop frame artists to be used on modern prehistoric dramas.

Another technique is to use a 'motion capture' system to obtain data about a subject's movement. This could, for instance, be a dancer who is providing the movements for a synthetic creature. These systems employ markers on the subject's body which can be tracked by a camera/software system. A series of Scotchlite disks on the relevant parts of a human for example, will be able to totally define how that person moves about. Equivalent points on the computer model can then be moved in an identical way. There are a number of different methods of tracking the subject but the principle remains the same.

Information about camera movement such as from a motion control system may also be imported into a computer to provide the necessary data about how the virtual 3D camera might move. Most MoCo companies can provide this information and have done so on many projects.

Whatever way data is captured and imported into the software it can always be modified thereafter to make it more appropriately fit the action required by the scene.

Rendering (getting the images out of the computer)

The final stage in computer graphics is to get the image out of the computer in a human viewable form. This process is called 'rendering' and a variety of formats can be output from the same original data since, in most CGI systems, the software produces information describing the construction and movement of the model but not a representation of it. During the process of modelling and animating, progress is viewed by the artist via a low-resolution and/or simplified render thus permitting fast feedback. For the final version much more detail will be required and it is important to make sure that the rendering process is set up to create an image of sufficient detail to be composited or matched in with surrounding material created conventionally. Thus for video one might be rendering at 576×720 pixels 8-bit/linear 50 fields interlaced and Y, U, V, but for film it might be 2048×1556 pixels 10-bit/log 24 fps progressive and R, G, B.

Rendering, like most other parts of the digital pipeline, is subject to the usual compromise between speed and quality. Even with the latest high-peed, high-power computers it is still possible to set up renders which take hours rather than minutes per frame! Given that there can be quality losses when converting from one image format and compression standard to another, it is most important to choose the correct system when rendering so as to avoid unnecessary losses in image quality at a later stage.

Most CGI systems have an integrated render engine but specialized high quality renderers such as 'Renderman' and 'Mental Ray' are often used to get the best looking image possible.